Feminist Definitions of Caring Communities and Healthy Lifestyles

Les définitions féministes des modes de vie sains et des sociétés sensibles à l'être humain

Canadian Research Institute for the Advancement of Women

Institut canadien de recherches sur les femmes

Feminist Definitions
of Caring Communities
and Healthy Lifestyles:
C.R.I.A.W. Conference 1999

Les définitions
féministes
des modes de vie sains et
des sociétés sensibles
à l'être humain:
Conférence de L'ICREF 1999

edited by
Gabrielle Lavigne, Tricia Burke,
Manon Lemonde

Your Scrivener Press

National Library of Canada Cataloguing in Publication Data

C.R.I.A.W. Conference (1999 : Sudbury, Ont.)
    Feminist definitions of caring communities and healthy lifestyles : C.R.I.A.W. Conference, 1999 — Les définitions féministes des modes de vie sains et des sociétés sensibles à l'être humain : Conférence de L'ICREF, 1999

Conference held Oct. 15-17, 1999, Sudbury, Ont.
Includes bibliographical references.
Includes 2 papers in French.
ISBN 1-896350-13-5

    1. Women — Congresses. 2. Women — Canada — Congresses.
3. Feminism — Congresses. 4. Feminism — Canada — Congresses.
I. Lavigne, Gabrielle, 1951- II. Burke, Tricia, 1969- III. Lemonde, Manon, 1955- IV. Title. V. Title: Définitions féministes des modes de vie sains et des sociétés sensibles à l'être humain.

HQ1106.C75 2001   305.4   C2001-902202-6

Book design: Laurence Steven
Cover design: Chris Evans
Cover reproduction of "June Geraniums" by permission of
    Mary Pratt; © Mary Pratt

Published by *Your Scrivener Press* 🌲
465 Loach's Road,
Sudbury, Ontario, Canada, P3E 2R2
scrivener@sympatico.ca
www3.sympatico.ca/scrivener

In memory of Karen Blackford
September 23, 1944 — January 13, 2000

Table of Contents

Feminist Analysis of Employment Trends

Community Awareness

Perceptions of the Body

Women in Isolated Communities

Defining Women's Health From Diverse Perspectives

Preface

After four years, we cannot help but reflect on all the steps taken to finally get this last piece of the puzzle together and put closure on what was a long process of getting this book published.

Our first and foremost recognition goes to Karen Blackford who, in the spring of 1997 asked Gabrielle Lavigne, as Chair of the Presidential Advisory Committee on the Status of Women at Laurentian University (SW), if she could have a few minutes at the monthly meeting to make a presentation on the Canadian Research Institute for the Advancement of Women (CRIAW). At the time, Karen, a professor from the School of Nursing at Laurentian University, was a member of the CRIAW National Board and wanted to find a host city for the 1999 Biannual Conference. The Status of Women Committee listened to her speak with passion about this group as she asked us to sponsor the conference. The Committee agreed "in principle" and somehow became the host for this worthwhile project — the first step to becoming involved in a project that would eventually take on a life of its own.

Second of all, we would like to thank the various Committees and their members, many of whom worked for almost two years preparing the groundwork for a conference that was finally called **Feminist Definitions of Caring Communities & Healthy Lifestyles / Les Définitions féministes des modes de vie sains et des sociétés sensibles à l'être humain.**

Special thanks go to Karen Blackford, founding chair; Andrea Levan, Conference Co-Chair and Paper Selection and Program Chair; Donna Mese, Finance Committee Chair; Cheryl Park, Child Care Committee Chair; Mila Wong, Publicity Committee Chair; Carole Trépanier, Entertainment Committee Chair; Mara Waern, Accessibility Committee Chair; Alison Fortier, Map Committee Chair; Marilyn Clulow, Telephone Committee Chair; Flo Carrière and her volunteers.

There are also project coordinators to thank, whose efforts lightened the task of Committee members and handled the complex day to day activities. Special thanks go to Mary Bedkowski, who successfully wrote our first proposals for funding; Ginette Graveline, who organized a fantastic Trade Show and prepared a conference video; Nicole Ladouceur who painstakingly oversaw registration; and Tricia Burke who wrote and processed proposals. Others who were our discrete readers include Gabrielle Lavigne, Carol Stos, Si Transken,

Manon Lemonde, Marg Kechnie and Tricia Burke.

Special thanks go to Andrea Levan and the wonderful team of volunteers on the Paper Committee who read all of the proposals and as a result were able to organize a program that met the needs of all the participants.

We also appreciate the guidance of special people at Laurentian University who were our invisible guides at different times during the initial stages of book editing: Marie-Luce Garceau, Jean-Marc Bélanger, and Jane Pitblado. Their advice, support and sources of expertise were extremely valuable.

In the community, we thank those individuals or organizations that made the conference as well as this book possible, they include, Paul Brokenshire, Convention and Visitors Service, City of Sudbury, the Sudbury Women's Centre, our numerous sponsors, Human Resources Development Canada, Industry Canada, Ministry of Northern Development and Mines, Ontario Lottery Corporation, Trillium Foundation, Social Science Humanities Research Council, Laurentian University, Cambrian College, Collège Boréal , Presidential Advisory Committee on the Status of Women (LU) CRIAW National, Centre familial de Sudbury, Canadian Centre on Disabilities Studies, Sudbury Business and Professional Women's Club, Sudbury and District Association for the Developmentally Disabled, Ontario March of Dimes, Royal Bank, students in the Daycare and Law and Justice programs at Cambrian College as well as our Trade Show exhibitors.

As the theme of our conference was broad in its application, proposals were solicited from women of all ages, from diverse backgrounds, academics in post-secondary settings as well as women affiliated with community-based groups. As we welcomed all these proposals, we also acknowledge that the book is a blend of academic and non-academic subject matter. Based on these premises, we did not alter the contents of most papers except for grammatical or typing errors and to change the format. We therefore, thank all our wonderful presenters who came from all over the globe — from Vancouver, to Quebec, Japan, Australia and England — to join us in this exciting conference and share their experiences with us. It has been our privilege to work with all of these wonderful authors, and to have the opportunity to put their words to print.

We also wish to thank the more than one hundred volunteers who worked with us before and after the conference on various

Committees. The words "thank you" do not seem strong enough to express our deepest gratitude.

We gratefully acknowledge Mary Pratt for allowing us to use her painting "June Geraniums" as part of our conference advertising and for our book cover.

Last but not least, we deeply thank Laurence Steven, from Your Scrivener Press, who was our wonderful mentor and guided us through the process of book publishing. We thank him sincerely for his patience and wonderful sense of humour as we muddled our way through deadlines and rewrites. We purposely chose a publisher from the north as it was important to us that we recognize our local talent. Again, we were well served.

With over three hundred people participating at our conference, there was a lot of discussion, a lot of laughter and some serious lobbying being done. It is hoped that this book will help those of you who attended the conference relive some of the excitement that took place that weekend of Oct, 15th-17, 1999 and that you have been able to bring to fruition some of the recommendations that were made during presentations. We hope that the feminist voices are still ringing loud and clear and that changes are being made around the world by those of you who are its leaders. For those of you who are with us for the first time, we hope that as you read this book you feel some of the excitement that we felt at the conference and that you take your own place in defining yourselves as feminists in your own lifestyles.

Merci, thank you, miigwetch

Gabrielle Lavigne, Conference Co-Chair (LU)
Registration Committee /
Administration /
Proceedings Co-editor

Tricia Burke, Proceedings Co-editor

Manon Lemonde, Site Committee Chair /
Proceedings Co-editor

Laurentian University, September 2001

Keynote Addresses

Women in the Global Economy: Can We Make a Difference?

Maude Barlow

CRIAW Conference Keynote Address:
Friday October 15, 1999

T hank you very much for the beautiful introduction. First of all I would like to say that it is just a joy and an honour to be here and what a pleasure it is to be on the same platform as Joan Grant-Cummings and Pat Armstrong, two women I enormously respect. I think you are going to have wonderful sessions with both of them, in addition to the wonderful papers in your program. I`m most impressed with what you've got planned.

Tonight I am not going to speak so much to the topic, instead, I want to speak about threats to the topic. In this country, we have a strong feminist legacy of claiming communities, claiming our health and having much more democratic control over our lives and the structures and institutions around us. A very big threat to this claim, I think, is coming from an economic and ideological system of which GE foods or genetically modified foods are a part. To explore the impact of the global economy, in general and specifically for women, I'm going to first take you away from Sudbury and away from Canada.

Economic globalization is the belief that a single, global economy with universal rules set by global capital, not government, for the global consumer market is the final destiny of humanity and our inevitable shared future — this has become a mantra. Economic freedom, not democracy, not ecological stewardship, has become the defining metaphor of the post Cold War period. As a result, I believe, the world is going through a watershed transformation as great as anything in our history. At the heart of this transformation is an all-out assault on anything left standing in the public realm, otherwise known as "the commons". Everything is for sale, even things that we thought would never be for sale, things we consider sacred like health, education, culture and heritage, genetic codes and seeds, and natural resources including air and water.

The state of Texas is currently working towards the privatization of welfare. Guess who they have given the contract to? Lockheed Martin, the world's biggest weapon manufacturer. The only question that remains is.whether Lockheed Martin will have the right to determine eligibility, or if eligibility requirements will remain with the state at some level.

We know that last year about $157 billion worth of public institutions, public assets were privatized, mostly to large transnational corporations. This represents an increase of about 70 percent in one year.

We have seen a company called Layman Brothers, a big stockbroker's house in New York, put out a publication saying that education is going to go the way of health care. This means that education will be privatized and commercialized, entirely within the next decade. They say just as they took what was left of public health in the United States and made it a big business, so too they will do with the privatization of education. You know how they have HMOs, Health Management Organizations in the United States? Well, now they are going to have EMOs, Education Management Organizations, which you and I know as schools. This publication is very, very frightening material.

Increasingly, services and resources are being controlled by a handful of transnational corporations who operate outside of the law, either domestic or international, and they are big. Of the world's 100 largest economies, 52 are now transnational corporations, which means that most countries are far smaller than corporations. In fact, WalMart is bigger than 161 countries, so I'm not kidding when I talk about the WalMartization of the world's workforce. The top 200 companies are now so big that their combined sales surpassed the combined economies of the GDP of 182 countries. Finally, 60 percent of all the holdings of private banks are now secured in tax havens; hiding this money is a bigger business than the global narcotics trade.

This system is dividing the haves and have-nots, within nation-states and between nation-states, as at no time in history. An entrenched underclass is being created in every society, along with an emerging elite, a global royalty, living in unprecedented wealth, who have more in common with each other than they do with the citizens of their own countries. When I think of the global royalty, I think of people like our Prime Minister; our media moguls like Conrad Black;

our senior bureaucrats; and, our senior business people. This elite group attends these international meetings and lives in a kind of style you and I will never see.

More importantly, this new global royalty now centrally plans the market, destroying lives and nature in its wake. Listen to David Korten who used to work with the World Bank:

> The world is now ruled by a global financial casino staffed by faceless bankers and hedge-fund speculators who operate with a herd mentality in the shadowy world of global finance. Each day, they move more than two trillion dollars around the world in search of quick profits and safe havens, sending exchange rates and stock markets into wild gyrations wholly unrelated to any underlying economic reality. With abandon they make and break national economies, buy and sell corporations and hold politicians hostage to their interests.

Canada Conforms

A striking feature of globalization is the creation of dramatic inequality. The United Nations Human Development Report recounts the latest statistics on the income gap every year. According to the UN's report, the disparity in the level of the world's top 20 percent and the bottom 20 percent is now 150:1 and has doubled in the last thirty years. In other words, we are going in all the wrong directions. The world's 225 richest individuals have a combined wealth equal to the annual income of half of humanity. The three richest people in the world, all working for Microsoft by the way, have assets that exceed the combined gross domestic product of 48 countries. I believe this to be an obscenity.

Economic globalization is also disenfranchising millions of workers in the global economy — an army of the desperate who have no access to the products they produce or assemble. The International Labour Organization declares that there are almost one billion, unemployed or severely underemployed workers in the world, and millions of others who are working in conditions next to slavery. Last year, Michael Jordan earned more money from Nike to shill for the company than the company paid all its workers in Indonesia combined.

Work occurs in "free trade zones", called Maquiladoras, some of which I have visited. There are about 500 of them in the world and although they're geographically located in a country, they really belong to transnational corporations. I have walked along the rivers in Northern Mexico, in Maquiladoras, near Tijuana and other places. In one location, residents gave me a pencil and told me to dip it in the river and it came out stripped of its paint. This is the river upon which people live and depend for their drinking water, their bathing water and so on, filled with toxins. This river happened to be downstream from a slaughterhouse, you cannot even imagine the pollution. In reality, there is no clean water left in Northern Mexico as a direct result of economic globalization. We simply do not care what happens to people as long as we get our product.

Moreover, the conditions for women are appalling. Most of the workers in these plants are young women, whom companies say are less trouble, are preferred and work until their eyes or their fingers give out. I have been in Maquiladora plants where women workers had to show monthly proof of menstruation or they were fired. Then, I have seen babies born with deformities from the chemicals that these women are working which are unspeakable.

Walking through the shacks and the desperately poor communities in these areas, I have also seen babies drinking Pepsi-Cola and Coca-Cola from Pepsi and Coca-Cola baby bottles. Nobody can tell me they don't exist, because I have seen them. This is the real Coke and Pepsi war, there is no clean water and nobody can afford the milk or juice. A recent survey of 5 700 teenagers in 12 Asia-Pacific countries found that McDonald's and Coca-Cola are consistently named as the most popular restaurant and soft drink. Coke now claims that 94 percent of the world's children recognize its logo. In Third World communities, Coke is all the people drink: the water is polluted absolutely beyond safe use.

I want to talk briefly about water, because it is such a big issue for us in Canada. Today, almost one billion people have no access to clean water and more than five million people, most of them children, die every year from drinking poor quality water. All over the world, industry is moving up precious river systems, drinking them dry as they go. To finance its so-called economic miracle and provide for the demands of the global consumer market, China has diverted its water usage from farmers to industry, leaving huge areas of desert in its wake and millions without access to water. The Worldwatch Institute, the World Bank and the UN say that if we don't change our use of the world's water pattern now — the amount of available fresh water is very finite, it's less than half a percent of all the world's total water stock — if we don't stop depleting, polluting and diverting it, by the year 2025, two-thirds of the world will be living in water scarcity, a full third of the population living in the absolute extreme condition of no clean water whatsoever.

Now let me turn to the issue of genetically altered foods, which simply did not exist a decade ago. However, backed by the governments of the industrialized world, Canada being absolutely top among them, a handful of food and chemical corporations has transformed the entire global food industry. Farmers are held hostage to companies like Monsanto, who force them to shift production to GE foods and to pay royalties for seeds impregnated with pesticides that only their own seed brand can withstand.

Consumers, who have had no warning about this, and no opportunity to decide on the merits of GE foods, are suddenly presented with GE potatoes, corn, soya, and a whole host of other products. Not only are we not given any choice in the decision, these corporations and our governments, particularly the Canadian government, are vehemently opposed even to labelling them. How can women "choose" a healthy lifestyle when we cannot even make this fundamental choice?

In India, where rural communities are being devastated by GE food corporations, there has been a rash of farmer suicides. The method of choice is swallowing Monsanto's Roundup Ready pesticide — a symbolic protest to show that these farmers would rather kill themselves than poison the earth or their families.

Businessman turned environmentalist Paul Hawken says:

> Given current corporate practices, not one wildlife reserve, wilderness, or indigenous culture will survive the global economy. We know that every natural system on the planet is disintegrating. The land, water, air, and sea have been functionally transformed from life-supporting systems into repositories for waste. There is no polite way to say that business is destroying the world.

Turning back to the global royalty for a moment, there is a story I want to tell you, a very strong image in my mind. You all know about APEC, the Asia -Pacific Economic Cooperation forum, from the pepper spray incident in Vancouver. Well, what you may not know is that every year the countries of the Asia-Pacific gather somewhere and talk about further trade liberalization. The year before it was in Vancouver it was in the Phillippines, and I attended the conference and I watched the global royalty and the global serfs going through the airport.

The global royalty including all our politicians and all our senior business corporations, CEOs and so on, walked through a very special line at the Phillippines airport and were whisked into limousines that were air-conditioned. Organizers did not want these people, including President Clinton and people from all over the world, to see the poverty in the Phillippines. It is pretty hard to miss poverty in Manilla as there are 1.5 million street children — that's not poor children — that's just children living on the street.

In order to ensure that the poverty was not visible to the dignitaries, organizers had a wall built, a big wooden wall, that would be at eye-level if they looked out of their limousines, to hide the city on one side. On the other side, they razed the homes of people living in the shanties and the shacks along Manilla Bay, and poured blue dye in the ocean. A lot of fish died, a lot of kids got sick, but they wanted the visiting delegates, whisked into these beautiful air-conditioned limos, not to see poverty on one side and to see beautiful Manilla Bay on the other side. When they arrived in the city, they were brought to a compound that was so beautiful, that the big story was that the Sultan of Brunei stayed and bought half of this compound when he was there.

Meanwhile, the rest of us were treated like dirt. We were there to protest what they were doing and to ask for environmental and human rights, social concerns and so on. The army was brought out against the Filipino people and people like ourselves just for being there. I didn't get clubbed, but I was with colleagues who did. So this global royalty is an extraordinarily real thing I can tell you.

The last night that we were there we were on a compound run by the Catholic Church. We were literally surrounded by goons outside with big fire trucks ready to hose us down, people with clubs, and people with bags of faeces and urine. I have never been so frightened in all my life as I was that night.

During the evening, a group of street children performed for us and it is safe to say, I'll never forget it as long as I live. The performers were all street prostitutes, kids who have raised themselves on the street who designed the costumes, wrote the material and performed for us.

The performance was based on the invasions of the Phillippines: the Japanese Invasion during the Second World War; the American Invasion, which was called an occupation, but they saw as a Sexual

Invasion because the children had been so terribly treated; and, the latest invasion by the global economy, the Corporate Invasion. These kids were dressed as McDonald's, Green Giant and Phillip Morris cigarettes and they understood. I thought would I ever like to take a brain transplant, and take their knowledge and their values, and transplant them into Jean Chretien's head. These children with their no grade anything education, street kids from Manilla, who went back out on the streets to earn enough money to live, taught us a stunning lesson.

So what does that mean back here in our own countries? Well in Canada we are like nation-states everywhere, responding to the "inevitability" of this global economy by slashing funding for natural resource protection. In the last five years together 60 percent from the federal level and 60 percent from the province of Ontario has been slashed, a double slash effect. Moreover, slashes to health, safety measures and social programs have occurred in order to attract capital and investment. In fact, federal spending on health care has been slashed by $36 billion in a decade. The government of Jean Chretien killed the Canada Assistance Plan, which was the standard we tried to establish for social assistance, so that people could live in some kind of dignity. The federal measure opened the way for Ontario to cut a further $1 billion from programs for the poor in the last year alone. In fact, Canada has cut funding to government social programs so deeply that we are now back to where we were in 1949, in terms of how much we spend on social programs as a total percentage of total government spending.

In the last decade, Canada has experienced the sharpest rise in child poverty in the industrialized world. Since 1989, when Parliament unanimously voted to abolish child poverty by the year 2000, the number of children living in poverty has grown by 60 percent, while the number of millionaires has tripled. The statistics for Ontario are even more desperate — 114 percent in those same years.

Furthermore, like most countries around the world, we have abandoned our once deep-seated belief in social equality. In this country, we used to see ourselves as a family, all of whose members counted, which I think is a feminist vision. Now, in many ways we have adopted Margaret Thatcher's notion that there is no such thing as society, only "individuals, looking out for their own self-interest."

In the new Canada, the poor themselves are responsible for their poverty. Young people are required to accept their lot in life — be it on the bread line or in the boardroom. This is, in my opinion, what the assault on public education and public educators is about; it's not because they've failed, it's because they've succeeded in turning out too many young people with a sense of entitlement. The world economy does not want entitled citizens. This is what the assault on our educators is about, a very political and devious assault, the goal being the legitimization of inequality and the privatization of poverty.

In the new world order, "the economy" — as defined by the new global corporate royalty including many of our political leaders — has a life entirely separate from the well-being of ordinary people. In this world order it is possible that we can see a rise in child poverty at the same time that we have this incredible wealth growing in our country because our definition of wealth has nothing to do with children and absolutely everything to do with corporate health.

The influential Vancouver think tank, The Fraser Institute, says that the issue of North American poverty could be solved by changing our standard measures — they suggest using China's. Their President, Michael Walker, likes to say and I quote: "Poverty is simply a reflection of the fact that the sufferers were dealt an unlucky intellectual or physical allocation from the roulette wheel of genetic inheritance." I bet he sleeps well at night. To be honest with you, I love my country, but lately I've been finding it harder to love because I've been finding it harder to find.

Trade Tyranny

Now, the glue that holds economic globalization together — embraces corporate rule, and keeps nation state governments in line — is international trade agreements. Please do not fall asleep now, I promise you, you have to hear this, it is like medicine, we have to learn this. My plea to you tonight is that as women, as feminists, as women who are leading the charge in so many fields, we have got to add to our economic and political literacy by becoming trade literate. A lot of what happens to us in our lives today, is now involved very deeply and explicitly with these trade agreements.

NAFTA, the North American Free Trade Agreement, among many other bad things, is the first treaty in the history of the world which allows corporations to directly sue the government of another country, if they feel a law that government brings in has cost them lost profits. Prior to NAFTA, corporations always had to get their own government to lay a charge.

Currently, we have a number of NAFTA Chapter 11 challenges. The first challenge occurred when Jean Chretien's Liberals, Jean Chretien himself, called MMT, Methylcyclopentadienyl Manganese Tricarbonyl, "a neurotoxin dangerous to children" and banned it. MMT is a gasoline additive that has been banned all over Europe and in California. This additive is a dangerous neurotoxin directly linked to ADD in children and to Alzheimer's and Parkinson's disease.

The company that makes MMT, the only company that makes it, happens to be American — Ethyl Corporation of Virginia. Two years ago, when we banned MMT in Canada, Ethyl launched a Chapter 11 NAFTA challenge and said to the Canadian government, "You owe us money." The government was so worried it would lose the case, that it backed off and reversed the legislation.

Today, MMT is not only in your gas, it is in all your gas, you can't even buy MMT free gasoline. Moreover, the Canadian government gave the company $90 million for their troubles, and the thing that bothers me the most, they gave them a letter apologizing for any negative statements that the government had made about MMT, which Ethyl is taking all over the world.

Under NAFTA Canada was forced to abandon its plans to make the cigarette manufacturers put their cigarettes in plain packages; reversed a law to prevent the export of PCB-laden waste; and, a United States water export company is now suing Canada under NAFTA because British Columbia banned the export of bulk water. The water company says that NAFTA has given them a say in Canada's water policy — they are absolutely right.

Now the threat to Canadian health care under NAFTA is very clear. Once privatized, no health service can be brought back into the public realm without government compensation to the private US industry that was denied their opportunity for profit, or even future profits. For instance, Ontario has entirely privatized home care, the fastest growing area of health care in Canada. If a future government in Ontario decided to make home care public, to bring home care into the public realm, we would have to be prepared to pay billions of dollars to the American for-profit home care corporations who are now operating here.

However, an even more immediate threat is upon us. In early December, the 135 countries of the World Trade Organization (WTO), are meeting in Seattle to launch a new round of negotiations called

"The Millennium Round". The representatives of these same 200 global corporations will be there as well.

The Seattle Host Committee is not made up of the labour movement or environmentalists; no the conference is co-hosted by Bill Gates, CEO of Microsoft and Philip Condit, CEO of Boeing. In exchange for a range of "donations" to the event, they have promised corporations direct access to these presidents and prime ministers, dependant upon how much money is given. There are emerald, diamond, platinum, gold, silver and bronze type donations and the more you give, the clearer the access to the more powerful heads of state. "The greatest possible interactions" are what these corporations have been promised. Needless to say, no such privileged access exists for civil society groups.

The WTO is the most powerful institution in the world and it enforces many, many trade rules from trading goods and services, intellectual property rights (a huge issue for educators), food safety, the global trade in food, and financial services. What makes the WTO so powerful is that, unlike any other global institution, it has the legislative and judicial authority to challenge the laws, policies and programs of countries that do not conform to WTO rules, and strike them down if they are seen to be too "trade restrictive." Cases are decided — in secret — by a panel of three trade bureaucrats and once a trade ruling is made, worldwide conformity is required. A country is obligated to harmonize its laws or face the prospect of perpetual trade sanctions or fines.

The WTO contains no minimum standards for the environment, labour rights, social programs or cultural diversity, and has already been used to strike down a number of nation-state laws protecting these areas. Wherever the environment and trade have clashed in a ruling, the environment has lost — in every, single, solitary case. An official with the WTO told the *Financial Times* and I quote: "The WTO is the place where governments collude in private against their domestic pressure groups."

In Seattle, the WTO is meeting to step up its agenda of trade liberalization and privatization in all the areas that we know. But here is what I want to say to you today, for the first time in history, they are talking about including health and education. The way in which they are including these topics in the talks is that preceding the WTO meetings, there is a meeting of the GATS: The General Agreement on Trade in Services.

The GATS is a body that meets to promote trade and services and it has very strong binding rules of enforcement. So far GATS agreements have included things like insurance, data processing, banking, telecommunications and so on and have been what they call "bottom up" agreements, meaning companies had to introduce the issue. Charlene Barsefsky, the United States Trade Representative, is promoting the notion that they should make it a "top down" agreement. This would mean that absolutely everything, all services including social services, water by the way, health and education would be included, and governments would have to fight to remove them.

The US have created a list of its "Negotiating Objectives" for the GATS talks, which includes "the need to encourage more privatization . . . promote pro-competitive regulative reform . . . and market access and national treatment". This means that governments cannot discriminate against the corporations of other countries for education and health care. Barshefsky also asked the powerful US business lobby, the Coalition of Service Industries, to supply her with a list of services they want included in the talks. The Coalition came back to Barshefsky with a 31 page document which included every facet of public education and health.

The WTO, on its web-site, describes the GATS as the first multilateral agreement to provide legally enforceable rights to trade in all services and boasts of being the first "multilateral agreement on investment"(MAI). Since the agreement covers not just cross-border trade of every possible means of supplying a service, it allows what they call "the right of establishment". What this means is that you could not stop big corporations like Columbia in the US—whose president says he wants to render every Canadian public hospital a private hospital within a decade—from coming across the border, the WTO would discipline this action.

I cannot overstate the danger to public education and health care in Canada if the GATS agreement and the WTO are allowed to start trade in these "services." Under the GATS agreement, countries are required to grant "national treatment" rights to foreign corporations, including the right to "set up a commercial presence in the export market." If the US is successful in including educational services and health care in the Millennium Round talks, Canada's public education system and our health care system will be forced to open up to foreign competition and the private sector, all without the knowledge of almost anyone in this country. Now I am not being alarmist, everything I have predicted in the past about these agreements has come true.

Women Must Act

In closing, I want to come back now to women and what this all means to us. The creation of "the commons" is a women's issue because without it, without our social programs, women in this country would not have advanced in the same way that we have. In this country it didn't matter whether you were rich or poor, you had access to basic facilities, and more importantly basic rights were built into our notion of whom we were as a country. To me, "sharing for survival" was the Canadian narrative. This is very different from the American narrative of "the deserving poor", you know where they say "everything's fine but we'll have a widow and orphan's fund over here." In Canada, we didn't believe that, we believed that as a right of citizenship you should be able to go anywhere in this country and claim fundamental rights. This tenet has been enormously important in building the women's movement in our country. I guess what I want to say here tonight is that as women, as feminists, as leaders as you all are in your communities, we need to come together and take what we learned in our fight for equality and use it to put our hands on these issues — these issues need our analysis, our work, our preparation.

As women, we have to become "trade literate". We have to take our place in this debate which, to date, has largely been the domain of men. I find it interesting that as we move into power — as authorities in education and health and politics at a domestic level — the real decision making has moved to other institutions, and believe me they are dominated by men. So its really an interesting scenario, it is almost as if someone is saying, "leave that to the women, because the power isn't down there anymore."

This phenomenon is occurring at the federal level as well. Yesterday, I met with Lloyd Axworthy, the Foreign Affairs Minister, on the issue of water. Axworthy basically admitted to my group that the WTO is out of their hands, like it is an institution that has it's own momentum. The Foreign Affairs Minister says that he feels powerless and he's a man and he's in power. So this is the situation we are dealing with. I think we need to name it; I think it needs women's hands; and, I think women have to help forge what I call a "moral alternative" to the brutal system that has grown up around us.

Tonight, I also want to honour my dad by thinking about the generation that so selflessly rose to a call against fascism, against tyranny and for something we have inherited, something I believe we are in danger of losing. John Ralston Saul calls this process a "coup d'état in slow motion." We might not see it, because it is in slow motion, but it is really, truly happening. We are losing our democratic rights everywhere.

So I want to end with the beautiful, beautiful words from the Women's Creed, from the Beijing Conference, not all of them, it is too long, but just to remember what it is we're for as well as remember and recognize what we're against. Just before I do, my plea is as a women's movement that we have to address these issues. Women's equality is deeply and inevitably and inexorably linked with class and equality and with the destruction of the environment. We have to put our hands to it, it needs us and we need it, and this is the next stage of our fight.

So hear from the Women's Creed:

> Bread. A clean sky. Active peace. A woman's voice singing somewhere, melody drifting like smoke from the cookfires. The army disbanded, the harvest abundant. The wound healed, the child wanted, the prisoner freed, the body's integrity honoured, the lover returned. The magical skill that reads marks into meaning. The labour equal, fair, and valued. Delight in the challenge for consensus to solve problems. No hand raised in any gesture but greeting. Secure interiors — of heart, home, land — so firm as to make secure borders irrelevant at last. And everywhere laughter, care, celebration, dancing, contentment. A humble, earthly paradise in the now . . . All this is political. And possible. We will make it real, make it our own, make policy, history, peace, make mischief, make a difference, the connections, the miracle, ready. Believe it. We are the women who will transform the world.

Thank you.

Caring for Women in the New Global Economy

Dr. Pat Armstrong

CRIAW Conference Keynote Address:
Saturday October 16, 1999

As Maude said last night, it is truly a privilege to be here with such a distinguished group of women, both up here and out there. I want to thank Karen Blackford, in particular, who I had the extra privilege of working with when she was at York University.

Health care is a women's issue — obviously don't have to tell you that. But, let me remind you that approximately 80 percent of the people who provide paid care, and a similar proportion of those who provide unpaid care, are women. The paid ones account for 16 percent of the female labour force. Women also account for the majority of patients and in some cases, like long-term care, account for more than 80 percent of the patients. Women are also a majority of the elderly poor, a majority of the poor in general, but especially those who are single-parent mothers. At the same time, women are almost half of the paid labour force, and when you get to some age groups, like the age group between 25 and 45, three-quarters of the women are in the paid workforce. Moreover, women are a minority of decision-makers, although they are not a minority of the critics of the way health care has been, or is now, delivered and organised. For any discussion of caring for women, this is the background and the starting point.

One of the things I want to talk about today is privatization by stealth, through a shift in paradigms and practices in health care. The other issue is the undermining of the public health care system that increasingly leads people to say that the only solution is the private one. It is hard to see, in part, because it is combined with promises to save health care and preserve the principles of the Canada Health Act. So what are the principles of the Canada Health Act? There are five of them: accessibility, universality, portability, public administration, and one that's increasingly hard to believe, comprehensiveness.

Today, new paradigms and practices are undermining women's possibilities for care, and to care. Now health care is about a reliance on a market. But, history tells us markets have never been kind to most women, especially to the most vulnerable women. John Kenneth Galbraith has said this notion of reliance on markets, is a notion of trickle down, that if you let the markets run, it's true some people will make a lot of money, but the benefits will trickle down to everyone. Galbraith's trickle down theory is very much like saying, "If you feed all the oats to the cows eventually some of it will reach the sparrows," or as a health care worker quipped, at a conference I attended at Harvard, "Don't pee on me and tell me its raining." The other issue I want to talk about is the form of privatization, that is shifting blame and responsibility to women.

At the same time, much of this reform is couched in feminist terms, and appeals to the critiques of current care practices that have a very feminist ring. As the Organisation for Economic Co-operation and Development (OECD) puts it, there has been "a perception that the public sector performance was inferior to that of the private sector," and growing, "citizen's demands for improved responsiveness, choice and quality of service." Many of the citizens making these demands are women.

Whatever the language of reform, and how authentic the promises to preserve the "sacred trust," as Brian Mulroney puts it, reforms have to be understood within an international and national paradigm — the kind of paradigm we heard about last night from Maude (Barlow). A paradigm that says the business of government is business and governments should act like businesses. This can mean even victories for women may, in practice, turn out to be losses.

Take for example the issue of reproductive rights. Rosalind Petchesky argues that the 1994 Programme of Action of the Cairo International Conference on Population and Development, "enshrines an almost feminist vision of reproductive rights and gender equality in place of the old population control discourses and retains a mainstream model of development under which that vision cannot possibly be realised."

Petchesky goes on to explain that the Programme represents the success of years of effort by women's groups, but it failed to address the real implication of privatization and even went so far as to make a commitment to increase privatization. Privatization is treated as the answer to the crisis in health care and especially the situation of women. In Petchesky's words:

> The Cairo document promotes the very privatization, commodification and deregulation of reproductive health services that, by its own admission, have led to diminished access and increasing mortality and morbidity for poor women who constitute "the most vulnerable groups" in both developing and developed countries.

Whatever the promises of health care reform, they may be undermined by efforts to support the market and, to quote a variety of government documents, "ensure that governments do not do what the private sector can do." Or, in the words of an American insurance executive, "the Canadian health care system is an unopened oyster, one that needs to be opened, so that it can be a source of profit."

Privatization and markets are being promoted not simply as the only choice—the global made me do it or the "TINA (There-Is-No-Alternative) Syndrome"—but also as the best choice. The assumption is that competition makes businesses more efficient and effective; promotes quality while reducing waste; increases choice; and, makes services more accountable, as well as more accessible.

Yet, in these times of commitment to evidence-based decision-making, indeed to evidence-based everything, it is perhaps surprising that there is little evidence to support these assumptions on which so much global and local change is based.

As John Ralston Saul has noted, the reforms to health care have taken the form of a religious crusade, with very little debate or evidence produced to support the claims. Let me briefly set out some of the evidence we do have, evidence that challenges the assumption that the private sector does all these wonderful things.

Access

The first issue I would like to address is the issue of access, so let's examine the evidence. New Zealand produced a two-tiered market system—on the basis of that religious crusade—in 1991. By 1997, waiting lists increased by 47 percent and public funding to hospitals alone had fallen by 13 percent.

Lately, I have been doing a lot of my research in the United States, because this is what our model is and this is where we are getting our practices from. They have a largely private system, yet the share of public spending as a proportion of the GDP is virtually the same as it is in Canada. For those public dollars, they only cover the very poor, the very old, the very disabled, and the military for some of their expenses.

According to the *Sunday New York Times* last week, there are 44 million Americans with no health care coverage at all, which is over 16 percent of the population. This represents a significant increase in the number of people without insurance over time, in the period of a famous economic boom in the United States. At the same time, individual insurance costs are going up and what gets covered by their insurance goes down. In the same *New York Times*, I found a cartoon that depicted two people begging on the street with signs. One sign said: "Need money to pay for an operation – no health insurance," while the other said: "Have health insurance, need money for an operation."

Recently, the United States federal government had to pass legislation requiring that when someone turns up at the emergency room, they have to be treated – they had to pass legislation to have this happen. But, the legislation does not guarantee patients will have access to care. The California nurses that we interviewed said that they, "Treat them and street them. Tylenol for your pain and off you go in a cab," or they close the emergency room completely in poor areas. The nurses also talked about how they spend a great deal of time trying to figure out how to get care for their patients. Understandably this process takes them a great deal of time and energy to accomplish. The nurses talked about whispering to patients, "Check yourself out of the hospital, come back into emergency and say you have a pain here," going on to describe the kind of pain that will make them eligible for admission.

Of course, undoubtedly, waiting times are increasing in Canada, although not as much as the Fraser Institute research claims. But I would argue, and I think I can back that up with evidence, that those waiting lists are best solved by a better public system, rather than by adding a second private one. Research by the Consumers Association in Alberta has shown that the longest waiting times were for those doctors who operated in both the public and private systems. The research also indicated that those people, who went to doctors operating in the public system alone, did not wait unreasonable times for cataract surgery, however, the cost went up significantly when a second private system was added. Women, of course, are the least likely to be able to afford that private system.

Selectivity, based on ability to pay, breeds contempt for public care and often leads to a second-class public system — we have seen this occur in countries where it has been happening. In such selections, women get relegated to the poor care in a public system. Access to health care has declined because we have cut support and introduced business practices adopted from the United States, in other words, a private system. We can change this by changing our practices, by changing the amount of money we put in. We do not have to go to a private system.

Similarly, user fees do not increase access and they do not reduce waiting times. What they do accomplish is to deter care for those people who cannot afford it and perhaps really need it, while not deterring at all, those people who have the money to pay for whatever they want.

Choice

The second issue to be addressed is that of choice. The question, quite simply is this: Does the private sector, as is claimed, offer more choice, even though it is a choice based on ability to pay?

Certainly feminists have been concerned about choice, the ability to seek out services that meet their specific and different needs, and have been critical of the way the public system responds to their needs. However, the fact remains our public system has allowed more choice, precisely because we are signed up to a provincial health care system, not to a single insurance company or single provider, and not as individuals the way it is done in the United States. Our choices are being reduced by cutbacks and by the reform practices that are based on a business model; they are not being reduced by the fact that we have a public system.

In the United States, choice has been dramatically curtailed by the new Health Maintenance Organizations (HMOs) way of organizing care, the new magic pill in the United States. The HMO system is the way the majority receive care, a type of 'one-stop shopping' for all health care services. But, as the *New York Times* puts it, it is a reform that "has been a top-down revolution that people never got to vote on." Americans continue to have very little choice in terms of what they can have covered and whether or not they can get care.

Recently, I was talking to a retired CEO from the United States, who was telling me what a wonderful system they have and how he had wonderful insurance after retirement. Then he went on to say, "Every month I'm afraid to open my mail, when I get mail from my insurance company or from my former employer because I'm afraid they've changed my coverage." The nurses also tell us that the HMOs change so often, and change so often what they cover, that they don't know the rules, but more importantly, their patients don't know what they have the right to.

In Canada, at least we have the choice of voting for those who manage this "top-down revolution," and in Ontario, of course, the "common sense revolution," and retain some possibility for stopping the erosion through public debate. Those with money in the United States do have choices, but very few have enough money for long term health care problems. Before Dr. Spock died, the man whose book sold next only to the Bible, his wife had to send out a letter asking for financial support from his friends because they'd run out of money to pay for his health care. As some California nurses told us, they see people trying to choose between having that cancer surgery for granny or sending the kids to college.

Efficiency and the Reduction of Waste

Third in my analysis, I want to challenge the notion that the for-profit sector is necessarily efficient and the notion that what works in the car plant can work in care provision. To this effect, I will offer three pieces of evidence, the first of which comes from England. When health services were contracted out, 20,000 more managers were hired—a number roughly equivalent to the number of nurses who were fired.

A second piece of evidence, on the inefficiency of applying business practices, comes from Ottawa. The compulsory contracting out of services, through the Community Care Access Centres (CCACs) in Ottawa, means that the region will pay $830,000 a year more for therapists and social workers than they did before the divestment and contracting out.

A third example, relating to efficiency and effectiveness, comes from the giant plants we are organizing as "mega hospitals with campuses." What is interesting to me about this type of organization is that we did it on the basis of a notion of business practices that a big factory produces more cheaply. Yet, big corporations are busy moving in the opposite direction, for example, the Benetton company does not have a factory. Technically, we are adopting *old* practices from the business sector. As of yet, there is no evidence that these giant hospitals are better: more efficient, have higher quality care, or reduce costs in any kind of way. In fact there is evidence emerging that this style of hospital achieves the exact opposite.

Moreover, there is proof emerging that women find it very difficult to travel to these giant hospitals, and even more difficult to find their way around them. Recently, we conducted an interview with a GP in Ontario who revealed that he is finding it very difficult to do any admissions to hospitals, in spite of the fact that we are supposed to have this new emphasis on primary care. If the GP's patients do get admitted to a hospital, the hospital is now so far away that he never sees his patients; moreover, he only receives $14 a visit—it costs him more to park and travel there.

The British Columbia nurses we have interviewed tell us that specialization does work in some areas, like eye surgery for instance. They say it makes sense to concentrate those high tech services for things like eye surgery that you plan ahead, you know is going to happen, and can be done on a short term basis. They also say it works in some cases like birthing centres, where you can provide the whole range of services. For example, a woman could start off seeking natural childbirth, but if that wasn't working, could go on to the most high tech facilities.

However, these mega hospitals are intended to be organised like production plants, specializing in specific parts to be fixed—an approach that increases the very medical model that feminists have been so critical of and rightly so, I would argue. As one nurse said, "You could be in the hospital having a hip done and you might end up having a heart attack, but it takes 45 minutes to get to the hospital that does that."

Similarly, the business practices seek to reduce women's care work time, by speeding up the work and by hiring more women on a casual basis, thus disrupting continuity of care. Now, less than half the nurses in this province are employed full-time, which has an impact not only on the care providers, but also on their patients. The nurses have "No time to care," they tell us, "No time to teach or to even do the necessary tasks." As one BC nurse said to us:

> They don't want us to spend time with the patients anymore. And I don't mean just time talking. I mean time changing a dressing that really should be changed. Yes, it could probably wait for another four hours but its mucky and its really

uncomfortable for the patient and it should be changed.

In Ottawa over Christmas, the for-profit company that took over home care only hired nurses on a casual basis and the nurses said: "We don't do Christmas." This is the only power you have as a casual employee, so the company could not provide the care. The company was forced to go to the Victorian Order of Nurses, that still exists in Ottawa and does hire people full-time, to fulfill their obligations to patient care.

Before I move onto quality and accountability, let me say a brief word about waste. We are told these new business practices will reduce waste, that all we are doing is getting rid of the waste in the system. But in a for-profit system, there is an excessive amount of waste. There is money wasted on profits that could go to care, and there is money wasted on advertising products and services to increase their use. Yesterday, I was watching television and I saw an ad for MRIs. The ad depicted a mother worried about her kid having something wrong with her ankle, and how you can come to the States and get an MRI. However, there are hardly any cases where you should have an MRI for an ankle injury. But the purpose of the advertising is to create health anxiety, which it efficiently does. You think to yourself "Oh my, I'm not properly looking after my child – I didn't get them an MRI."

Beyond the wasted services, wasted by those who believe the ads, there is wasted money on extremely high executive salaries in the millions of millions of dollars, and wasted money on duplicated services that are necessary to competition. You cannot have competition without duplication. Waste of this kind leaves less money to pay women to provide care and less money for care provision.

Quality and Accountability

Finally, in terms of privatization through the market, let me look at quality and accountability. There is very little evidence that quality in a private system is better. Certainly, the mainly private system of the United States has more technology, but what this means for care quality is unclear. For instance, in the United States you might have an MRI on every corner, but the question remains: Does it make a difference to health?

OECD data for 1989 indicates that the incidence of abnormal reactions and misadventures during medical care in Canada was half that of the United States. A more recent comparison of surgery outcomes in Western Manitoba and an US Eastern Seaboard state indicated that in 9 out of 10 procedures, Canadians had better long-term survival rates, and better maternal mortality, infant mortality and women's longevity rates than in the United States. According to a California nurse we interviewed:

> In their system every patient is neglected. That's the irony. And that's what most of our legislators don't understand — most people in general — is that when it gets to the level of the nurse in the hospital, the person who is taking care of the patient 24 hours a day — our neglect is not selective. Everybody gets neglected.

Most of those neglected are women.

Certainly, women in Canada have been critical of the quality of care they receive, but there is little evidence that they would fare better in a private system; that either quality or survival rates would be better if we went for a two-tiered system, or an all private system. Women have also sought to make care providers more accountable, more responsive and the new practices promise to do that. However, in business terms accountability is mainly about counting.

A study by the Prairie Research Centre of Excellence on Women's Health, about to come out, shows that counting is precisely what accountability means, in the regional health authorities throughout Manitoba and Saskatchewan. "If you can't measure it, you can't manage it," is the rallying cry in management circles. The new systems seek to measure and manage everything from the time it takes to clean a bed to the time it takes to heal from hip replacement. Under this system, these measurements can be used to manage both patients and providers.

Once again, feminists have supported the collection of evidence and have used such counts to show, for example, that there are enormous variations in caesarian rates, perhaps indicating that they are wrongly used. However, feminists have not supported the translation of these data into formulas for care. A midwife told me recently that at the same time as she is saying to a patient, "Don`t feel badly about having a caesarian, don't feel badly at all," she is saying to herself, "Oh my God, there go my numbers. I can't have more than 15 percent caesarian." These rates can be important to know, and can be important in terms of questioning whether you should do it or not, but they can also limit care.

I recently read an interview done with a nurse responsible for implementing a new care pathway for hip replacement. The span of time they indicate that a hip replacement should take is five days and so she told the nurses on staff that this was the care pathway that you had to follow to get patients out in five days. Two weeks later, after she had explained all this, they were still seeing patients staying longer than five days. She said the nurses simply did not understand that the answer was now five. The numbers become answers rather than guides, and a means of control, rather than evidence on which decisions are based.

Now I don't think we have gone nearly down that road here in Canada, as they have in the United States. Yet, I was equally amused at this woman implementing care pathways who said that they had bought the computer program software from United States and had customized it—they had the name of their institution throughout.

In using these programs, there is no time for the nurses to exercise their skill and judgement based on individual patient needs, and there is no diversity of care to reflect the diversity of the patients. This is the direction in which we are moving. Indeed, you may have 'one-stop shopping', which is what I hear all the time, but there is only one size left in the shop and I keep feeling that my body doesn't fit the formula. Let me read to you briefly from one of the California nurses interviews in which this new managerial practice is commented upon:

> I come into work today after being off one day and there are five new pieces of paperwork on my patient's chart. I had eight pieces of paperwork to fill out on that patient that I was getting ready for surgery, five of which were new, and they were telling me I should be able to get three patients ready in the course of an hour and that is without a clerk. I got to put the charts together, do a full assessment, fill out eight pages of paperwork, start IVs, put on compression stockings, answer the telephone (because they only have a unit assistant) and some mornings I come into no beds clean and I have to clean those beds and in an hour do all that. If the patients aren't ready then they are writing me up because the patients were late for surgery. You are just frantic and you cut corners wherever you have to and you are praying that you are not going to overlook something either something you've missed or that you've done a thorough assessment. You never feel good you know. There is always something not done. You live

in fear.

Similarly, the measurement of cleaning is intended to be used to constantly reduce the time needed to clean, primarily through control over the cleaners. The result, women tell us, is that the "dust bunnies" have become "dust cougars" and there is "blood on the rails" in the emergency room.

Food and cleaning services, contrary to what the literature on health determinants tells us and contrary to the way the women who do that work in health care define themselves, are increasingly being called "hotel services," to indicate that this has nothing to do with health. The determinants of health literature tell us that food and a clean environment are an essential part of health care, after all Florence Nightingale's big contribution to the health profession was cleaning up the hospital, opening windows and giving people good food. Indeed, a friend gave me a story from the *National Post*, about how a hospital in Toronto is sending their volunteers to a hotel to get training.

The emphasis on numerical measures often denies women's experiences, whether they are patients or providers. Moreover, this stress ignores a central claim in feminist approaches, that experience is expertise, and it provides no way to count care. Furthermore, it also denies another tenet of feminism, namely that difference and location matter.

When it comes to markets then, the most vulnerable suffer more and most of these vulnerable are women: particularly, women with disabilities, women who are very poor, Aboriginal women, and women in rural areas. Also, there is little evidence that there is any widely shared gains in terms of quality and accountability; reduced waste and greater efficiency; and, more choice and access for providers and patients.

Let me turn briefly to the second area I wanted to talk about—the privatization of responsibility and blame. Today, we are shifting responsibility for health care provision to patients and to unpaid care providers. Now some elements of this shift may be good, I want to say that about all of these reforms, and reinforce that point.

However, within hospitals, we have redefined what hospital care means for patients. Patient care now is equated with a nano-second of care, or what the California nurses called "drive-by surgery." Anyone else is a bed-blocker, an abuser of the system. Most of these bed-blockers and abusers are women, and the accusation is made without any accompanying provision of good, alternative care services.

Moreover, this redefinition of care defines the patient out from under the protection of the Canada Health Act. The Canada Health Act, remember, applies more clearly to doctors and hospitals, as soon as you move out that door, you move out of that protection for the most part.

At the same time, we are also building up a hysteria around aging. We experienced "deficit dementia," an induced illness a number of years ago, which we seem to have cured. It has now been replaced by fear of seniors, most of whom are women, senior women who will overload the health care system. According to pundits, these greying heads will put so much pressure on our services that we have to cut back now so we can provide care in the future, or we have to go to a private system so that we can provide care for the future. But let me provide for you three kinds of evidence to suggest that we cannot blame it on the elderly women.

First, when baby boomers become seniors it is estimated that the proportion of the population that is aged will be 16 percent. This is the same level currently experienced in Sweden and Germany for example, and they don't have a healthcare crisis.

Second, many of these baby boomers are well-educated, fit and relatively rich — all factors that lead to good health in old age. If we are really concerned about the cost of caring for the elderly, what we should be doing is caring for the young. We should make sure that this young generation grows up to be healthy in their old age. What we are doing instead, I think, is the reverse, evidenced by the fact that social programs for the young and pensions for those who are still in their twenties and thirties and all those kinds of supports are disappearing. So in the future, we are going to see an increase in costs, induced not by growing old, but by the reduction in our social support.

Third, the real issue is how we treat the elderly, rather than whether they are old and expensive. As Barer points out, "the medicalization of elderly women is not a necessary fate nor tis their high cost." If we really want to address that cost, then we should do something about pharmaceutical prices and pharmaceutical prescriptions. In short, women are being wrongly held responsible for current or future health costs, and for the need to make the kinds of reforms we see now.

But women are also being blamed on another level: for failing to take care of those bed-blockers, those abusers of the system, those people who don't belong in institutional care. The movement of care "close to home" is closer to unpaid care, mainly performed by women. While the phrase "closer to home" is from British Columbia, my example about this phenomenon comes from Ontario.

According to the January 1999 Ontario Health Coalition Fact Sheet, the "underfunding of in-home services is forcing providers to ration the services for which no fee is charged." Even though the Community Care Access Centres (CCACs) reported a $34 million deficit in 1997/98, the CCACs were, even with that deficit, following Government guidelines setting "a maximum of 4 nursing visits per day and 80 hours of homemaking per month, for the first month, and 60 hours of homemaking per month thereafter" — whatever your health problems. The Ontario Ministry of Health guidelines for 1998 on long-term care, also states that to be eligible for public services, namely home care, people must have first exhausted — *exhausted* — the care giving and support capacities of their friends, relatives and other community services. For example, the Brant, Ontario CCAC guide states that "individuals who have a capable caregiver are not eligible for home support services. This includes caregivers who work outside the home." Needless to say, women are the most likely to be classified as capable caregivers.

The implication is that women are not now doing their share, or as much as they could, in spite of the evidence indicating that most of the disabled and frail elderly are being looked after at home, mainly by women. Not only do women take a much greater part of the unpaid care workload, but recent research by Jay and Avison indicates that women are more affected than men by events occurring to their significant others, suggesting that they bear more of the psychological costs as well.

Conclusion

In conclusion I would like to put the following questions forward for consideration: What exactly are our choices? What are our alternatives here?

I'm reminded of a story Marshall MacLuhan used to tell about a diver. This diver was sent off a ship in the middle of an ocean to go diving. When the diver reached the end of the line, the diver got a message saying, "Surface immediately. Ship sinking."

Well, I don't think those are our choices. I don't think our choice is the old system of which we have been very critical, or a private one, or a two-tiered one, nor do I think nothing can be done. Indeed I think that we have had some successes. The introduction of funded midwifery in Ontario is, for instance, an example of how change can happen within the system. But there are more ways forward.

One of the things that I think we need to do is demand the evidence before the change happens: demand that the research and the exploration happen before we go for these single solution plans that have such massive cost, like single mega hospitals. This research must be sound research, rather than research based on assumptions that have long been held, the research must be long-term, and very importantly, it must be gender based.

The Prairie Research Centre Study I referred to earlier, surveyed the regional health authorities in Saskatchewan and Manitoba and found that some of them didn't even segregate data by sex, let alone do research on gender. Women's health service was defined as "boobs and babies and unpaid care," period. We have to make sure that the evidence is much, much more than that. Moreover, we have to recognize in doing research that all bodies and all research is social located, reflects and enforces values.

Second I think we should at the very minimum, make privatization a question rather than the answer. Today it is being offered as the only answer.

Third, I think that we should demand multiple strategies rather than single solutions or simple dichotomies like the assumption that homes are havens in a heartless world for everyone. We have to be able to respond to individual needs and we have to recognize difference, which means leaving more choice for both patients and providers.

Fourth of my five, is that we need to apply what we know about the determinants of health to care provision, to the institutions, to the people who work in the institutions, and to the people who provide care in homes. Recently, I saw some research, done by a student at the University of Toronto, on the health impact in the home of sending all this care home. You know how I said a few minutes ago, that the most important thing that Florence Nightingale did was clean up the hospital? Think about where we are sending people with all these tubes, and open wounds and bandages. What is that environment like? And what happens to that stuff?

In the hospital, as anyone who works in a hospital knows, you have to very carefully treat all this stuff. Do you know what happens to it in the home? You don't wear gloves and you throw it in the garbage and it goes out in the street—that's where it goes. In fact, when this student decided to look in Ottawa to find out about what happens to needles, she was told "Well several drug stores will take your old needles." So she said "Can I have a list?" To which they responded, "Well, we don't have a list. But you can ask individual drug stores if they would take those needles." This is just talking about needles, not bandages etc. So we have to think of the determinants of health in terms of where care is provided.

Fifth, we know that health is about food, shelter, jobs, joy, social support and social security. We need to apply that to the providers of care, not just outside the health care system. Health care is not simply another determinant of health, the determinants of health apply within and we have to demand that this be recognized.

Finally, Maude was talking yesterday about a home care issue, a topic in which I've been extremely frustrated. The National Forum on Health Care Conference stated that its time for a public plan for home care in Canada, a home care act based on the principles of the Canada Health Act. If we are going to move care closer to home, and move it out of the hospital, where the Canada Health Act applies, it is essential that we have a new act which applies to this other area.

As far as I can determine, this is a dead issue at the national level and I think we need to revive it. One idea I had was to demand a Royal Commission on home care. I don't know whether that is the appropriate strategy, but it is something I would like to be able to talk to people about as a strategy of bringing attention to what I think has been a crisis issue, and definitely a women's issue.

Often I feel, when I do this research on health care, like it's a silent war on women. Is it intended? I don't know, and frankly I don't care. But I keep thinking about what the Supreme Court of Canada has said about discrimination, namely that it doesn't matter if you intended to discriminate, it is the result that counts. The result of what they are doing in health care, both in terms of reducing the amount of money and shaping reforms according to for-profit business practices, and even handing it over to the for-profit sector, is harmful for women and I think we have lots of evidence that indicates that this is the case. So my final word on that comes from an old feminist line which is "Don't go mad . . . get angry."

Thank you.

Women's Organizing in a Climate of Cutbacks

Joan Grant Cummings

CRIAW Conference Keynote Address:
Sunday October 17, 1999

T hanks very much. Actually, I want to start out by sharing with you one of the many quotes that I use to give myself sustenance while I do this work. This quote is from Frances Harper, a self-described black abolitionist feminist, and is taken from a work that Harper wrote, about one hundred years ago, that speaks to state responsibility. Harper's point was that what women were fighting for, blacks were fighting for, and so on, directly linked up with state responsibility. Harper believed that we cannot let the state off the hook stating:

> A government which can protect and defend its citizens from wrong and outrage and does not is vicious. A government which will do it and cannot is weak. And where human rights are insecure through either weakness or viciousness in the administration of the law there must be a lack of justice. And where there is wanting, nothing can make up the deficiency but the rising of the people.

These words speak to where we are right now, today.

I also want to go back to our history as feminists in this country, because I think, on occasion, that we, ourselves do not understand the value of our feminist history. A very disquieting feeling is revealed when you go across the country and speak in universities, colleges and high schools. It is there you see how feminists are conscientiously being written out of the history of Canada; how feminism is being undermined and devalued and how that relates to the way young women see feminists; how the majority of the women in the middle class see feminists; and, how the media sees feminists. Sometimes we forget what a wonderful thing feminism is, and that it is a revolution we have put in place.

The Women's Movement in Canada

Thirty years ago, when most feminists historians will say the second wave started, we started out with a process. There was a Royal Commission on the Status of Women and we outlined our agenda, in which we talked about critical mass mobilization. We wanted to have at least 50 percent representation in federal, provincial and municipal level politics. We wanted to eradicate violence against women. We wanted pay equity. We wanted employment equity. We wanted not just public services, but *well-funded* public services, because we understood this as an affirmative, equality-seeking measure. We wanted to have a fully funded public health system, another equality-seeking measure. We wanted to have a National Day Care Program, a major affirmative, equality- seeking measure that we still need to have in our country.

The Commission came out with four pillars that they said had to be observed if women's equality was even going to be dealt with in Canada. The first pillar was the need for a Ministry, not a Department, a Ministry, responsible for the status of women. We needed to have a Minister, not a Secretary of State, a Minister.

Secondly, we needed to have a Women's Program Fund set up, not to provide services or education, but to do political organising. This fund was to be in place for grassroots women's organisations to have access to state resources to do political organising. So we should not apologize for accessing state funding for political organising, because the state has already recognized how they undermine our lives by not having resources accessible to us, to impact public policy.

The third pillar was the organization of an independent national lobby group. The National Action Committee on the Status of Women (NAC) was organized to do that, to act on the behalf of women's groups and women in Canada.

Finally, the fourth pillar was that we needed to have a research, monetary and evaluation body, so the government set up The Canadian Advisory Council on the Status of Women to accomplish these goals. However, the Council was dismantled in 1995, the same year we went to Beijing and the same year, our government told Hilary Clinton about the Council. The Council was adopted in the United States as their way of tracking their response to Bejing +5, while Canada no longer has any comparable body to track our government's record on Bejing.

When you look at the four pillars in today's context, what you notice first are the deficiencies. The Canadian Advisory Council is gone and we do not have the Women's Program Fund. NAC and other women's groups are under attack, consistently being defunded and marginalised. We have a Secretary of State, not a Women's Ministry, and we have a junior cabinet person, called a Secretary of State, not a Minister.

So, women are working in their communities, rejecting the crap that the State tells them, rejecting what companies are telling them should be the way; and are finding other mechanisms and alternatives within the economy in terms of how they teach their children all of these things. But it takes time and we do not have easy answers, because they are no easy answers. As Maude Barlow said yesterday, "we are fighting the gap but we are wearing Gap shorts," there is a lot of ambiguity about our fight.

As a movement, we have to understand what our goal is because I think this goal is what will end up impacting how we make the decisions. We need to understand as well, that regardless of who we have leading our movement, there is a particular goal that women need to support. We have to do that—we cannot decide that we are sick and tired and that's it. As Fanny Lou Hamer said, "I'm sick and tired of being sick and tired."

When I get tired, I remember to ask: If Hamer had said that she was going to sit down and die and not get up the next day—where the hell would I be? This is the only way to see it, because each of us, each generation, has a responsibility to advance the struggle. For our generation, the questions surrounding our movement are: How do we make our struggle anti-racist? How do we make it anti-ablest? How do we make it anti-agest? How do we create the most cohesive force? How do we ensure that lesbians and trans-gendered people are integral to the struggle? For it is our mobilisation, as a critical mass, that is going to create the movement against what the other side is doing.

I have to call some of you to get travel points to see Paul Martin, to give him our agenda, while the Business Council on National Issues has their plane waiting at Pearson International Airport, at any given moment in time. Sir Thomas Aquinas has an appointment with the Finance Minister at the drop of a hat. These are the kinds of resources that we are dealing with, in terms of this struggle. Accordingly, I can have the most progressive analysis, I can have the best research at my disposal, but if I cannot get it out and if it is not being heard, it may never go anywhere. This is where we need to have our forces mobilised.

When we talk about 30 years ago, we talk about a specific agenda. Where we are today, in terms of that agenda, indicates that in some places we are actually regressing rather than progressing. We are regressing in the area of violence, we are regressing in the economy, and we certainly are in terms of where women are now being placed. The whole issue of how we mobilise forward is of paramount importance to pick up the agenda again. Women's groups have not been sitting back on their hands. We have women's groups, shame of all shame, where executive directors are working unpaid, and women's groups that have had to take operations into their own homes; or, we have women's groups who have decided that they cannot do without corporate help, and have ended up setting aside their agenda just to have corporate sponsorship, to do pieces of the work, and found out how it impacts them. There is this whole turmoil going on amongst us.

Furthermore, many of us are letting the state off the hook by default, because we feel to raise a clamour about the funding means that we are saying we are victims and we are helpless. This is exactly what the state likes to hear, because it lets them off the hook. When the Reform party talks about taxpayers—do you think you are not a taxpayer? Why shouldn't women's groups be supported by your taxes? Tax support is, in some cases, the only political representation that some women have. When women's shelters have to close and you have, in Ontario alone, 66 percent of women polled saying, "I'd rather stay in this abusive relationship because there isn't a women's shelter in my community and I do not want myself and my children to live in poverty," what exactly are we condemning women to? A state responsibility is to eradicate violence against women, beyond being a women's issue, it is a human rights issue.

Issues for Tomorrow

There is a lot of work to be done. One of the ways in which we can accomplish this is, of course, by combining our forces. I know, for sure, that amongst national women's groups, networks and coalitions, are mechanisms that we have increasingly turned to in our organising. This manner of organising has tensions as well. NAC for example, has always been seen as the big bad bull group, and the group that grab the most media, even though we are all members of NAC. But, I think we have reached a point now where we recognize that all of us have different pieces of the strength to add to the movement, and we have to apply that in one place to have any kind of impact. We have to deal with the game that the government plays with us around co-optation — I'll fund you to do this, I won't fund them to do it — that set up a tension. Another co-opting game is evident in the scenario where the government funds an individual feminist researcher this money to do something that another women's group had asked for ten years ago.

So there are all kinds of coopting games being played. I was really horrified to read the government's response to the Bejing Platform, in terms of what it is they claim that they have done in the last five years. Guess what they have done? They have used feminist researchers' papers to validate their stance of how they have complied with the Bejing Platform for Action. So, I look at the names of feminist researchers who are named in this response, and I think, oh my God! If you are reading that as a woman from another country, what you think is that the Canadian government is progressive by having feminists do this research on their behalf.

But nothing has come out of the research papers. Nothing has come out of those papers that clearly said that within the economy, within foreign policy, within the environment, these are supposed to be the policies. There has been no action on the papers, but there they are, sitting in the government's response, as action that has happened after Bejing +5. So we are in quite a dilemma over how we are seen around the world.

However, the Canadian women's movement has as a strength that I do not see internationally, that international women's groups tell us about, in how we see our democratic movement forming. When we formed our national women's organizations, we came up with a kind of a blueprint of how it should be done. In this plan, the executives would be elected, there would be representatives from provinces and territories and later, with all the struggles about inclusion, we would have to be representative in particular groups of women. Additionally, the blueprint included an annual general meeting, or a meeting to hash out our agenda, by debate, by resolution, and so on. Another national structure of a women's movement does not exist globally. While you have women who have strong provincial or strong local networks, there is not another country where you have an actual national group that actually endeavours to act so that rural women are involved.

Many women's groups say to us, if we could employ that kind of system globally, it would really create a mass global feminist movement.

On some levels, we are seeing this kind of organising in the Women's World March. The greatest difficulty in planning is that many women, many communities of women in different countries, will never get the information because the national groups are located in the urban centres. It is only if someone from the country's national group happens to travel out, or have connections out, that the women will hear about the event. In Canada, we have a structure that we can actually support and enhance in our movement towards how we democratise our movement. Grassroots mobilising is important for us to do, because we have a way of doing it, and we need to apply it. In some cases, we have forgotten just how to apply it.

So we see the march against poverty and violence as an organising tool as well, because it is a way to get women back in touch with the movement. We are becoming disconnected from the movement. We are starting to act in silos. There is a whole wealth of information within the academy, within the community, that is not coming together in the way that it should. There is a whole host of things being researched that are not starting out, from the beginning, framed in the way they should. What we are missing is the fact that women in the community have come up with alternative strategies to some of this stuff, which is not informing our research and is not informing our solutions.

Even if Status of Women Canada asks us to do a research document, how we do that research, and who we connect with, could be very, very different. In some ways, the research could actually come with more power, because it has that grassroots alternatives inculcated into the paper, or into the research model, and in terms of the strategy. There is so much power here in Canada, because we have so many grassroots women's organisations. If we could bring that power together, it would really push us forward and we would feel more connected to, not so isolated and alienated from, the thing that is the women's movement.

As well, we have to think of a conscious way of making sure feminist history is heard—we just have to. When Environics and Angus and all the polls taken say that the largest group of people who see themselves as feminist are women over 45, this is a real, real problem. For some reason, there is a group of women in that range under 25 who also see themselves as feminists, but in the 25 to 45 age ranges, it is only 3 or 4 percent of the group. So there is something seriously, seriously wrong there that we need to fix in terms of how as women we see ourselves.

When we are fighting the fight, around cuts to public services, we need to really frame our arguments from a perspective of health and equality. All through this conference we have asked the question: What is it that makes women healthy? Beside food, water and shelter, access to services, which must be publicly funded, is essential for women's health. The provision of services is a state responsibility that advances women's equality. Affirmative action, pay equity and employment equity should not be dirty words in a feminist book. They should only become dirty words when they are applied in a way that keeps out the most vulnerable of women — that is when we should react, and say, "Our system is not working — it needs to be improved."

These terms need to come back into our vocabulary. We should always remember, as activists, that everything we have won, we need to win three or four times over. None of this was given to us. We did not 'get' medicare, we had to fight for it; the little day care we had, we had to fight for; and, we had to fight for the Women's Programs Fund. These are our state`s responsibility. They are our entitlement, they are not charity, they are our entitlement.

If there is one lesson that, I think, I can say I have learned from young women, it is their strong sense of entitlement. Now it is our role to shape that entitlement within a feminist perspective. To decide to stay in a relationship where you are beaten is not a choice. The definition choice has to be framed within an equality perspective, instead of the debate we always end up having, regarding the definition of choice — because you people, meaning feminists, told us we had choices, I can choose to stay, this is my choice.

The whole issue of child care and mothers who stay at home, and women who are mothers and work in the work force, is another sticky area that we have never quite resolved as a movement. Indeed, we are as ambiguous as the government about the issue. We have to be very, very clear in our position. If we are going to value women's unpaid work, value motherhood, we should not feel or say, "Oh my God why would you want to do that? The work force is a lot better." If a mother decides that she is going to stay home and raise her children for 18 years, we should recognize that this a strong statement about valuing that role of parenting. Moreover, what we should examine is the question: What is the state's responsibility in terms of recognising women's unpaid work? Our government was one of those who said that the recognition of unpaid work should be a top priority in women's fight for equality. This issue should be included in public policy around pensions, day care, public education, public health and we have said it should be included in tax law. So that women who do stay at home up to 18 years, do not end up being automatically poor women when they are older women, because of pension laws and the fact that there are no guaranteed income or old age security because they were 'just' a mother or a homemaker.

This is where the focus should be: What is the state doing to recognize this piece of work? Most of us who decide to go back into the work force, after the birth or adoption of our children, say that we want at least two years before we go back. The question of what happens during this two-year period, in terms of our access to pension, public services, and so on, need to be addressed. Therefore, the National Child Care Strategy is essential to all of us, whether or not we are in the work force. Moreover, it has to be a whole composite of services that we demand from our government. We should clearly, clearly say we will not support capitalism if all we're doing is just being breeders for transnational and multinational corporations – this is not a reason to support capitalism.

So the questions that must be asked are: Where are we in the capitalist system? And, Who is getting the benefits from this? So far, the only benefactors are the Trans-National Corporations that roam the globe, pillaging here, raping forests there. We should reject this system and we should be very, very clear about it. Yes, we may be participating in the system but we're also fighting to revolutionise it; we are not talking reform, we are talking revolution.

Conclusion

I want to end today's talk with one of my other favourite quotes, which speaks to women`s courage. But, before I do that I want to address another issue and share another quotation. I know a lot of people are talking about how tired we are, tired of the struggle. Back in 1955, Rosa Parks said that, "Even if we don`t have the alternative, the fact is, it`s better to protest than to accept injustice;" moreover, she repeated these same words just this year.

Finally, this is a quote from Toni Cade Bambara, in which she

talked about women as feminists — black feminists, and all feminists.
Bambara stated:

> We have rarely been encouraged and equipped to appreciate
> the fact that the truth works — that it releases the spirit and that
> it is a joyous thing. We live in a part of the world, for example
> that equates criticism with assault, that equates social
> responsibility with naive idealism, that defines the unrelenting
> pursuit of knowledge and wisdom as fanatism.

Thank you very much.

Government Cutbacks
and Restraints

Home Care and its Impact on Women's Vulnerability to Poverty

Marika Morris
Ottawa, Ontario

Abstract

This paper is an overview of CRIAW's research on the effects of home care on women, published by the Status of Women Canada in December 1999. The research was based on the fact that governments do not engage in a gender analysis of the home care system, yet women comprise the majority of home care recipients, paid workers and unpaid caregivers. Interviews of all three groups, as well as of home care agencies were conducted in St. John's, Newfoundland and Winnipeg, Manitoba. Policy developers and national organizations concerned with home care were also canvassed. The research concludes that the design of home care programs has a negative impact on women and presents a series of recommendations for change.

Introduction

The study entitled *The Changing Nature of Home Care and its Impact on Women's Vulnerability to Poverty*[1] finds that current home care policies and practices have a negative financial impact on women, who make up the majority of home care users, paid workers and unpaid caregivers. The researchers interviewed home care recipients, paid workers, unpaid caregivers, managers in public and private home care agencies, regional health officials in Winnipeg, Manitoba and St. John's, Newfoundland, as well as people with expertise in home care policy issues from across Canada. Despite the different systems of the two primary provinces of study, the results were similar concerning the impact of home care on women. The following is a summary and brief analysis of the results of the study presented at the CRIAW Conference in Sudbury.

Summary of Findings

Women make up the majority of the poor in Canada. A Statistics Canada study found that the primary factor in the income gap between women and men is not education, age or marital status, but the presence of children. Women are expected to reduce or eliminate hours of paid work, often resulting in reduced or eliminated pension accumulation, benefits and advancement opportunities, in order to provide care. The same expectation holds for care of ill, disabled or senior family members. Men are not expected to quit their jobs to provide care for relatives.

The study finds that current home care policies and practices, instead of being viewed as an integral part of an accessible, publicly-funded health system, rely on women's unpaid work, personal sacrifices and financial contributions in order to function. Among other things, the study found evidence that some paid home care workers were downsized hospital employees who had well-paid, unionized jobs and are now providing the same services in homes for lower wages. Many are subsidizing their own work by paying their transportation to the homes, by providing necessary care which is not covered under the limited hours of publicly-funded home care and by buying food out of their pockets for poor clients. The study also documents the fact that some home care workers are unqualified to do the work expected of them. Furthermore, a comparison of wages paid in various agencies clearly shows that wages are highest in not-for-profit, unionized agencies and lowest in private agencies, particularly with no unions. Low wages, irregular hours, inadequate training and high turnover of home care workers result in lack of continuity of care, staff shortages, waiting lists, health risks to both workers and recipients and impoverishment. Some home care workers had to work several jobs to make ends meet while others were living below the poverty line.

In order to make up for inadequate hours of public care, informal family caregivers give up jobs or full-time hours, promotions, opportunities and pension benefits; decisions which have a lifelong financial impact. Unpaid caregivers are not always aware of respite care, feel too guilty to use it, or simply cannot afford it. Recipients of home care (the majority of whom are also women), subsidize the system at their own cost, by paying for medical and other services not covered by public insurance, which would otherwise be covered in an institutional setting; or may go hours without the care they need.

Inadequate income support programs keep unattached women over 65 and women with disabilities in poverty. Almost half (49%) of single, divorced and widowed women over 65 are living below the poverty line. The average income of women with disabilities under 35(those that have any income at all) and are living in a home setting, was $13 000. These women represent the two largest user groups of home care and the least likely to be able to afford to supplement inadequate care hours with private care and to pick up uninsured costs. Some of these women are in their current financial situation because they themselves had been unpaid caregivers to spouses who have since died.

Other issues discussed in the study included:

- **Isolation** of women in private homes made it more difficult for paid workers to get to know each other, exchange knowledge, benefit from a colleague's experience or expertise, or unionize. Isolation frequently results in depression for unpaid caregivers, particularly those who are the only adult in the household caring for a relative or friend with Alzheimer disease. Isolation of home care recipients, some of whom report that seeing the home care worker is the only social contact in their life, is debilitating. This is especially relevant given the fact that social support is one of the determinants of health. Furthermore, the isolation of women as recipients, informal caregivers and paid workers obscures the gender imbalance. These women may feel they are alone in their situations instead of as part of a systemic problem that relegates women to low or no wages for caregiving work and financial insecurity in old age. This isolation impedes them from organizing together to pressure policy-makers for change.

- The recipients, paid workers and unpaid caregivers interviewed had health and human rights concerns. Some caregivers were subjected to **violence or harassment** by recipients, particularly those living with mental illness. Some recipients reported financial abuse, robbery and harassment by paid and unpaid caregivers; and all groups reported physical safety concerns due to the overwork and inadequate training of both paid and unpaid caregivers.

- Services were not culturally sensitive, leading to under-use of services among urban Aboriginal peoples and some ethnic, racial and linguistic minority communities. Women in these communities frequently *are* the home care system. Both home care recipients and caregivers experienced **racism**, such as the case of a disabled w,oman of colour being told by a worker, "as an immigrant you should be grateful that you are here and for the services you receive". In the course of our study, no agencies which offered anti-racism training or had harassment policies were uncovered.

- Other forms of discrimination, included **stigma** associated with certain diseases and conditions; such as HIV/AIDS, socioeconomic status and sexual orientation. Some women workers were treated as servants, or referred to as "the cleaning lady" or "the girl".

- Home care has up to now, not been taken into account in the transfer of health services from the Medical Services Branch at Health Canada to some **First Nations** Bands. Those who have agreements which do not include home care funds cannot now obtain those funds; leaving some communities with no resources for home care.

Home care is an important part of a comprehensive health care system. Although provincial governments have increased funding for home care, the increases have not come close to meeting the demand. The need for home care will increase with the rapid aging of the population, the tendency toward shorter hospital stays and pharmaceutical rather than surgical treatments. Access to home care depends on where you live in Canada. Overall, there is poor (or no) service in rural areas. Moreover, access to publicly funded service also depends on what province one lives in, eligibility requirements and maximum hours of service. Whether or not and how much the recipient is required to pay varies from province to province.

Conclusion and Recommendations

The study concludes that equality for women cannot be achieved by impoverishing women through an underfunded system that relies on women's unpaid work. Some of the study's key recommendations include:

- Provide the provinces and territories with ongoing funds for home care at levels significant enough to ensure access and cover psychiatric/psychological services, drug costs (pharmacare) and other currently privatized costs essential to the health and well-being of elderly, disabled, chronically ill and recovering persons;

- Restore full rather than partial funding for health care services;

- Work to develop a Canada Home and Community Care Act based on the principles of the *Canada Health Act*, ensuring accessibility, portability, universality, comprehensiveness and public administration. Other principles of the act should include access to coordinated, appropriate, publicly accountable and culturally sensitive services;

- Establish a national inquiry into wages and working conditions of home care workers and unpaid caregivers; which will among other topics, explore the issue of remuneration for caregivers;

- Review income/tax programs and policies to alleviate poverty using a gender analysis;

- Eliminate fees for service where they exist, as these affect poorer people most, the majority of whom are women;

- Establish or facilitate provincial professional associations for home care workers for the purposes of accreditation, training, ongoing skill and career development, provision of information regarding employer and employee rights and responsibilities, and negotiation of wages, benefits and working conditions;

- Review and streamline the assessment process with a view to eliminating gender bias and ensuring recipients get all the care they need;

- Require any public or private agency receiving public funds for home care to be transparent and accountable to the public;

- Invest in respite care for unpaid caregivers with no user fees. Ensure caregivers are aware of services available and how they can benefit themselves and ultimately, the recipient of care;

- Implement the recommendations of the Masuda Report[2] on women with disabilities; and finally,

- Develop quality standards for home care where they do not already exist. Audit and evaluate home care programs and agencies to ensure standards are being met with real consequences for agencies which do not comply.

Endnotes

1. The full title of the study is *The Changing Nature of Home Care and its Impact on Women's Vulnerability to Poverty* and will be hereafter noted as simply "the study". The work was completed by Marika Morris, Jane Robinson, Janet Simpson, with Sherry Galey, Sandra Kirby, Lise Martin, Martha Muzychka, for the Canadian Research Institute for the Advancement of Women (CRIAW) and published by Status of Women Canada Policy Research Fund in November 1999. The paper is available from the Status of Women website, or for a hardcopy send e-mail to research@swc-cfc.gc.ca or write to: Research Directorate, Status of Women Canada, 350 Albert Street, 5th floor, Ottawa K1A 1C3.

2. Masuda, Shirley. (March 1998) The impact of block funding on women with disabilities. *Status of Women Canada Publications*. Available: http://www.swc-cfc.gc.ca/publish/research/bfdis-e.html. (September 12, 2000)

References

Morris, M., Robinson, J., Simpson, J., Galey, S., Kirby, S., Martin, L. & Muzychka, M. (1999). The Changing nature of home care and its impact on women's vulnerability to poverty. *Status of Women Canada Policy Research*. Available: http://www.swc-cfc.gc.ca/publish/research/morris-e.html (September 12, 2000)

Immaculate Deception: The Quiet Conspiracy Against Women's Hospital Health Care Rights

Louise A. Edmonds
Pembroke, Ontario

Abstract

This paper explores what has happened to women's health services under health care restructuring in Ontario; specifically, the role of religion in hospital governance and its impact on women's health care access. Tracing the impact of the Health Services Restructuring Commission (HSRC) in five communities across Ontario the author examines the policies and decisions of the HSRC in terms of its authority as a non-political government body that denies women access to legal, public health care in favour of denominational health care. This paper provides evidence of the power wielded by the Committee to close publicly owned institutions in the face of massive public opposition. Finally the role and particular problems of feminist activism in a rural community setting are addressed.

Introduction

Few, if any local institutions play a greater role in the health of their community than the local hospital. In today's world of health care, hospitals have become multi-million dollar enterprises. But cutbacks and restructuring have alerted local taxpayers to questions around hospital accountability, particularly the community hospital component of women's health services. In one area of Eastern Ontario, the provincial government's Health Services Restructuring Commission (HSRC) ordered the local public hospital closed, leaving the entire region to seek hospital services at the one remaining hospital—a privately owned and religiously controlled institution operated by a Roman Catholic order. The public hospital closure divided the community and highlighted many troubling issues for local women. This situation has very serious implications for issues around access to women's health services as legal health services and medical procedures are no longer available in this community (or are shrouded in secrecy) because they conflict with the values of the Roman Catholic Church.

This paper will explore the emasculation of women's health

services under the guise of health care restructuring and "rationalization" in Ontario. More specifically, it will look at the role of religion within hospital governance in determining women's health care access, both in a rural setting and in larger centres in the province. The duplicity of the government's role in undermining that access will also be revealed. In terms of healthy, caring communities, this study will provide informative instruction for women across Canada regarding the power of hospital boards and the larger issue of hospital governance and public accountability. To conclude, a brief summary of the special problems associated with feminist activism in a rural community setting will be specified. Here, the feminist adage 'the personal is political' assumes a whole new meaning when the political becomes very, *very* personal.

Hospital Restructuring

In March of 1996, as part of its rationalization of hospital services the Ontario government established an independent body named the Health Services Restructuring Commission (HSRC). The Commission was given a four year mandate to close, merge and otherwise streamline hospital services in the province. Several examples of the restructuring process experienced in Pembroke, Sudbury, Cornwall, Kingston and Toronto will be reviewed below. These restructuring cases are instructive for several reasons. First, they illustrate the relinquishing of democratic political control by the provincial government in the handing over of multi-billion dollar health care decisions to unelected and unaccountable officials at the Health Services Restructuring Commission; a body which had no rigorous reference framework. The enabling legislation stated that HSRC could implement local hospital restructuring "in the public interest"(Ontario Regulation 87/96, 88/96). Access to a range of women's health care was not guaranteed—even if it has been historically provided— because the Ontario government did not implicitly or explicitly identify women's health care services as being in "the public interest."

Secondly, these cases also reveal that an arms length, non-political government body was legally capable of playing politics with community health care across the province. The HSRC forcibly closed publicly owned institutions despite overwhelming opposition from local residents, elected politicians at all levels, and in some cases, the government's own district health councils. More importantly, these cases reveal that while the HSRC had no overt policy directives on denominational health care at the outset of the restructuring process, religion played a defining role in the restructuring of hospital health care in Ontario, much to the detriment of Ontario women. The current government at Queen's Park was not only guilty of duplicity in denying women access to legal, public health care in favour of more restrictive denominational health care, but this government was doing so — at public expense — in the absence of any constitutional obligation.

Pembroke

In the small rural town of Pembroke, Ontario (pop. 14 000) the Commission ordered the closing of the public Pembroke Civic Hospital with all hospital services for the catchment area of approximately 55 000 to be provided to residents by the one remaining hospital. The hospital was privately owned by the Grey Sisters of the Immaculate Conception, a Roman Catholic order. The Sisters currently control hospital services through their Roman Catholic Mission Statement and hospital by-laws; appoint all hospital board members; and hold veto over board decisions. The Catholic Hospital receives over 90% of its operating budget from public funds[1].

The public was stunned by the decision of this very powerful arms length government agency. Local protest developed quickly following the public release of the HSRC's recommendations. An overwhelming number of public and elected representatives expressed concern over the governance issue (see Appendix A). The creation of the Committee for Public Governance for Pembroke's Only Hospital was almost immediate; busloads of protesters travelled to Queen's Park; and this quiet rural community raised $280,000 to take the Province of Ontario and the HSRC to court on grounds which included Charter Rights of Freedom of Religion and procedural fairness. Although the courts granted a stay of the directives to close the hospital while the court case was being heard, they later ruled against the public hospital. They found that the powerful HSRC did have the authority to forcibly close this institution, although they admitted that "[on] the spectrum between political decision making and judicial decision making, the Commission is close to the extreme political/legislative end of the spectrum"(*Pembroke Civic Hospital v. Ontario:* 3). On the issue of denial of health care services, Justice Archie Campbell said in his decision that this question was "premature and speculative". The time to bring a case about denial of service, according to Campbell, was when actual services had been denied (i.e. *after* the public hospital was closed and service denied at the Catholic hospital).

One of the central arguments of the court case was that the HSRC remained, as Michele Landsberg described it, "privately determined to offer up the Civic on the alter of [Catholic] appeasement"(1997). Substantial lobbying of all three major political parties by the Catholic Health Association of Ontario (CHAO) had occurred prior to the provincial election and all had recognized the contribution of denominational hospitals to health care in the province. But statements made by HSRC Chief Executive Officer Marc Rochon also suggest that Pembroke may have been a pawn in a larger strategy to ensure Catholic health care for Ontario following restructuring.[2] In Sudbury where the Sisters of St. Joseph of Sault Ste. Marie were told to merge their Catholic hospital (the Sudbury General Hospital) with the two other public city hospitals, the Sisters launched a court case in protest. In his affidavit in the Sudbury case, Marc Rochon stated that it was not the intention of the Commission to close Roman Catholic hospitals in the province. He stated that in fact the HSRC "contemplates changes . . . that will see public hospitals run by Catholic organizations assuming a larger role". As an example he gave the Pembroke situation, where he said the HSRC would close the public hospital and the Catholic hospital would remain open. However, at the time of his statements, the HSRC had only handed down their *proposed* directives on Pembroke and they were still hearing public submissions before issuing their final report. Also, the HSRC held private meetings with the Catholic Health Association, discussions which were not made public nor revealed to the Pembroke Civic Hospital in their bid to keep the local public hospital open.

Further statements made by HSRC commissioners at the time of the interim report confirm the theory of a predetermined Catholic outcome for Pembroke. The following is an excerpt from the local newspaper at that time:

> The one area the commission said they responded to in reply to public concern was the governance issue. "We think it is vital that the community should have a voice in this process and that the new board should reflect the community served by the hospital," said commissioner George Lund. But whatever the outcome of the governance discussions, the General Hospital will still be owned by the Grey Sisters. "The

facility is owned by the Grey Sisters and will continue to be run by the Grey Sisters," [Commissioner Maureen] Law said. ("HSRC will stick to deadline")

In written presentations and personal meetings with the HSRC, the Pembroke Civic Hospital had on numerous occasions outlined the restrictions on public health care that would result from the decision of the HSRC to keep the Catholic hospital as the only hospital serving the area. Furthermore, at the same time as the interim report in Pembroke was being debated, the Sisters of St. Joseph in the Sudbury case had filed their legal action against the HSRC. The legal brief they presented to the HSRC was infinitely detailed as to why the Roman Catholic Mission of their hospital could not be accommodated within a public hospital. The document outlined Canon Law and stated specific medical procedures and services which could not be accepted by the Sisters. It was very clear that full regular public hospital procedures and services could not be provided in a Roman Catholic hospital.

The Sudbury legal action outlined the following:

> Health care in the Roman Catholic Church is governed by the relevant provisions of the Canon Law of the Catholic Church, and by the moral and ethical tenets of the Catholic faith . . .
>
> To be consistent with the requirements of Roman Catholic belief and practice, The Sisters of St. Joseph of Sault Ste. Marie, both individually and as a congregation (a group of members), must comply with Canon Law so to ensure the ownership, sponsorship, and control of the ministry is under the Church's authority . . .
>
> In the same way they must practice the basic tenets of morals set down by the Church in their day to day ministry. In this regard, the Church has developed health care ethics guides which spell out certain criteria which are fundamental to the Roman Catholic health care ministry. In Canada, this document is, in fact, known as the *Health Care Ethics Guide.* Failure to observe these guidelines would constitute a failure to comply with the requirements of Church teaching . . . . *The Guide* is to be operative in all Catholic health care institutions.

Moreover, the Mission Statement of the Pembroke General Hospital itself, outlines the hospital's religious mission: "Pembroke

General Hospital, a person-centred Catholic facility committed to the healing mission of Jesus, provides the best possible health care for all people of Pembroke and area in the tradition of the Grey Sisters of the Immaculate Conception". One of its five Mission Values states: "Sacredness of life ensures the dignity of life from *conception* to *natural* death" [italics mine]. These statements have obvious implications for reproductive services for both men and women and certainly end of life issues. Ironically, during the Pembroke court case proceedings, HSRC Chief Executive Officer Marc Rochon stated that he was unaware of the Pembroke General Hospital's Roman Catholic by-laws which clearly restrict hospital activities not in compliance with the teachings of the Roman Catholic Church.

A predetermined outcome for Pembroke was also indicated by the HSRC's actions regarding the local health council's recommendation. It had been the stated objective of the HSRC to find local solutions and to abide by the recommendations of the local district health councils.[3] But the HSRC willfully and purposefully ignored this advice in the Pembroke situation. For example, the Renfrew County District Health Council had recommended using the Catholic hospital's building, but suggested "a single administration, single medical staff and single governing body"(HSRC,1996:19). The Council's intention was that it would be a public board which would oversee the new hospital. When it became clear from the Interim Report that the HSRC had ignored their recommendation, the local Health Council passed an enabling resolution further detailing their desire for a public, non-denominational board: "This could be done by establishing a new regional public hospital corporation with membership open to all residents of the service area. These members would then elect the first board at a public founding meeting" (Renfrew County). The HSRC did not change its decision. When the government was criticized during Question Period at Queen's Park for its handling of the Pembroke situation, Finance Minister Ernie Eves responded that the government was only following the recommendations of the local Health Council.

Finally, a number of compromises were proposed by the Pembroke Civic Hospital, to the HSRC including a shared hospital—a condominium model. This was denied by the HSRC. Then Pembroke Civic Hospital suggested that the Grey Sisters hand over sponsorship of the hospital to a public corporation who would run the hospital, allowing the Sisters to maintain ownership, but be removed from any religious conflicts. The HSRC said this option was not up for discussion. Moreover, at the time of its forced closing, the Pembroke Civic Hospital was the only case in Ontario where, when two hospitals were reduced to one, there was no opportunity to merge. Furthermore, Pembroke was the only municipality in Ontario where, following restructuring, and despite great community resentment, people were left with a single denominational hospital to serve a pluralistic community. These and other actions by the HSRC and Ontario Government show convincingly that Pembroke was indeed a pawn in a much larger strategy to ensure Catholic health care for Ontario. While protection of Catholic health care was not a stated guiding principle of the restructuring commission, it has become obvious that Catholic health care has been accommodated at the expense of women's health care rights throughout the province and has even "trumped" public health care in some instances. Whenever restructuring decisions about public health care clashed with Catholic health care, the integrity of the Catholic system was maintained by the HSRC — in Pembroke, Sudbury, Cornwall, Peterborough, Toronto (St. Michael's - Wellesley) and more recently in Kingston — in most cases at greater public expense — in many cases through denial of services to women.

The regulations for Catholic Hospital restructuring are quite explicit:

> The Catholic Health Association of Ontario and Alliance of Catholic Health Sponsors has established "Guidelines on Collaboration" which stipulate the policies and procedures to be met by all Catholic hospitals in order to be in compliance with Canon Law corporate responsibilities of a Catholic health institution. This includes the requirement that while entering collaborative relationships with others, Catholic hospitals must have: their own corporate entity; their own Board of Directors; and appointment of their own CEO. The basis for these requirements is to ensure that they have control of their mission . . . (Sudbury Restructuring Report:4)

The HSRC was fully aware of these extensive restrictions as it set about its task to restructure Ontario's hospitals. In Sudbury, the Sisters of St. Joseph's law suit never reached the courts. The HSRC offered the Sisters a compromise wherein a wing of the public hospital would be governed by a separate Chief Executive Officer and Board appointed by the Sisters of St. Joseph "for the fulfilment of their Catholic mission and the provision of health services" (HSRC (March) 1997:13). The

Sudbury Public Hospital Corporation would then contract with the Sisters of St. Joseph to supply health care, "provided that the contract is consistent with their Catholic mission" (HSRC (March) 1997:13). Such a "condominium model" of hospital administration is not only a costly duplication of bureaucracy in many respects, but it is also an example of government sanctioned discrimination against women. Unlike examples in the past where governments allowed privately owned hospitals to refuse medical service that ran counter to their own religion, housing a restrictive religious institution within a publicly supported hospital validates the moral judgements of the Roman Catholic church. This decision is saying it's OK to deny a woman a tubal ligation or an IUD contraceptive **in a publicly funded health facility** because it offends one particular private religion. Thus, religious doctrine has, in fact, triumphed over public health care.

Later in Cornwall, the HSRC ordered the small, public Cornwall General Hospital to close and the larger Catholic Hotel Dieu Hospital to remain open. While size and obvious cost savings would play a convincing role in determining that the larger site would remain open, the Cornwall situation was complicated by the fact that the public hospital also performed abortions. In the absence of any local organized lobby effort, the HSRC quietly reversed their initial decision and decided to keep *both* hospitals open. They are now run by two separate boards. Again, religion played a defining role in hospital restructuring, regardless of financial implications.

In Kingston Ontario, the HSRC mandated the closure of the Roman Catholic Hôtel Dieu Hospital, with its services and programs to be transferred to the public Kingston General Hospital. The Hôtel Dieu filed legal action against the Province of Ontario and the HSRC, but lost in two court challenges. The hospital had argued that the HSRC directives violated their freedom of religion under the Charter by ordering the termination of their religious mission. The courts ruled against them stating that "the crucial word here is 'public' . . . the great principle of freedom of religion does not guarantee public funding for denominational public hospitals" (Lukits,1999b).[4] HSRC lawyer John Laskin stated in the Kingston legal case:

No matter how my friends seek to package their claim, it's a claim for continued public funding for their mission. It's a claim for government support for the exercise of their religion . . . The Sisters remain free to carry out their health-care mission. The only thing they can't do is operate a public hospital with public funding. They have no charter claim to do this. (Lukits,1999a)

But, having established that the province had no constitutional obligation to fund denominational hospitals, the Ontario Government has now decided *not* to close the Hôtel Dieu hospital in Kingston, at least in the interim stage and possibly indefinitely (Lukits,2000).[5] Premier Harris himself announced the concession to the Hotel Dieu during a visit to Kingston on March 8, 2000. Hospital restructuring in Pembroke, Sudbury, Cornwall and Kingston clearly reveals the government's priority in protecting Roman Catholic denominational hospitals in the province even in the face of women's health care rights and higher financial costs.

Access to Women's Health Services

Apart from abortion, the women's movement has not often explored the role of the community hospital in providing access to women's health services. Women's greater proportional use of the medical system has been well documented and women are both formally and informally principal caregivers (Canadian Woman's Health Network). Today, the care of children and aging parents remains primarily women's responsibility. Moreover, the average Canadian woman herself will experience a number of significant hospital medical procedures — some of which are *only* available at a hospital depending on her location: her birth, birth control procedures[6], ultrasounds, xrays, childbirth, aftermath of any miscarriages, tubal ligations and end of life procedures. While clinics and free standing laboratory facilities are available in major cities, in small rural communities most of these services and procedures can only be found at the local hospital. Furthermore, medical walk-in clinics that may exist in urban centres are not an alternative to the local hospital: they do not provide the range of hospital services listed above; and they cannot provide emergency or after hours medical services.

Hospital health care becomes even more critical as the physician shortage in rural and small urban areas becomes more acute. Residents begin to use the Emergency Department of the local hospital as their doctor's office because they have no where else to go.[7] Access to a local family practitioner is particularly critical where there is a concentrated migrant population such as a Canadian Forces Base or a local college.[8] The local hospital, then, is a very important component of women's health care, and for rural women, possibly their only choice for some procedures and services.

But hospital health care is proscribed or denied when medical procedures and services are filtered through the doctrine of the Roman Catholic Church. The lack of national standards for women's health care rights means that health services that are legal, have been deemed "medically necessary" in the province, are billable under the Ontario Health Insurance Plan (OHIP), are not available to all women in the province. In fact, access to many legal health services is dependent on the by-laws, mission statement and board membership of a community's hospital. In many respects, "Catholic doctrine, not the patient and her doctor, will determine a woman's medical options"(Landsberg, 1997).

In the Pembroke situation many local women were outraged that services formerly available at the public hospital, such as the morning after pill, abortion referral, family planning (eg. IUD insertion), AIDS education and palliative care,[9] would not be available after the public hospital closed.[10] Unrestricted access to other medical services such as tubal ligations and vasectomies, prenatal screening and services associated with reproductive technologies were all in question, as these procedures conflict with the religious values of the hospital owners as set out by the Roman Catholic Health Association in their *Health Care Ethics Guide (1992)*.[11] Also in question is whether or not the Hospital will honour living wills.

The Guide is very explicit in its religious philosophy:

> In health care and in society at large the Catholic health care institution is a voice expressing a vision of life based on the moral and religious values of the Roman Catholic tradition ... Our Roman Catholic faith can further specify what is morally proper . . . (Ethics Guide: 20, 64)

Prior to the closing of the public hospital in Pembroke, one court case affidavit documents the situation of a young teenager who sought emergency birth control at the Catholic hospital after a failed contraceptive incident.[12] Due to the fact that she lived a half hour's drive from the hospital and had no transportation of her own, the teenager was near the end of the 72-hour window of effectiveness for the morning after pill when she arrived at the Catholic hospital. According to her statements, the nurses at the Catholic hospital refused her service and made her feel very uncomfortable. The physician on call in the Emergency Department told the young woman to meet him four blocks away at the public hospital, where he then provided her with the requested emergency contraception. Unclear to this day is whether the now sole remaining Catholic Hospital will provide full access to this medical service and if the public pharmacy, located within the hospital, will be allowed to dispense the prescription.[13]

What is "morally proper" (Ethics Guide: 64), according to the Roman Catholic faith becomes not just a right to deny service, but an appalling moral judgement test for local women. One woman complained that in written documentation to be completed by couples before a vasectomy, the Pembroke General Hospital states that the hospital "tolerates" this procedure (Edmonds, Personal Correspondence). These moral judgements are not just visited on local Pembroke and area women, but are applied to most women in the better part of the county. Due to earlier hospital rationalization, all women from neighbouring towns and villages (even those with a hospital) must seek obstetrical/gynecological services at the Pembroke General Hospital. Ironically, the entire region has only two obstetrician/gynecologists — both of whom work out of offices located at the Roman Catholic Hospital, thus subjecting themselves, their patients and the services they can provide to the bylaws and Mission Statement of the hospital.[14] Effectively, women's rights have been abandoned.

Sexual assault is another hospital based service in the Pembroke area. In 1998-99, 1 275 local residents sought counselling at the Sexual Assault Counselling Centre located within the Catholic Hospital (Pembroke General, 1999a:36). Once again, anecdotal evidence from a former employee suggests that a full range of options cannot be presented to women who have been sexually assaulted because of the application of the Roman Catholic mission statement to the Centre housed within the publicly funded General Hospital.

Mental health counselling is another crucial service for women housed in the Catholic Hospital in Pembroke. In fact, all mental health services for the entire County of Renfrew (population 92 547) are now coordinated from the Pembroke General Hospital. While the *Code of Ethics* of the Ontario College of Certified Social Workers requires a social worker to counsel her/his client according to the *client's* values and not those of the social worker or the institution, several examples in Pembroke have proven otherwise. Local residents are concerned that neither the religious based treatment nor the conflict of interest is being declared by hospital social workers. Some types of counselling — particularly that around divorce, sexual orientation or termination of a pregnancy — could be constrained and has, in fact, been denied based on the Catholic Mission Statement of the Hospital. In October 1999, a local woman with an addiction problem who sought counselling around the issue of terminating her pregnancy was refused counselling at the Pembroke General Hospital because of its Catholic Mission Statement; moreover, due to this religious constraint on hospital employees, she could not be referred to any other counselling service. If indeed she had been referred, her only options would have been to pay for private counselling locally, or travel to Ottawa (100 miles away) for OHIP funded counselling help as the Pembroke General Hospital operates all provincially funded adult mental health services in the entire county.

Several employees at the Pembroke General Hospital have admitted that behind closed doors they counsel their clients as they see fit (Personal Correspondence). Ironically, during the court case the chief of Obstetrics and Gynecology at the Catholic Hospital admitted under oath that he had never read the Roman Catholic Mission Statement of the Hospital and that he provides whatever services and procedures he sees fit in his office within the hospital (Affidavit of Dr. Sharma). Yet the Pembroke General Hospital continues to defend its Catholic mission in the community and even demands that its board members sign in writing to respect the Roman Catholic Mission of the Hospital — a demand sanctioned by the HSRC (HSRC, June 1997:15). Most troubling however, is that this "don't ask, don't tell" provision of service model places women in a health care roulette wheel where care and procedures are dependent upon the physician one sees,[15] or the local bishop.[16] In fact, Pembroke General Hospital Executive Director Sheila Schultz told reporters that many of the issues dealt with in the *Catholic Health Care Ethics Guide* are not "black and white", and are "open to interpretation by leaders of the local church" (Pembroke's Unhealthy Situation). This has led one critic to comment that "it seems the bishop has as much of a say in your health needs as does your doctor" (Blizzard).

The Pembroke General Hospital is currently being sued by a woman who became pregnant after a failed tubal ligation. The lawsuit claims that the Hospital knew there was a problem with the procedure but failed to warn her and other patients of the risk of pregnancy. According to Dr. Sharma, between July 1, 1996 and March 31, 1998 about 300 women had a surgical sterilization using Filshie clips at the Pembroke General Hospital. While the normal rate of failure is two or three per 10 000 procedures, Dr. Sharma and his colleague Dr. Onochie, both had four or five of their patients become pregnant. Despite the fact that the hospital suspected a problem with the clips or the applicator and stopped using the instruments in April 1998, hospital officials did not send a warning letter to patients that they could still be fertile until January, 1999 — a full nine months later. Moreover, Dr. Sharma revealed that he had informed the Hospital of some failures in late 1997. One must ask whether religion played a role in the hospital's overt negligence in informing its patients. According to the Roman Catholic Mission and by-laws, direct sterilization is formally prohibited: "sterilization procedures . . . are expressly forbidden in a Catholic health care ministry and are fundamentally contrary to the tenets of the Catholic faith . . . "(Sisters of St. Joseph). Furthermore, full disclosure of the failure of their tubal ligation procedures would have called public attention to the fact they were performing this forbidden procedure and could have prompted the termination of several pregnancies.

St. Michael's Hospital, Toronto

As well as in the smaller centres, women's health services have been affected by religious overrides in major centres in the province following provincial restructuring. For example, in Toronto the HSRC mandated the merging of the downtown Wellesley Hospital under the governance of the nearby Roman Catholic St. Michael's Hospital. Public outcry ensued as the Wellesley Hospital had been the main hospital used by the largest gay community in Toronto and moreover, the Wellesley Hospital had performed abortions. Almost immediately after the takeover of the Wellesley Hospital, a memo was circulated to all staff at the new St. Michael's Hospital - Wellesley Central Division. The memo said that as of midnight April 6, 1998 no therapeutic abortions would be performed at the amalgamated Saint Michael's Hospital - Wellesley Division and that all tubal ligations must be approved by the hospital's ethics committee (see Appendix B): an appalling reversion to health care of the 1950s.

One of the arguments used to defend the actions of the HSRC was that women and homosexuals could seek hospital treatment at other hospitals in Toronto. Surely the more obvious question is: why should they? Why should taxpayers be denied medical services because their private medical choices are not "moral" in the eyes of hospital owners?

Besides, why is the Ontario Government continuing to provide public funding to hospitals governed by an exclusionary and restrictive Catholic ethics guide? This Guide bans the obvious procedures, but also sterilization, some parts of artificial insemination (e.g. for single women or lesbians), in vitro fertilization, birth control (apart from the rhythm method) and any prenatal diagnosis procedures which might affect a pregnancy. Once again, despite denial of services to women, the religious restrictions on public health services at St. Michael's hospital were not challenged by the HSRC but, in fact, were defended by the Minister of Health herself (Artuso).

Unquestionably, women's health care rights have been denied, proscribed and unabashedly forced back behind 1950s style closed doors as a result of provincial hospital restructuring. It would be difficult to argue that these actions could have been accomplished without the overt approval of the Harris government and their not so subtle support of Roman Catholic health care and its restrictive doctrine. The issue is clear: "It is noble for an institution to have ethics and morals. The big question is this: in an institution that serves a multifaith, multicultural society and that is funded by public money, whose morals and ethics should reign supreme?" (Blizzard).

The Power of Hospital Governance

Hospital restructuring in the province of Ontario has highlighted the powers of hospital boards and the larger issue of hospital governance and accountability. For instance, critics point out that the newly restructured mega-Ottawa Hospital has a budget greater than that of the City of Ottawa and yet the hospital has no elected board members. Similarly, the City of Pembroke's annual $23 million budget is easily exceeded by the $32 million budget of the Pembroke General Hospital; tax dollars spent by unelected, unaccountable officials and lay people.

According to the Ontario Hospital Association (OHA) there is no one model of hospital governance in the province. A number of municipalities actually elect hospital board members on the municipal ballot. There are other localities, Arnprior for instance, where there is a mix of an elected board with nominated municipal representation. Most hospitals however, follow the model which was in place at the Pembroke Civic Hospital: local taxpayers buy a membership in a hospital corporation for a nominal fee, entitling them to vote for elected board members on an annual basis.[17]

At the outset of the HSRC's mandate there were 32 denominational hospitals in Ontario: 29 Roman Catholic, 2 Salvation Army and 1 Seventh Day Adventist. While the board structures of many of the province's hospitals are a matter of tradition, the structures of Roman Catholic hospital boards are by design. Mr. Ron Marr, former president of the Ontario Catholic Health Care Association has stated that in order for a hospital to maintain its mission and values as a Catholic hospital, it must have control over its corporate structure — namely the members of the corporation — the chief financial officer and the board of directors("Prognosis unknown for Catholic hospitals"). Clearly outlined in the published documentation of Roman Catholic hospitals is the fact that they must maintain religious control over their institutions through the hospital administration and the board:

> The healing ministry of the Catholic health care facility is an expression of the ministry of Christ and of the church . . . In order for this to happen, the total atmosphere of our institutions needs to be permeated with the love of Christ and with the visible signs of faith that characterize the authentic Catholic tradition. Some tangible signs of Catholic identity include . . . Catholic ownership and/or management and recognition by the bishop of the diocese of the institution as an integral part of the apostolate. (Ethics Guide:11)

Within these parameters, it is difficult to envision any truly public hospital board of directors which could reflect a diverse pluralistic society. In fact, in the Pembroke case, all prospective board members must agree to sign in writing that they will respect the Roman Catholic Mission, values and goals of the Hospital.[18] This requirement was actually sanctioned by the HSRC and amounts to blatant religious screening, presenting a strong argument in favour of elected hospital board membership with no religious overrides.

Surprisingly, the provincial government exercises very little control over the administration of these multi-million dollar publicly funded institutions. For example, in the Pembroke situation, following the announcement of the forced closure of the public hospital, the HSRC in December 1996 directed that the new board of the Pembroke General Hospital must reflect the community. The Pembroke General did not comply with this directive, but no reprimand was sent by the HSRC or the Ministry of Health. Then, due to the continuing, fractious governance issue, the HSRC sent a facilitator to Pembroke in June of

1997. He mandated that the new board must "be representative of the communities served and reflect the demographic, cultural, linguistic, geographic, ethnic, religious and social characteristics of Pembroke and Renfrew County and to the extent practical, shall be reasonably gender balanced"(HSRC,1997:16).[19] There was no follow-up or compliance mechanism, and indeed, the hospital proceeded to nominate a board with only one community female board member.

Today—two years later—Pembroke has a taxpayer funded institution which is privately owned and whose hospital board members are personally selected by the Roman Catholic Grey Sisters. There are no visible minorities on the board despite the fact that qualified candidates have applied. The new board is predominantly Roman Catholic with no Native representation (although the hospital's catchment area includes the Golden Lake Indian Reserve and the hospital was mandated to include ethnic and cultural minorities). The board is not geographically representative: being heavily weighted in favor of the City of Pembroke; and omitting practically any representation from the outlying areas that had opposed the choice of the Pembroke General Hospital. On a nine member board, only two women sit as community representatives. Two Grey Sisters sit on the board as *voting* ex-officio members representing the owners of the hospital. Those members required by law include the Chief of Medical Staff and the President and Vice-President of Medical Staff—all of whom in this one hospital town, owe their employment directly to the Grey Sisters. Nothing prevents the hospital administration from nominating more ex-officio members—all of whom would have full voting privileges.

Public Accountability

Elected and fully accountable hospital boards are necessary to safeguard women's hospital health care rights and to ensure public confidence, public fundraising and transparent spending of public taxpayer dollars. In an era of cutbacks and rationalization, individual communities are being asked to raise funds locally for crucial hospital machinery, renovations and expansions. Volunteers are being called upon in even greater numbers to supplement cutbacks to staff. However, where public confidence has been undermined, public fundraising will suffer and local health care as well.[20] [21]

On a final financial note, the proposed renovations at the

Pembroke General Hospital have now far exceeded the cost savings of closing the public hospital. In fact, the current capital investment requirement ($24 million) at the Pembroke General so far exceeds the initial estimate ($5.5 million) as to bring into question the integrity of the original consultant's report. For the amount of money it will now take to restructure the older Pembroke General Hospital, the province could have renovated the public hospital (capital cost $23.4 million) (HSRC,1996:52). Moreover, by doing so could have side-stepped a costly and bitter court challenge and averted splitting a community which will now not raise the required $6 million in local fundraising necessary to ensure complete restructuring. Ironically, cost — and not religion — was the major factor stated in the HSRC's decision to choose the Roman Catholic Pembroke General Hospital over the public hospital located mere blocks away.

Rural Feminist Activism

Several lessons can be learned from these case studies regarding special problems associated with feminist activism in a rural community setting. While the feminist adage 'the personal is political' was evident from the outset of this debate, the political became very, *very* personal for almost anyone who wished to join the debate. From the outset, the General Hospital tried to portray any opposition to the hospital's governance as anti-Catholic sentiment ("Sister Marguerite Hennessey explains Grey Sisters role . . . ", Snowdon). While this clearly was not the case (the President of the Civic Hospital's board was himself a Roman Catholic), it was difficult for local activists to get beyond charges of bigotry and anti-Catholicism.

Furthermore, with only one hospital to serve this small community, residents were reluctant to speak out against the hospital administration and local activists were afraid to get sick.[22] Local Roman Catholics who were sympathetic to public governance were afraid to be seen siding against the owners, the Grey Sisters. Moreover, as the only hospital employer within 60 kilometers, employees were afraid of losing their jobs, being reduced shifts, or losing promotions if they spoke out. Only a handful of physicians were vocal before the closing of the public hospital and once the General Hospital became the sole hospital employer, physician criticism effectively vanished. The local ministerial association would not make any public statements despite the fact that some of its members publicly sided with the local Public

Governance Advocacy Group (see Ferrier). Local politicians within the City of Pembroke and the provincial representative, afraid of offending Roman Catholic voters, quietly faded into the background after the first initial public protest.

Rural feminists face additional burdens above and beyond their urban counterparts in their attempts to effect change. Queen's Park is not as sensitive to injustices occurring in remote or northern areas; and fewer media outlets exist for rural activists. In addition, as Pembroke organizers learned only too quickly, when religion plays a role the media can back off a divisive issue. Moreover, the Toronto media is not as interested in issues outside the metropolitan area. Another issue facing rural feminists is that fundraising is more difficult in small communities and activating older citizens requires more resources. Unfortunately, few urbanites can really appreciate the lack of choice dictated by rural geography. Unlike the argument used to defend the actions of the HSRC in Toronto, Pembroke residents cannot get on the next subway to another hospital just down the line. Seeking alternative hospital treatment requires great effort, both personal and financial, all at the risk of a loss of privacy. Furthermore, because of the familiarity amongst small town residents, rural feminist activists wage a more personal campaign and must risk more personal repercussions than activists in big cities. Finally, fewer organizations exist in the rural east to lobby on behalf of women. Therefore, rural-urban connections must be strengthened so that women can lobby effectively to protect their rights, no matter where they live in the province.

Conclusion

Health care continues to be a heavily politicized process. One casualty has been the HSRC itself. Ironically, the all-powerful HSRC was demoted to an advisory body midway through its mandate; which many attribute to the fact that the HSRC ignored the political realities of the province. But the actions of the provincial government and the HSRC prove that we must press to have women's health services fully protected by the five fundamental principles of the *Canada Health Care Act.* We need health care that is universal, *truly* accessible, comprehensive, portable and publicly administered; substantive protections which, on many accounts, are not met by denominational hospitals.

Moreover, it is time to recognize that denial of publicly funded and medically sanctioned health services by private denominational hospitals is indefensible. Hospitals are no longer private charitable institutions funded exclusively by religious owners. They are multi-billion dollar public institutions funded by taxpayers dollars. Public funds should no longer go to support hospitals that discriminate against women; hospitals heretofore protected by a shield of religious dogma. The very viability of these hospitals depends entirely on public funds. If the government stopped funding these hospitals tomorrow they would be forced to close immediately. Furthermore, unlike education in Canada, the courts have stated decisively that there is no Charter guarantee of publicly funded denominational hospitals.

Finally, we must all be vigilant in the face of government rationalization and restructuring to protect women's hospital health care rights. This means fighting the quiet conspiracy, be it in small town Ontario or in large urban centres. According to Landsberg, "this cold carving up of women's health services begins to feel more and more like the 1950s . . . As hospitals rush to consecrate their medical marriages of convenience, women's rights and freedoms could be thrown to the winds"(1996). In many instances, the damage has already been done.

APPENDIX A

"I told the commission it had failed to address the governance issue in its preliminary report and it is very important that it deal with that in its final report," he said. "We have to incorporate public control of the millions of dollars of public money into the governance structure."
    - Sean Conway, M.P.P. Renfrew North
    ("Conway has 'constructive' meeting with commission". *Pembroke Observer*, December 23, 1996, A1)

"Most especially, there is very little support, none that I can find, for the governance model that they have proposed. I told the commission quite bluntly, and I hope I represented most if not all of my constituents, that for the kind of health and hospital restructuring to occur in Pembroke and area and elsewhere in the province, there must be a broad base of public support for those changes."
    - Sean Conway, M.P.P. Renfrew North
    ("Hundreds of residents protest health care issues in Pembroke," *Eganville Leader*, January 7, 1997, A11)

"[T]he majority of members must be elected or appointed by municipalities, but it must be a democratic procedure."
  - Mayor Les Scott, City of Pembroke
  ("Hundreds of residents protest health care issues in Pembroke," *Eganville Leader*, January 7, 1997, A11)

"Pembroke city council and its residents are not prepared to accept any lesser services for the citizens of the City of Pembroke and the surrounding communities that was available prior to this report. The restructuring plan of the HSRC included inaccuracies of data, impossible time lines, illusive governance issues, and depths of cuts that go beyond the mandate of this commission. The report is absolutely unacceptable in terms of meeting the health care needs of our citizens now and in the future, and is in no way supported by this community."
  - Mayor Les Scott, City of Pembroke
  ("City says it will go to court, if it has to," *Pembroke Daily News*, December 28, 1996, page 4,5)

"Recognizing that it is very unlikely the commission will withdraw its decision to close the Civic, Stewart said it is paramount for the new hospital to have a board of directors that truly represents the population at large. 'It should be a public board that operates the hospital,' said Stewart."
  - County Warden David Stewart, Renfrew County Council
  ("County joins hospital fray," *The Pembroke Daily News*, December 18, 1996, page 4, 24)

"Izett McBride, a member of the DHC, explained that last fall a resolution was adopted by the DHC calling for the establishment of a new public hospital corporation made up of a public board whereby anyone who lived in the community could buy a membership. He said the group would have an initial founding meeting of that corporation and elect a board that would carry on from that time. 'That group would become the governing group of the two existing hospitals. Take over full operation and work towards establishing one-site model from that vantage point.' . . . He said unfortunately that section of the report was not adopted by the commission. 'We think they've made a grave mistake both for the current situation for the labour groups involved and for the long term as well. It's something we're not really happy

about.'"
> - Izett McBride, Vice-Chair, Renfrew County District Health
>   Council
> ("Hundreds of residents protest health care issues in
> Pembroke," *Eganville Leader*, January 7, 1997, A11)

"Our council is very concerned that there is indeed, a religious overtone to the governance issue which will affect the level of health care accessibility in the future . . . We feel that "religious grounds" should be eliminated as a *potential sole determinant* of which medical services we will or will not receive." (June 4, 1997 letter to HSRC)
> - Petawawa Village Council

Endnotes

1. While the province also funds other religious hospitals — the Jewish Mt. Sinai in Toronto for example, this hospital, unlike Roman Catholic ones, does not require its physicians to sign any documents forcing patients, nurses and doctors to adhere to any religious principles (see Blizzard).

2. This is also the stated public view of the longtime local M.P.P. — a Liberal member of the Official Opposition provincially.

3. "The Commission will have regard to DHC hospital restructuring plans, the Ministry's analysis of DHC plans and any other information that it considers to be appropriate to enable it to make good faith decisions in the public interest" (Ministry of Ontario).

4. Ironically, the exact same HSRC lawyer who had argued to protect a single Catholic hospital in Pembroke argued in Kingston that the state had no obligation to fund religious health care. The Hôtel Dieu was later denied leave to appeal to the Supreme Court of Canada.

5. The legislative mandate of the HSRC expired in the spring of 2000 and it is unclear whether their orders to hospitals, now stale-dated, are still in effect. Some speculate that political deals may see the Hôtel Dieu remain open indefinitely.

6. The insertion of IUDs is usually performed at a hospital due to the risk of perforation of tissue and the resulting bleeding.

7. A survey of local general practitioners in the City of Pembroke revealed that only two GPs were accepting new patients: of these two, one did not have admitting privileges to the Pembroke General Hospital. Further, in one part of the catchment area of the Pembroke Hospital, the population ratio is one physician for every 7,765 residents; the yardstick used by the Ministry of Health's Underserviced Area Program is one physician to a population of 1,380 (Edmonds,1999).

8. In the Pembroke case, while members of the military have access to the medical centre at CFB Petawawa, their family members (the majority women and children) must use the facilities at their local hospital—the Pembroke General. The hospital itself anticipates an increase in the CFB population from 5,000 to 20,000 over the next 5 years (PGH Capital Campaign). Further, an Algonquin College campus is located in Pembroke signalling another migrant population base.

9. The hospital offers pastoral care only.

10. Evidence during the court case revealed that written AIDS education materials provided to the Pembroke General Hospital by the local Health Unit had been returned by the hospital. The Health Unit's pamphlets counselled condom use as a method to prevent AIDS. A palliative care worker with the AIDS community locally admitted that most gay men do not seek medical care at the Pembroke General Hospital due to the Roman Catholic church's views on homosexuality. Most AIDS patients are registered in programs in Ottawa, a one and a half hour drive away (Personal Correspondence).

11. *The Health Care Ethics Guide* is an embodiment of "criteria which are fundamental to the Roman Catholic Health Care Ministry" and "failure to observe these guidelines would constitute a failure to comply with the requirements of church teaching" (Affidavit of Cheryl Lowe:6). The issue is further complicated by the fact that the Pembroke General Hospital refuses to state clearly

which procedures it outlaws and which procedures it allows. The Pembroke Civic Hospital board requested this information in writing but the administration at the Catholic hospital responded that the issue was [then] before the courts and therefore they could not comment on this question.

12. Affidavit of Kimberly (name withheld), Sworn June 13, 1997, Divisional Court, Ontario Court (General Division) Pembroke Civic Hospital and Cheryl Lowe v. Health Services Restructuring Commission and the Minister of Health (Pembroke General Hospital, Intervener).

13. The executive director of the Catholic hospital had stated to the public in 1997 that all procedures offered before the closing of the public hospital would still be available after it was closed. When asked whether the morning after pill would then be provided she responded: "that is not a procedure; that is a prescription" (Personal Correspondence).

14. The Preamble to the Roman Catholic *Health Care Ethics Guide* states the following: "It [the Guide] is addressed, specifically, to the owners, boards, personnel, and residents/patients of all Catholic health care institutions in Canada and to Catholics who work in or are patients/residents of other health care facilities." The Guide further notes: "Throughout this guide the term "personnel" includes all those who serve patients/residents, e.g. administrators, physicians, nurses, other health professionals, staff and volunteers." Later in the Guide under Employer/Employee Relationships it states: "All members of the institution's health care community are to respect the basic orientation of its mission in their work for the institution" (Guide:25).

15. The Canadian Abortion Rights Action League (CARAL) has established that Canadian physicians are under no obligation to refer patients to other physicians or institutions if the physician's conscience prevents them from offering a patient service.

16. The Catholic *Health Care Ethics Guide* states that: "the local bishop has the responsibility to provide leadership and to collaborate with the mission of the Catholic health care institutions.

In fulfilling his role as the primary teacher and pastor of his community, with the assistants of specialists in different health care disciplines, he has the task to ensure that the constant teaching of the church is reflected faithfully in the context of rapidly developing medical advances and of the increasing complexity of human sciences" (Health Care Ethics Guide:12).

17. Personal correspondence, Brian O'Riordan, Ontario Hospital Association, 9 December, 1996.

18. To be eligible to be a candidate for Director of the General Hospital Board, "a person shall be required to formally commit to comply with the obligation to respect the [Roman Catholic] mission, values and goals of the Pembroke General Hospital."

19. The facilitator dictated that there would be a Nominating Committee composed of three members from the Civic Hospital, three from the General Hospital, two from the County of Renfrew and one from the City of Pembroke. This Nominating Committee would then choose a two-year Interim Board for the Pembroke General Hospital. The Interim Board was also charged with determining the selection/election/nomination formula for subsequent boards. The Pembroke Civic Hospital refused to participate because the Grey Sisters retained the power to veto any new selection/election/nomination formula put forward by the Interim Board. The Grey Sisters could also veto any new board members following the Interim Board's two year expiry. Despite the absence of one of the two major players, the process continued uninterrupted and undisputed by the Ministry of Health and the HSRC.

20. Such is the continuing case in Pembroke where fundraising has now become an issue. The HSRC mandated that local municipalities pay 30% of new renovations. Yet public confidence has been undermined by a series of actions by the hospital administration. For example, local pharmacists were outraged when—without any public notice or tendering process—the Pembroke General Hospital sole-sourced a pharmacy in 1998. The hospital provided no convincing rational for this breach of public tendering. Greater still, in June of 1998 the General Hospital handed over corporate

sponsorship and control of the hospital to the newly created
Catholic Health Corporation of Ontario (CHCO) located in Guelph.
However, it was not until six months later, when local critics
brought the matter to the media's attention that the community was
made aware of this important transfer of control. The hospital's
Executive Director is quoted in the local media as saying that the
board of directors at the General Hospital are 'answerable to the
corporation and not the public at large' (Uhler:3).

21. Not only is this religious imperative detrimental to public
confidence and fundraising, it is also an impediment to
municipalities seeking to attract qualified doctors — a chronic
problem in many rural communities across Ontario. As one critic
has pointed out: "Why should Jewish and Muslim doctors be asked
to sign a Catholic document that really belongs in the last century?"
(Blizzard).

22. While residents with their own transportation could drive the 60
km. to the Renfrew Victoria Hospital or the Deep River and District
Hospital, many local residents were concerned that in an emergency
situation the ambulance drivers must take a patient to the closest
hospital (i.e. for Pembroke and area residents, the Pembroke
General Hospital) despite patient protestations. Further, obstetrics
and all but minor surgery are no longer performed at the Deep
River Hospital and these residents must go to the Pembroke General
Hospital or drive one hour further to the next available public
hospital.

References

Affidavit of Cheryl Lowe. (April 22, 1997). Divisional Court, Ontario
    Court (General Division) between Pembroke Civic Hospital and
    Cheryl Lowe Applicants and Health Services Restructuring
    Commission and the Minister of Health Respondents.
Affidavit of Kimberly (name withheld). (June 13, 1997). Divisional
    Court, Ontario Court (General Division) between Pembroke
    Civic Hospital and Cheryl Lowe Applicants and Health Services
    Restructuring Commission and the Minister of Health

Respondents.

Affidavit of Dr. Som Dutt Sharma. (June 5, 1997). Divisional Court, Ontario Court (General Division) between Pembroke Civic Hospital and Cheryl Lowe Applicants and Health Services Restructuring Commission and the Minister of Health Respondents.

Anderssen, Erin. (1997). Hospital makes case for secular control. *Ottawa Citizen*, 22 July 1997, A5.

Artuso, Antonella. (1998). NDP raps Tory hospital reform. *Toronto Sun* 21 June, 1998.

Blizzard, Christina. (1998). Public funding, private morals. *Toronto Sun*, 14 June, 1998.

Bohuslawsky, Maria. (1999a). Couple sues hospital. *Pembroke Observer*, 29 March, 1999, A1.

Bohuslawsky, Maria. (1999b). Mother sues hospital over pregnancy after tubal ligation. *National Post*, 27 March, 1999, A4.

Canadian Woman's Health Network. (2000). *Women's Health Research and the CIHR: A Backgrounder*. Winnipeg: CWHN.

Catholic Health Association of Canada. (1992). *Health Care Ethics Guide*. Ottawa: Catholic Health Association of Canada.

City says it will go to court, if it has to. *Pembroke Daily News*, 28 December, 1996, 4-5.

Conway has 'constructive' meeting with commission. *Pembroke Observer*, December 23, 1996, A1.

County joins hospital fray. *The Pembroke Daily News*, 18 December,1996, 4,24.

Doctor shortage looms. *Pembroke Observer*, 29 March, 1999, A1.

Edmonds, Louise. (1999). *Care in the Community: Establishing a Community Health Centre for the Whitewater and Bromley Region* report presented to the Ontario Ministry of Health, Whitewater and Bromley Region Rural CHC Steering Committee, Westmeath, ON.

Ferrier, Reverend Mark. (1997). Different moral choices must be respected. *Pembroke Daily News*, 16 July, 1997, 6.

Fraser, John. (1998). Wellesley decision monstrous. *Toronto Star*, 7 June, 1998.

Health Services Restructuring Commission. (December 1996). *Pembroke Health Services Restructuring Report*. Toronto: Health Services Restructuring Commission.

Health Services Restructuring Commission. (March 1997). *Sudbury*

Health Services Restructuring Report (Supplemental). Toronto: Health Services Restructuring Commission.

Health Services Restructuring Commission. (June 1997). *Report of the Facilitator, Hugh Kelly*. Toronto: Health Services Restructuring Commission.

Hooper, Lewis. (1999). Health Services Restructuring Commission, Personal Correspondence, 18 June, 1999.

HSRC will stick to deadline. *The Pembroke Daily News*, 26 February, 1997, 1,3.

Hundreds of residents protest health care issues in Pembroke. *Eganville Leader*, January 7, 1997, A11.

Landsberg, Michele. (1996). Back to the '50s as hospitals slice up women's services. *Toronto Star*, 12 May, 1996.

Landsberg, Michele. (1997). Women's health is threatened in Pembroke. *Toronto Star*, 7 June, 1997.

Landsberg, Michele. (1998). St. Mike's religious rules undemocratic. *Toronto Star*, 30 May, 1998.

Lindgren, April. (2000). Glitches delay closing of 26 Ontario hospitals. *Ottawa Citizen*, 24 January, 2000, A4.

Lukits, Ann. (1999a). Decision on Dieu coming shortly, says judge. *Kingston Whig Standard*, 9 June, 1999.

Lukits, Ann. (1999b). Hôtel Dieu appeal denied. *Kingston Whig Standard*, X June, 1999.

Lukits, Ann. (2000). Personal Correspondence, 17 April, 2000.

Martin, Sheilah. (1989). Women's Reproductive Health, The Canadian Charter of Rights and Freedoms, and the Canada Health Act. Ottawa: Canadian Advisory Council on the Status of Women.

Ministry of Health. (1996). *Health Services Restructuring Commission Mandate (Backgrounder)*. 28 February, 1996, Toronto.

Myers, Terry. (1998). Grey Sisters hand over control of hospital. *The Pembroke Daily News*, 2 September, 1998.

O'Riordan, Brian. (1996). Ontario Hospital Association, Personal Correspondence, 9 December, 1996.

Pembroke Civic Hospital v. Ontario (Health Services Restructuring Commission). (1997). (No. 2) 102 O.A.C. 207 (Ont. C.A.).

Pembroke General Hospital Inc. (1997). *Pembroke General Hospital Inc. Administrative By-Laws*.

Pembroke General Hospital Inc. (1999a). *Annual Report 1998-1999*.

Pembroke General Hospital Inc. (1999). *Capital Campaign: The Right Care at the Right Time.*

"Pembroke's Unhealthy Situation". (1997). (editorial) *The Ottawa Citizen,* 9 October, 1997.

Petawawa Village Council. (1997). Letter to Health Services Restructuring Commission (June 4, 1997.)

Prognosis unknown for Catholic hospitals. *Kingston Whig Standard,* 11 December, 1996.

Province of Ontario. (1996). *Ministry of Health Act, s.8(1) Health Services Restructuring Commission.*

Province of Ontario. (1996). Ontario Regulation 87/96, 88/96, Authorization to Issue Directions Under Section 6 and Subsection 9(10) of the Act, Health Services Restructuring Commission.

Renfrew County District Health Council. (1995). Resolution. 18 September, 1995.

Sarick, Lila. (1998). St. Michael's philosophy causes controversy. *Globe and Mail,* 27 May, 1998.

Sister Marguerite Hennessey explains Grey Sisters role . . . (1997). *Eganville Leader,* 31 December, 1997.

Sisters of St. Joseph of Sault Ste. Marie v. Ontario (Health Services Restructuring Commission). (1997) Notice of Motion, Application for Judicial Review, Ontario Court (General Division), 14 January, 1997.

Snowdon, Shelley. (1996). Sisters are upset with the rumors being spread. *Eganville Leader,* 31 December, 1996.

Uhler, Stephen. (1999). Governance issue over General Hospital begins again. *The Pembroke Daily News,* 18 June, 1999,1,3.

Impact of Migration on Immigrant Women's Health

Methchild Meyer
Ottawa, Ontario

Abstract

This article presents some results from three studies conducted by Gentium Consulting over the last three years.

I   Violence Against Domestic Workers

This study, undertaken on behalf of Status of Women, Canada aimed at documenting what is currently known about violence against domestic workers, particularly those coming to Canada through the "Live-In Caregiver Program". The results confirm that the economic exploitation, and physical and sexual abuse of domestic workers is also widely experienced by live-in caregivers in Canada. Perhaps the only significant difference between domestic workers and the immigrant women who become live-in caregivers is the age of the latter, since those applying to come to Canada are not children, but women of a certain age. The three components of this study, which is soon to be released by Status of Women, Canada are composed of: 1) a consultation process with domestic workers' organizations from across Canada; 2) a review of the literature, including community-based studies and court cases brought against employers by domestic workers; 3) a survey of community organizations serving domestic workers.

All three sources of information confirmed that because domestic workers are required to live in the employer's home they are extremely vulnerable to all forms of abuse. Almost all domestic workers are exploited, most frequently in an economic sense, but physical and sexual abuse is not uncommon. This has tremendous consequences in terms of their physical and emotional well-being. It was also revealed that live-in caregivers also fall through the cracks of the various types of legislation that might be applicable to their particular situations. Who is responsible for protecting these women from abuse? Is it the task of Immigration Canada? Or that of Provincial Labour Relations? Or should it be the responsibility of Human Rights Tribunals or Criminal Court? What are the implications when your workplace is also your home?

II   Infant Care Survey

This study is the analysis of results of an evaluation conducted by the "Healthy Babies–Healthy Children Program" of the Ottawa-Carleton Health Department. It illustrates how women who are not sufficiently fluent in either French or English might fall out of the assessment process with potentially harmful consequences for their health and that of their children. The evaluation was conducted by telephone with women who had given birth three months previously. We were delighted to find that the percentage of women in this survey who spoke a language other than French or English (twenty per cent) was comparable to the population in Ottawa-Carleton. Unfortunately, this statistic reveals a serious problem as well. In assessing post-partum depression, women in the survey who showed signs of depression received a follow-up phone call and a visit by a public health nurse. However, the interview data showed that twelve of the women surveyed were not assessed for post-partum depression because of "language problems". This amounts to one-fifth of the women surveyed whose home language is neither French nor English.

What are the implications? First of all, the accuracy and reliability of the assessment tool detecting signs of depression is called into question when applied to women with different backgrounds. To what degree has it been tested with different populations? Even those women who are able to answer the questions may not understand them in the same way. This also makes the validity of the instrument questionable. Women who cannot answer at all may not get the support they need and this may lead to neglect in the care of their babies and young children. This, in turn, creates the potential for intervention by the Children's Aid Society. It is easy to see how a simple and routine evaluation still leaves a group of women out of the loop, with direct consequences on their health and well-being.

III Immigrant Women and Substance Abuse

This study, initiated by Health Canada, was undertaken because there was a lack of information about the extent of substance abuse problems among immigrant women. A comprehensive review of the literature revealed problems with the data collection regarding this issue within national Canadian samples. For example, new "ethnic" groups were constructed to overcome small sample sizes, lumping Spanish and Portuguese respondents into one group, but reporting results separately on the English, the Welsh, the Irish and the Scottish.

The national survey, which included interviews with health services, immigrant women's programs, women's programs, substance abuse programs and other health services, revealed that there were very few indications of problems. This was particularly surprising since immigrating to a new country is extremely stressful, and stress is often associated with substance abuse in the North American context. The study also revealed that there was a considerable amount of stereotyping among service providers about the extent to which immigrant women were abusing drugs. For example, a number of workers stated that substance abuse was a big problem, but when asked how many women they or their program had served or assessed, they had to decline to answer.

In situations where a service provider had actually encountered a women with a drug problem there was a real ping-pong effect of back and forth referrals. The immigrant serving agency might refer the woman to health services, but they would refer her back to the agency since they did not know how to serve her or because they were unable to speak to her in her language. As well, many immigrant women's programs felt that the issue needed to be addressed within the broader context of health promotion.

These three studies illustrate the many layers impacting on the health of immigrant women. The impact may be embedded in the immigration policies allowing women to come to Canada, as demonstrated with the Live-In Caregiver Program. There may be consequences because these women fall out of routinely-used assessment tools, or immigrant women may slip through the cracks of the health service delivery program altogether. A further consequence is that migrant women may not show up in any data or studies: this has serious implications for policy development and the resulting program development that is supposed to address their health needs.

Teaching / Learning / Researching

Empowerment as Healing: Experiences of Nursing Faculty

Marilyn Chapman and Maureen Parkes
Nanaimo, British Columbia

Abstract

In this paper the authors explore the introduction of a new concept, in teaching nursing, to the Malsapina University College Nursing Program. Chapman and Parkes worked as part of a team that introduced new nursing curricula, which promoted empowerment as an essential tool for nursing, and at the same time, experienced profound professional and personal growth in their own lives. As part of this program Chapman and Parkes learned that dialogue is "a process in a journey in self growth and learning about self." This study also focusses on understanding the nature of self-empowerment, the implementation of a feminist perspective in the classroom, and how the new experience of shared governance in the classroom is both exciting and liberating. Finally, the authors address their introduction to and exploration of alternative healing practices, triggered by one woman's cancer experience, which heralded much broader and unexpected outcomes.

Empowerment as Healing

T rue personal empowerment leads to engagement in community and social action. More and more, nurses are involving themselves in community development and social action aimed at changing social inequities which have an adverse impact upon health. These shifts have provided the impetus for modifications within nursing education, directed at viewing the learner/teacher relationship as foundational to curricula and designed to promote personal and professional empowerment. Although the learning outcomes for such nursing curricula primarily relate to students, ultimately the teachers experience profound personal and professional growth.

In this paper, the authors will share their research and their personal experiences as teachers in an emancipatory nursing program; as part of a working team trying to implement a feminist perspective;

and, as women trying to make sense of being women. The experiences of the predominately female nursing faculty, teaching in an empowerment-focussed program have led to the exploration of alternate healing practices. This movement, initially triggered by one woman's cancer experience, has had broader, unexpected outcomes for all involved.

Historical Context

In 1992, five educational institutions in British Columbia implemented a new nursing curriculum. This implementation came from identifying changes in societal health concerns, requiring nurses to have higher levels of competence and critical thinking skills. These skills are needed to address these changes, and to practice within a caring perspective at a time of fiscal restraint.

In this curriculum, the student/teacher relationship and interactions are viewed as the core of the curriculum, rather than the course of studies or behavioural objectives that have traditionally been so highly valued in nursing education. Teachers are considered to be expert learners working with students in an empowering partnership, drawing on student experiences and the necessary theory to develop the content to be learned. Bevis (1989) discusses how teachers and students incorporate feminist scholarship and teaching techniques in order to empower and emancipate students. In turn, students within this model become more autonomous and critically reflective of their practice in the increasing complex role of a nurse in western society.

The aim of the first study, conducted in 1993, was to extend the knowledge and understanding of the student/teacher relationship and what the new curriculum meant to four teachers as they implemented the changes at one site. The study was timely, as few studies on the student/teacher relationship had been particularized to a nursing curriculum.

The second study considered the teachers' and students' perspectives on empowerment while teaching and learning in one particular course, in the new curriculum. In reviewing the background and findings of these two studies, the reader can consider some of the factors which might affect the teachers' experiences more recently, as they have been exploring alternative healing practices and its effect on their lives both personally and professionally.

STUDY ONE:

Faculty Experiences Teaching in a New Curriculum

The major findings involved change for the participants and the struggle to conceptualize these changes within the context of their own value systems. All participants indicated that the change was profound, but qualified this with different reasons. It was important to them not to have to know all the answers; however, they struggled with conceptualizing the student/teacher relationship.

Participant Quotations:

> "I give more responsibility to the student. I am trying to feel comfortable that students can choose."
>
> "I am more assertive. I struggle with how much choice and practicality."
>
> "I reflect more so I can move forward. I question more to work through difference."
>
> "I consciously reflect perceptions to the student. I need to be flexible with individuality."
>
> "Part of the learning or the essence of the learning is the teacher/student relationship and I think we have been struggling with what does that really mean? So we have had to talk about what does that really mean. What are the repercussions and implications of that. And, because the philosophy talks about each individual being different, then that also spills over into every teacher being different and every student being different, so you have to be able to go with what you think is right there. The student/teacher relationship is really the realization of a lot of things I always believed in and tried to do. I always believed in freedom of the student to go where they wanted to go."

Another revealing aspect of the research, that came out of completing it over a semester, was that three of the four participants stated that they felt like either quitting or not coming to work when they were being interviewed during the middle of the semester. When the researcher discussed this disclosure with the participants at the end of the semester, they expressed surprise that they had felt that way and indicated that their perspective had since changed. This severity and effect of change from the old paradigm very much related to the change in stress level throughout the semester.

Faculty Communication

The faculty needed to discuss philosophical differences to understand, for themselves and to have other faculty understand, the meaning of the student/teacher relationship and the context of the changes for them individually, and as a group. Time is needed to develop a trusting relationship within the faculty and with students, and lack of time was viewed as a detriment in faculty learning and the development of student/teacher relationships.

All of the participants saw learning about themselves and being on a life-long journey of learning as a big part of this process. They felt a profound need to discuss changes with other faculty, develop trust, and listen to each other — just as students are expected to do. This detail related to the same characteristics and factors seen as important in the student/teacher and nurse/client relationship by the participants.

Participant Quotation:

"It almost seems like the students are more open than the faculty. The restrictedness that I used to feel with the students, I sometimes feel with the faculty, because we are all in kind of different places it seems...maybe if we talk and find out that we really aren't but we are all so busy we don't have a chance to hash that out. So we say to the students, 'discussion is really important and listening to other people and working it out together', and then we don't do that...maybe it doesn't feel safe for some people or it is not a priority. It will be really interesting to read your paper and maybe I will find out I am not as alone as I think...should be respect for faculty philosophical differences, same as for students."

Use of Power in the Relationship

The participants mentioned a sharing of power with the students, a mutual decision-making, but also a mutual responsibility and the need for clear expectations. Friere (1970) addressed the traditional power relationships between students and teachers describing the transformed relationship as

... problem-posing education. Through dialogue the teacher-of-the-students and the students-of-the-teacher cease to exist and a new term emerges: teacher/student with students/teachers. The teacher is no longer merely the one-who-teaches, but one who is himself taught in dialogue with the students. They become jointly responsible for a process in which all grow. (p. 28)

Participant Quotation:

"We didn't give up all the power yet and I think to give that power we have to be comfortable in the standards and guidelines for us, for our responsibility as teachers and that is what holds us back…we haven't set all the safety nets in place yet. We need to be more articulate of the bottom lines…the standards. What do we see our responsibility toward that…there has to be a shared power but there still has to be a teacher and student and I think sometimes we really have to question how is that working because I still have a responsibility to be a resource person because I have been in some of the places the students haven't and I have to take a leader's role and that is not taking the power away…not that we know better but we have been there before. We can't say this is a self-directed problem and I will see you now and in December and it is up to you to get there. I think we have a responsibility to help them."

A Journey in Self-Growth: Learning About Self

The teachers saw the process as a journey in self-growth and learning about self. The findings give a sense that the students were asked to question, reflect, be vulnerable, be lifelong learners and ask for feedback; but more importantly, that the teachers need to do the same. Also, the data showed that the teacher needs time to develop trust, be able to not be right all the time, and to know the bottom lines — just as students did this.

Teachers should model trust and empowerment, and be able to question and reflect. Watson (1985) states:

A goal of nursing is to help persons gain a higher degree of harmony within the mind, body and soul which generates self-knowledge, self-reverence, self-healing and self-care processes. This goal may be achieved through the unique relationship that the nurse enters with a client. This relationship is most effectively taught through modelling the preferred nurse/client behaviours via the faculty/student relationship.

The findings of the study suggested that there is a profound interdependence of students and teachers in the relationship, and highlighted the importance of ongoing faculty communication during the implementation of the new curriculum.

This inquiry included the personal stories of nurse educators in which they questioned where they came from, where they are, and where they hope to go. Many of the principles outlined in the curriculum revolution were modelled by these teachers.

STUDY TWO:

Empowerment: Perspective of Students and Teachers Within this Curriculum

This study was an action research study. The study focussed on the nature of the classroom relationships; the teaching strategies that contributed to the evolution of the learners' understanding about the nature of empowerment; and, the participants' own sense of personal empowerment. Serendipitously, the study revealed the relationship between the teacher's growing sense of empowerment and that of the learners, and the healing nature of personal empowerment.

The course that was central to the study, and my own personal experience, was called "Empowerment". The course was, and remains, part of a four-year baccalaureate degree program in nursing, offered in the fifth semester of the program, during the fall of year three. The learning goals for the Empowerment course were listed as follows: to explore,

- personal meaning concerning gender relations in both the personal and professional life of the learner;
- historical attitudes and perspectives shaping the current status of women in the caring professions;
- selected current women's issues and issues for other oppressed, or marginalized, groups; and,
- the social actions appropriate for remedying gender, and other, inequities.

Most nurses are women and for this reason, ideas about the status and empowerment of women and the relative standing of the female dominated professions are considered important to the understanding of the evolution of nursing as a profession.

The curriculum, of which the Empowerment course is a part, is grounded in a philosophy of caring, where caring as the foundational underpinning of nursing practice is emphasized. In addition, the curriculum is grounded in feminism, humanism and critical social theory, as well as the natural sciences. All of the philosophical components lead to an overall curriculum design that encourages the development of both personal and communal empowerment.

Although the medical emphasis in Western health care still tends to place the physician in a dominant position in the health care hierarchy, a more team oriented approach to health care is becoming more prevalent. Nurses are taking on expanded roles in the community by providing health counselling in private practice, and by assuming more independent practice positions within health care institutions. Nurses are beginning to speak out loudly about the independent nature of nursing practice and the health promotion services that nurses are capable of providing in diverse practice settings.

However, Mason, Costello-Nickitas, Scanlan and Magnuson (1990) maintain that nurses are often frustrated by their inability to bring about change in the workplace or the community, therefore an education program that promotes empowerment is essential for nurses. Mason et al contend that such a program should include:

- the development of a strong, positive self esteem;
- the development of self-efficacy skills required for the attainment of personal and collective goals; and,
- consciousness-raising about the interlocking political and social realities that are the context of one's life and circumstance.

My study was carried out over a two-year period, during which there were two offerings of the Empowerment course. In designing the course, I was greatly influenced by Hezekiah (1993) who proposes five feminist goals for the classroom, namely:

- the creation of an atmosphere of mutual respect;
- the development of trust and community;
- the development of shared leadership;
- the presence of a cooperative structure that leads to the integration of cognitive and affective learning; and,
- the implementation of some form of action-oriented course work.

The course was designed as a series of learner-driven seminars. I provided some foundational readings and facilitate initial discussions, but the majority of the classes were student facilitated. I stressed the idea that the classes were to be seminar format, that groups were to prepare background material and to seek out videos and other stimuli to initiate dialogue.

In addition to the student-facilitated seminar format, I employed a process of collaborative decision-making about assignments and grading. The learners and I struggled as we tried to let go of some preconceived notions about grading in a formal education setting. My challenge was to develop some internal consistency within my philosophy of teaching and learning and my evolving understandings about empowerment.

The specifics of the course will not be considered in this paper, instead the list below describes some of the themes that became apparent through a narrative analysis of the journal I kept while teaching the course. The themes include the following:

- the role of power in relationships and the impact of the misuse of power.
- getting it clear: What I believe about teaching and learning.
- the impact of the positioning of individuals within society and within narrative and discourses.
- the importance of being in tune with the rhythms of learning.
- the relationship between development of a comfort with criticism, and the development of critical thinking.
- the impact of the writings on feminism and feminist pedagogy upon my practice (both teaching and nursing).
- the importance of a safe environment for learning.
- the healing associated with a growing sense of empowerment.

Instead of addressing all of the themes, I will develop the themes which had the most impact on me as a faculty member.

Nursing is a discipline with a large body of knowledge, a certain proportion of which practitioners must acquire before they graduate from nursing school. Faculty members can easily be pulled into a model of teaching that marks them as the expert, and the content as more important than the learner. In teaching the Empowerment course, I had to confront my own needs to be in control and found the experience of shared governance in the classroom both exciting and liberating. Once such a philosophy is embraced, it spills over into other areas of your life: working with faculty, interacting with your children, working in the community, etc. My journal revealed my struggles as a teacher in a university-college setting; as a part of a curriculum founded on caring; and, as a feminist pedagogue who desires to share power with the learners. Eventually, I realized that often learners want choice, but they also want structure, particularly when venturing into new and potentially anxiety-provoking areas that have the potential for transformative learning. In the delivery of my course, I feel I was able to reconcile these warring perspectives. In addition, I came to realize the impact of my upbringing upon my ideas about power, and in particular, male power.

Frequently, the misuse of power results in teachers not creating a safe place for learners to learn. As part of the action research study of the Empowerment course, I asked the learners what they needed in order to be safe, and how I did, or did not, contribute to that sense of safety. The learners told me that the "teacher needs to share themselves." Such sharing involved telling stories about their own lives and learning. The learners told me that teachers needed to be humble about what they knew and provide structure along with freedom. For the learners this meant that they could share their ideas without censure, but needed to know the limits of behaviour within the classroom. For example, the learners in the Empowerment course said that they appreciated being able to swear occasionally without being judged.

As a teacher and learner, I too, found that I needed to feel safe. My reflections upon how I like to receive feedback helped me to be responsive to how learners said they wanted to receive feedback. In turn, this reflection on the nature of feedback helped me to be clearer when other faculty required a response. I found that rather than "hedging" around, if I address my perceptions and offer them as not necessarily the only way to see things, I am much better received. Moreover, I have found that I need to feel safe with a group of learners in order to be effective. For example, my effectiveness increased over the semester as I came to know the learners and we collaborated on how to work together. I tried to be honest with the class, at all times, particularly when I struggled to create a safe climate for all and I tried to be honest with the faculty team when I did not feel safe or felt threatened.

Finally, in reviewing my journal I was struck by the number of times my experiences in teaching the Empowerment course led me back to disempowering experiences from my childhood, and the disempowering messages I still sent myself. I was over forty and still dealing with issues of power, and in particular, men and power. Readings on healing, forgiveness and feminism began to reveal new ways of approaching my experiences. I was encouraged by reading Brooks' book *Feminist Pedagogy: An Autobiographical Approach* (1992). Although I did not experience incest as Brooks had, the text helped me to identify blocks to my learning and personal growth that remained from my past. Through this process, I realized that I had created boundaries and continued to do so to protect myself.

In many ways I experienced what Mezirow (1978) calls a "perspective transformation" while teaching the Empowerment course. My learning was as profound as that experienced by some of the students in the class. At times I found that it was difficult to distinguish between teacher and learner in a class that had an emancipatory and transformative agenda.

In conclusion, I would like to add a personal note about the connection between healing and empowerment. For a number of years, I have suffered with rheumatoid arthritis. My dawning understanding about the connection between my fear of power and control, my need to control, and my growing understanding of the true nature of empowerment, has been accompanied by a remission in my arthritis. Recently, I have observed that when I get anxious about power and control issues my arthritis flares up. Many noted healers have written about this phenomenon, or a closely related theme. Believing in self, yet looking outside of self to contribute in some way to the greater good, allows for healing. Healing is not about being disease free, instead healing is about trusting in whom you are on a psycho/spiritual level.

Recent Faculty Experiences of a Healing Circle

"The professional is personal" is a philosophical stance the Nursing Faculty has become very conscious of in recent months. Caring and the relationships between faculty members became more important than ever, due in part to the fact that one of our members became ill with cancer. As a way of reaching out to her, and each other, we as a faculty, have been holding a healing circle. The woman diagnosed with cancer was very clear that the healing was to be shared, and that healing in its many guises was to be explored and be available to every person present at the healing circle. Teaching in an empowerment-focussed program had, in part, led these women to explore alternate healing practices.

In preparing for this paper, we asked several faculty members who participated in the healing circle to talk about their experiences. They shared with us how the experience impacted upon them both personally and professionally. The themes that arose in the reflections they shared are as follows:

- *Women are different at the healing circle than they are at work. People seemed able to come outside self to give to others.*

One faculty member indicated that she thought that at the healing circle women connected without words, with a deeper meaning, taking time for the self and appreciating others. She believed that this was very different from what happened at meetings. At the circle women came with the intent of pure, spiritual communication, while at meetings, the intent was not always clear.

- *Women were able to heal self with support from others.*

One woman said, "I have done a lot of my own healing, but I don't know if people at work could have helped with that. They can help make it work and set the setting, but I have to do the work myself just like her."

- *The experience of the healing circle allowed women to return to their bodies.*

On this theme, a woman shared that the group had a purpose, allowing her to be in her body rather than her head, which was where she spent a lot of her time. Another participant said that "we can't depend on technology to tell us how we feel." She suggested that women have been disconnected from our bodies, and alternate, healing modalities can give us control of our bodies and healing.

- *Life is short and fragile.*

The essence of this idea was captured by a participant who suggested that we live with the illusion of life, of many tomorrows. Another woman said that the experience of the circle grounded her in the sense that life was short and fragile.

- *Talking and experiencing alternate healing approaches brought connectedness and helped build relationships.*

This sentiment was echoed by one woman who stated that the experience of the healing circle allowed the participants to be more real and connected with each other, initially altruistically, and then for self and others. Another faculty member felt that attending the healing circle allowed people to drop their facades and get outside of self to give to others.

- *One woman's cancer experiences were the impetus for reflection and perhaps change.*

According to one member, the experience of cancer for one person was sad, but tragedy brought us closer and was the instigation for team healing. Another member said that she felt like an outsider before she joined the healing circle. While a third person reported that the circle allowed time for appreciation of self and others.

- Women questioned whether the healing circle was for the woman with cancer, self or both.

All of the faculty members with whom we spoke brought up this idea in some way. The women said that they came initially to assist the person with cancer with her healing, but that ultimately they experienced some form of healing themselves, not necessarily dramatic or physical, possibly relational, but healing nevertheless.

- *The perception that the faculty group needed a purpose for meeting outside of work time.*

It was interesting that it took one person's crisis to bring a group of nursing faculty together. Most of the faculty members attended the healing circle at some point, some more able to attend on a regular basis than others. This membership seems to attest to the nature of the relationships between faculty members.

- *The need for faculty to be trusting of each other, safe, and tolerant of differences in how each works with students and how students then work with patients.*

There is a tendency for divisiveness between faculty members: a tendency for faculty members to judge their merit one against the other. One member said that she thought that at the healing circle, the agenda was pure, spiritual communication, while at team meetings, she felt that the individual agendas were not as clear. She shared how she thought that we needed feminist healing and empowerment to move from the healing circle to the day-to-day working of faculty members.

- *The healing circle brought openness and healing.*

A strong theme was that we heal ourselves but that others can help us along that path.

Looking Forward: Personal Reflections
Maureen Parkes:

My experiences teaching in an emancipatory program and trying to make sense of being a woman has led to broad and unexpected learning. At times, I found it very difficult to be part of the healing circle. I thought that others would judge me, but found, in fact, that others were as vulnerable as I was. Since the healing circle began, I think that our Faculty Team Meetings have changed. People seem more willing to talk about basic concerns, let some things go and set priorities on important issues. I would like to undertake another research project with faculty members to identify how they have changed and developed in their values and beliefs. This research would be particularly interesting to pursue as we face increasing acuity of patients in the hospitals in which we work, expansion in numbers of students in our nursing program, and increasing needs for faculty members to undertake professional development. It is a circular process: teachers need to role model to students trust, empowerment, caring, and tolerance of others beliefs, and yet they need to learn how to support each other in a safe environment. I appreciate the importance of life long learning and I continue to strive for growth. I am thankful for my own journey of understanding and it is with confidence that I realize my own growth as a woman and teacher since the days of my research. I like me. I have more confidence, but retain the humble part of my character. I value students and faculty members as vulnerable people. I look after myself and try to stay in tune with my body, especially when I am feeling anxious and tired.

Marilyn Chapman:

I felt very honoured to be part of the healing circle. Unfortunately, I was not able to attend as often as I would have liked, but when I did it felt very comfortable. The circle was a way for me to put into practice much of what I believe about healing and health. I too felt vulnerable at times, as we ventured into uncharted territory for us as a group. Some days I attended and really felt the energy created by a group of women dedicated to helping each other, while at other times I arrived and found it very difficult to set aside the concerns of the day in order to be a conduit for healing energy. I believe that the group was very understanding of this, and each time we met, tried to use what each person had available that day. I do think that there has been a change in how we work together as a faculty team, as I think we speak more openly and identify when something is upsetting us or making us angry. This way of being is different for us and is, I believe, an indication of the increasing trust between us. Do not misunderstand me, we still struggle to put into practice some of the philosophical underpinnings of our curriculum. As Maureen says, we should be role-modelling the caring, tolerance and nurturance of feminist thought that directs the curriculum. I think that the healing circle has helped to put us back on track in this endeavour, but we still have work to do!

References

Bevis, E. O. & Watson, J. (1989). *Toward a caring curriculum: A new pedagogy for nursing.* New York: National Nursing League.

Friere, P. (1970). *Pedagogy of the oppressed.* New York: The Continuum Publishing Company.

Watson, J. (1985). *Nursing: The philosophy and science of caring.* Boulder, Colorado: Colorado Associated University Press.

Participatory Action Research: Feminists Conducting Research

Gayle Broad and Linda Gordon
Sault Ste. Marie, Ontario

Abstract

For the past three years, the authors have studied worker ownership and participation at Algoma Steel Corporation Incorporated located in Sault Ste. Marie, Ontario. They conducted related research over a two-year period with employees involved in a worker buyout of the company in which they worked. The research examines the spillover effects of employee participation in the community and evaluates the employees' ability to bring quality of life issues into the newly organized, joint decision-making process of a large corporation undergoing radical changes. In this paper, Broad and Gordon explore their experience as feminists conducting participatory action research in a male-dominated workplace, as well as the added dimension that feminist theory and practice have contributed to the knowledge created.

Introduction

In June 1992, Algoma Steel Incorporated located in Sault Ste. Marie, Ontario was purchased by the employees, and has since been co-managed by unionized and management personnel. For a number of years we have conducted related research at the company. Gayle's research has explored the experience of steelworkers engaged in the change process: the changing structures, the changing workplace, the changing work and the changing relations of employees as owners and decision-makers. While Linda's research has looked at the result that the employees' buyout has had on the community, namely the spillover effects of changes in one part of people's lives into other areas. Linda has also examined the changing role of workers in their interaction with families and community organizations as a model to others of changing workplace relations.

Based on our research from the past three years, four general areas of focus, of particular importance to feminists, have emerged:

- The way that relationships have been key to our learning, and to the learning that we hope to pass on to others;
- Concrete examples of feminist practice that contribute to making participatory action research work as a methodology;
- The unique interpretations that the application of feminist theory to a male-dominated workplace provides; and
- Recommendations for those feminists, who like us, are integrally engaged in praxis.

Relationships and Relational Learning

In a research methodology praxis, there is an image of a researcher as being an isolated, solitary individual with an immense capacity for knowledge that eradicates any hope of forming close, intimate relationships. This image is reinforced in academia by the stress on "original thinking" that every graduate student must illustrate before being considered for a degree; the emphasis on attributing every thought that is not "original" to the author(s) who previously identified it as their own; and, by the resistance to recognizing that ideas usually do not leap full-blown from the forehead of the researcher, but rather are often the results of discussions, readings and comparing notes with other researchers and friends.

Our work has provided proof that researchers do not have to live a life of isolation or solitary despair, and we fully expect to destroy the myth that only a few select people can do research of value. In the work that we have done in the past three years, our connections with each other and with other people stimulated the research, sustained the research, and we believe, led to a degree of excellence in the research that could not have been achieved without relationships.

When we began this journey, we knew each other only through our community activism, in that we were both members of the local social justice coalition and the local health council. Through a casual conversation after a meeting, we discovered that we shared a mutual interest in returning to school. But we were both confronted with no access to a postgraduate programme in our community and due to family commitments, we were both unwilling to relocate. Shortly afterwards, Linda found a university that could accommodate these needs—through another friendship—and our research partnership began.

The partnership flourished initially because of the interests we shared — our interest in worker ownership and participation, our interest in community and community economic development, and our active commitment to feminist socialist principles. But in many ways, our differences contributed most to our learning — our different life experiences and academic backgrounds, our different personality types, our different approaches to solving problems, and our different comfort levels with theory and practice.

A common interest in Participatory Action Research (PAR) led us to select it as our research methodology. PAR provided an opportunity to continue promoting social change while also conducting research. During the process we were able to include and involve the people whose voices are not usually heard in the research process; and, were able to expand our research partnership to include the people whose lives and community were altered by their participation in worker ownership.

We believed that PAR is particularly suited to the study of complex phenomena, and we shared a common vision of a world where social, economic and environmental issues were all indivisibly linked. However, our different life experiences gave us varying perspectives of the aspects that needed study; and, as our research participants added their views, the dimensions of our understanding became larger and larger.

Walking around an object placed in the middle of a circle gives the viewer a different perspective from each angle. We found that posing a research question to people with varied life experiences provided the same. Even though the participants involved in our study were all affected by worker ownership and participation, each had different perceptions of that experience, and each enlarged on the "truth" of what that experience entailed.

As feminists, we know that each person's experience is their own 'truth' and we draw our conclusions not from challenging an individual's experience, but rather from the accumulation of similarities and differences that arise when we share that experience. By viewing research as an inclusive process it means that the more people involved in the process, attempting to discern the 'truths' that the shared experiences reveal, the better the quality of the research. In reference to the contributing authors of *Beyond Economic Man,* Rebecca Blank (1993) states:

> Through feminist theory, the authors argue for making

economics more inclusive, both in theory and in its methodology. These authors argue that there are many paths to truth, and that economics would be better off if it recognized and encouraged more of those paths. (p. 143)

Our recommendation to other feminists engaged in the research process is this: work collaboratively, find partners, build support circles, include the people engaged in the work under study, and by doing so, you will improve the quality of your research, deepen your analysis, and may even expand your conclusions.

Feminist Practice Contributes to PAR as a Research Method

Including other people in the research process means that there is a different set of skills required of the researcher. Instead of the ability to sustain long periods of time alone, the researcher requires the ability to establish, sustain and nurture relationships; a skill set which feminists have historically been required to develop in order to sustain themselves!

In our research, there were a number of very significant relationships. Beyond our own partnership was a small group of family and friends that we referred to as our 'book club', although we never actually read books together. Instead, our book club was a group of about six people with whom we spoke regularly, off whom we bounced ideas, and who patiently listened to our long, involved explanations of what we thought our research might be telling us. The group included two people working with a number of Algoma Steel employees, who often provided us with a secondary confirmation, or produced questions about some of the issues raised in our research. The group also included a person who made what he thought was a rhetorical statement one night — 'You can't really value the workers if you don't value the work' — which led Gayle's research down a whole new path of exploration. The book club provided sustenance to us as researchers, not only through cooking for us occasionally (which they did), but also through making our research a priority in their lives. They were constantly interested, assuring us that what we were doing was important and valued by a group of well-respected friends and colleagues.

We, in turn, developed relationships with a whole new group of people — the voluntary participants. These people committed themselves to spending enormous amounts of time educating us about the work they were doing: patiently explaining the processes of making steel, of making decisions in a co-managed workplace, of the vagaries of the steel market in a global economic crisis, and of the effects of all these changes on themselves, their families and their communities. As we worked with our groups—about sixteen people in all, although many more participated on an occasional basis—we were constantly challenged to re-evaluate our assumptions, question our motives and expand our understanding.

We were also challenged by the intimacy and trust the participants extended to us; and in turn, by the responsibility we felt to ensure that our research reflected the truth of their experiences. On one occasion, Gayle spent almost forty minutes on a telephone call from Bristol to Sault Ste. Marie with a research participant, verifying that quotes she wished to use did not contravene the confidentiality of the participant and that the quote and context accurately represented his experience.

We tried to develop relationships in which the participants would feel comfortable enough to challenge our ideas and action plans. At one point, Linda spent a month developing an action plan to propose to the research group, writing and rewriting, struggling to find options that would accurately reflect both the researchers' and the participants' objectives. When Linda presented her action plan at a meeting, it was dismissed by the group in less than ten minutes. By the end of the meeting the group had developed an entirely new plan that was quite ambitious, yet which they carried out in a systematic and rewarding manner. Clearly the participants were comfortable challenging the lead researchers!

Feminist Theory Contributions

A question we were frequently asked is: "Why are feminists studying steelworkers at Algoma Steel?" The implication was that feminists can only make contributions by studying women and so-called 'women's issues'. What we found was, in fact, quite the contrary for a number of reasons.

We chose worker ownership/participation at Algoma Steel Inc. as our research topic because of our shared belief that this model has the potential to promote the socialist principles of redistributing wealth and democratizing both the economy and the community. As feminist socialists we found that our analysis of the data collected in the research required us to find writings on economics, the value of work, holism, social psychology, sociology, theories of the family and theories of change. Feminist theorists have shown a willingness to tackle issues in a cross-disciplinary way that utilizes a holistic view of the world. Marilyn Waring (1998), Marilyn French (1986), Dorothy Smith (1987, 1999), Patricia Maguire (1987) and a number of other feminists, do not hesitate in taking issues, explanations and experiences from one part of life and apply them to another. A feminist lens applied to a male-dominated workplace exposed a whole new dimension, while the research done by women such as Pat Armstrong (1994) and Meg Luxton (1980) around women's work added another. Each additional theorist supplied another layer to our understanding.

We chose PAR as a research methodology because our personal commitments to making change had to be an integral part of anything to which we allocated this much time. Feminists have provided leadership in developing this approach to research, as well as contributing new consideration to the inclusion of voices not usually heard in the research process. In this area, the writings about action research by Canadian authors Ristock and Pennell (1996) and Reitsma-Street (1996) were particularly beneficial.

Feminist theories exploring the value of work have shown that relational work — the work of caring for others — is not valued/ devalued in society. Yet we know that in making and sustaining change, this kind of work is essential. Therefore, in the male-dominated workplace of Algoma Steel which was attempting to achieve a major cultural shift, the relational work should have been a crucial part of the infrastructure. Without the feminist recognition of relational supports as work, this whole area of endeavour "disappeared" (Fletcher, 1996).

Value of work theorists have also demonstrated that work tends to be evaluated only in terms of dollars — that unpaid work, or work that is paid at a lower scale, is not valued as highly, nor is the worker who performs the work, considered as valuable. In a workplace where all workers owned equal shares in the company, but were still being valued within the old hierarchical structures, it was not surprising to find discrepancies between the power and influence of workers.

Feminist economists have long recognized the fact that the way in which we measure the success of the economy has historically overlooked assigning a value to the sustainability of the planet, or indeed, the sustainability of any particular endeavour. Our research discovered that when a feminist lens is applied to the success of worker ownership/participation at Algoma Steel, the determination of whether the endeavour is a 'success' became a very different process. Currently, the standard method of evaluating a company's 'success' tends to be based entirely on its profit and loss statement. The evaluation does not even attempt to measure quality of work-life issues, numbers of employees, environmental sustainability, training and education of its workers, yet all of these factors are important in determining the company's continued viability.

Feminist sociologists and psychologists recognize the need for a holistic analysis of the person, and the interconnectedness of the many different spheres of people's and communities' lives. As Ann Jennings (1993) states:

> . . . the solution to "economism" is a cultural reconnection of home, workplace, and polity that recognizes the reproductive, productive, and political aspects of most human activities . . . Only when this happens can established beliefs in the essential dissimilarity of spheres, pursuits, and social groups — the precondition for devaluation — be transformed. What is separate is rarely, if ever, equal. (p. 126)

Our research partnership — based on the close collaboration and investigation of what are usually considered separate spheres — allowed us to connect Gayle's research in the public sphere of the workplace to Linda's spillover research about the private sphere and what Moore Milroy and Wismer (1994) call the third sphere of community work. By conducting these two pieces collaboratively, we followed the feminist approach of challenging the false dualism of different spheres.

A few examples from Linda's findings (Gordon et al, 1999) illustrate the blending of spheres. According to some interviewees, many of the steelworkers have learned to listen more. This was often attributed to the fact that the steelworkers were required to attend meetings and training in communication skills. The steelworkers felt that as a result of this training, they dealt in a more positive way with their families. One steelworker stated:

> It used to be the attitude that children are to be "seen and not heard". Now there's more of an attitude that kids are not just kids, that they have ideas, opinions and so on. Through training we have learned to respect other opinions. Their opinions are not just discounted arbitrarily. I think we carry that home. (p.12)

Another employee echoed this idea stating:

> At home with my kids, in my whole life with all the people I'm in contact with, training has helped with better listening skills, just understanding people better and being able to put myself into others' shoes, to have empathy. (p. 13)

The use of problem solving, communication and conflict resolution skills in personal relationships was part of the findings from the perspectives of not just steelworkers themselves, but from those of family members, friends, co-workers, service providers as well. A very clear example of this was given by a local social worker who said:

> The person was having a family problem, and . . . he was talking about the things he was learning at work . . . how he had the opportunity to have some training. He just lit up when he talked about it, whereas he definitely wasn't lit up when we were talking about the problems he was experiencing. So when he lit up, I said "Tell me more about this." And so he went into detail about the skills he was learning around problem solving and communication at work and working with a team. And so then I said to him, "Can we apply some of what you learned at work to this problem you are having at this time with your family?" And so we did. We looked at the family problems he was having, and I said "How can you use what you learned in the course to solve this problem?" What had happened is he had learned a problem solving skill and we applied it to the communication process with this particular family member. (pp. 12-13)

Finally, feminist theory was one of the main contributors to our notion of praxis. The statement 'the personal is political' encapsulates for feminists the inseparability of people's everyday experience from the theoretical conceptualization of the 'relations of ruling' (Smith, 1987), which both create and are created by those experiences. As our participants tried to improve (take action to change) their realities inside and outside the Algoma Steel workplace, they understood those realties better. Praxis, or action + reflection (Mies, 1986, p. 53), was at the heart of our participatory action research about Algoma Steel.

Recommendations and Conclusions

For feminists engaged in using research as a change process, we provide the following list of recommendations:

- Work collaboratively, enjoy the process of including yourself and others in your journey of discovery;
- Bring yourself into the research — understanding your own biases and being able to identify your values in what you are learning is at least as honest as trying to maintain objectivity;
- Cross disciplines as you would cross a street — if you feel a need to go there, it is because there is an aspect of understanding to be found;
- Apply feminist theory — the feminist lens — in whatever field you have an interest; feminists have a different way of looking at the world, and we need that dimension added to all facets of life including areas that have until now been the domain of traditional male thinkers;
- Include people with perspectives other than your own — learning is about questioning our own assumptions, seeing the world through the eyes of others, understanding how our own beliefs have evolved; and finally,
- Have the courage to let go of the process — learning and engaging in change is a process which cannot be controlled.

This type of research contradicts the script of traditional academia. We never pretended to be 'objective observers' engaged in some kind of ultimate discovery of absolute truths. Instead we used a democratic, inclusive approach that demystifies knowledge creation because the knowledge sources, the people engaged in the work under study, were integrally involved in the discovery and recognition of their own knowledge. In this type of protocol, if the researcher is successful, the participants realize that they are indeed the experts and that the researchers are merely the facilitators. In this model the researchers become space-makers, persons who make space and time for the participants to examine their experience and make sense of it.

The *Stone Centre Papers*[1] refer time and again to the "mutuality of learning". This is the exciting process in which both (or all) of the people involved in a discussion build on one another's ideas and concepts, respect their different approaches, and recognize that they are learning from one another. Our research process was like that; we questioned one another, we challenged one another to take more steps, and then we supported each other when we thought that the last step took us over the edge. The process was and remains an exciting, stimulating, and incredibly rewarding experience.

When we finish writing up our research, we know that the process is not complete. We remain in fairly frequent contact with our participants, who are themselves engaged in continued research in an informal way. Our actions are not finite, not closed by the conclusion of this phase of the research process. One of the great contributions of PAR is that it is a continuing cycle, so that it does not end with us. Our participants now understand and are capable of using PAR themselves, therefore we cannot predict where the cycle may go next, or whether the ripples and effects will even be visible to us; but, we do know that we have been profoundly changed by our experience, and cannot wait to find out what happens next.

Endnotes

1. We extend our thanks to Dr. Jennifer MacIntyre and Dr. Susan Garrett for introducing us to this series of "Works in Progress". Discovering these papers through them is yet another example of relational learning.

References

Armstrong, P. & Armstrong, H.(1994). *The Double ghetto: Canadian women and their segregated work.* Toronto: McClelland & Stewart Inc.

Blank, R. (1993). What should mainstream economists learn from feminist theory? In Marianne A. Ferber and Nelson, Julie A. (Eds.), *Beyond economic man: Feminist theory and economics.* Chicago: The University of Chicago Press.

Ferber, Marianne A. and Nelson, Julie A. (Eds.). (1993). *Beyond economic man: Feminist theory and economics.* Chicago: The University of Chicago Press.

Fletcher, J. K. (1996). Relational theory in the workplace (The Stone Papers no.77). *The Wellesley Centre for Women Publications [online ordering].* Available: http://www.wellesley.edu/wcw/stone/stonewo.html. (August

31, 2000)

French, M. (1986). *Beyond power: On women, men and morals.* New York: Ballantine Books.

Gordon, L., Amaral, J., Boissoneau, B., Carricato, M., DelVecchio, K., Greaves, E., Principe, J., St. John, R., and Zore, B. (1999). Joint Process and ownership: Benefits for life outside the plant. Unpublished summary of findings of Algoma Steel Spillover Research Project, Sault Ste. Marie, Ontario.

Jennings, A. L. (1993). Public or private? Institutional economics and feminism. In Marianne A. Ferber and Nelson, Julie A. (Eds.), *Beyond economic man: Feminist theory and economics.* Chicago: University of Chicago Press.

Luxton, M. (1980). *More than a labour of love: Three generations of women's work in the home,* Toronto: Women's Press.

Maguire, P. (1987). *Doing participatory research: A Feminist approach.* Amherst, Massachusetts: Center for International Education.

Mies, M. (1991). *Patriarchy and accumulation on a world scale.* London: Zed Books.

Reitsma-Street, M. (1996). Activist research contributions to shutting down a welfare snitch line. *Atlantis, vol 21,* no 1, Fall, pp 123-132.

Ristock, J. and Pennell, J. (1996). *Community research as empowerment: Feminist links, postmodern interruptions.* Toronto: Oxford University Press.

Moore Milroy, B. and Wismer, S. (1994). Communities, work and public/private sphere models. *Gender, Place and Culture,* vol 1, no 1.

Smith, D. (1987). *The everyday world as problematic: A feminist sociology.* Boston: Northeastern University Press.

Smith, D. (1999). *Writing the social: Critique, theory, and investigations.* Toronto: University of Toronto Press.

The Stone Papers. *The Wellesley Centre for Women Publications [online ordering].* Available: http://www.wellesley.edu/wcw/infopub.html (August 31, 2000)

Waring, M. (1988). *If women counted: A New feminist economics.* San Francisco: Harper & Row.

Heart Wise Women: The Sudbury Experience

Ellen Rukholm, with Jean Hyland,
Judy Courtemanche and Judy Poupore
Sudbury, Ontario

Abstract

The major cause of death and disability among women in Canada is cardiovascular disease, accounting for 47% of deaths in women in Ontario and 53% of deaths in women in Sudbury. In reaction to these statistics, a Sudbury committee was formed with the aim of raising awareness and educating women about this critical health issue. The committee's first activity was to host a breakfast event, in conjunction with the local Heart and Stroke Foundation Chapter. The committee's strategy was to combine a presentation of local and provincial cardiovascular statistics, an explanation of cardiovascular risk factors including pertinent lifestyle behaviours with a dramatic, personal-political story of a female stroke survivor. This paper will feature an account of the theoretical basis of research as well as a description of the learning gained from this event.

Introduction

Until very recently few people have been aware that women are susceptible to cardiovascular diseases. In fact, almost as many women as men die because of cardiovascular diseases each year in Canada. Although deaths from cardiac disease in both men and women have been diminishing since the 1960s, the rise in tobacco use by young women is a cause for considerable concern in the future (Eaker, Packard et al, 1989).

In the Spring of 1996 a group of Sudbury women, in collaboration with the Sudbury Chapter of the Heart and Stroke Foundation of Ontario, hosted a Breakfast Information Event for women in Sudbury. Over 500 women attended the event and 383 answered an evaluation questionnaire. This article provides some background information on cardiovascular risk factors in women and presents the results of that evaluation.

Risk Factors in Women

The following is a listing of specific risk factors for women along with an explanation of the factor, statistical analysis of the factor, and a brief description or reference to the research performed in each area.

- ## Smoking

Smoking is a major preventable risk factor of cardiovascular diseases in women. According to a Health Canada survey conducted in 1994, since 1991, cigarette smoking has increased by about 5%, most notably among young women.

- ## High Blood Pressure

Blood pressure increases with age in both men and women. Although more men than women experience high blood pressure, after menopause more than one third of Canadian women have high blood pressure (Joffres et al, 1992). Compared to women with normal blood pressure, the risk of complications is increased 5 to 6 times in women with high blood pressure. Only a few studies of women have been done on the effects of treatment. In particular, women have been under-represented in studies of the effectiveness of medications for hypertension.

- ## Cholesterol

Total cholesterol above 5.2 mmol/L occurs less in women under 45 years of age than in men of this age group (Connelly et al, 1992). However, after menopause women undergo a rapid increase in total cholesterol, acquiring levels higher than in men by 55 years. The 'good cholesterol' HDL-C, tends to be high in pre-menopausal women and low in postmenopausal women. The findings to date on hormonal replacement therapy following menopause are controversial and more research is needed in this area.

- ## Diabetes Mellitus

Diabetes mellitus (5%) in women is not as high as smoking (28%) or elevated blood cholesterol (43%), however, it is often seen with being overweight (27%) and having an inactive lifestyle (85%) (Health Canada, 1995; Reeder et al, 1992). The relative impact of diabetes on death from ischemic heart disease and acute myocardial infarction is greater in women than in men (Barrett-Connor & Wingard, 1983). Diabetic women have ischemic heart disease rates that are like those of non-diabetic men. Furthermore, studies of prognoses after a heart attack (myocardial infarction) have shown that diabetic women have a worse outcome than diabetic men (Abbott et al, 1988).

- Physical Inactivity

The Campbell's Survey of the Well Being of Canadians examined physical activity. According to this survey, only 10% of women aged 20-64 years of age are regularly involved in aerobic activity (30 minutes or more every other day, at 50% of individual capacity or greater). Thirty percent (30%) of women over 65 undertook aerobic activity, usually walking (Stephens & Craig, 1990). Only 41% of women in the Canadian Heart Health Survey mentioned lack of exercise as a risk factor for cardiovascular diseases. Even in women with a high degree of education, lack of exercise was mentioned by only 52% as a risk factor. The majority of women did not see regular physical activity as important for heart health (MacDonald et al, 1992).

- Obesity

There is a relationship between obesity and cardiovascular health (Reeder et al, 1992). Results from the Canadian Heart Health Survey, released by Health and Welfare Canada in 1981, indicate that for women, mean Body Mass Index (BMI) increases steadily to age 55-64 years of age, and then reaches a plateau. Obesity (BMI > 27) was evident in 27% of women ages 18-74. Of all women, 5% had a BMI > 35 compared to 9% of women aged 55-64 and 8% of women aged 65-74. Despite many attempts to promote healthy weight over the past twenty years, obesity continues to be a problem amongst women.

- Hormonal Risk Factors

Hormone replacement therapy and oral contraceptive are issues of central concern for women. Early studies of oral contraceptive use with higher hormonal dosage, showed a two to four times increase in risk of both fatal and non-fatal heart attack (e.g., Eaker et al, 1989; Ockene &Ockene, 1992; Stampfer et al, 1990; Wynn, 1991). However, lower dosages and careful selection of candidates for treatment have reduced the risk (e.g., Thorogood etal, 1991; Mant et al, 1987; Baird & Glasier, 1993). The risk increases, when combined with other risk factors. Combined smoking and oral contraceptive use, substantially elevate the risk of myocardial infarction (see: Croft & Hannaford, 1989; Thorneycroft, 1990). Although some evidence suggests that there is a residual risk of heart attack for up to six years after stopping oral contraceptives, most recent studies do not show a significant risk for those who have used oral contraceptives in the past (see: Vessey et al, 1989; Stampfer et al, 1990; Roseberg et al, 1990).

In contrast to oral contraceptives, post-menopausal estrogen replacement therapy seems to have a protective effect. According to research conducted at the Lipid Research Clinics in 1987, women who used estrogen for menopausal symptoms have one-third to one-half the risk of fatal and non-fatal heart attacks of those who do not. But estrogen taken alone seems to increase the risk of endometrial cancer, so estrogen combined with low dose progestin has been recommended to diminish the risk (La Rosa, 1988).

Symptoms of Ischemic Heart Disease in Women

Angina is the most common expression of ischemic heart disease in women. Interestingly, the expressions of symptoms of a heart attack in women are thought to be different from those of men. Angina seems to have a better long term prognosis in women than in men (Lerner & Kannel, 1986). Angiographic studies have shown that 50% of women with angina have minimal or no obstructive coronary disease, thus explaining the relatively benign outcome (Kennedy et al, 1982).

Because of the lower over-all prevalence of ischemic heart disease in women, the predictive value of any diagnostic test is lower in women than in men. Exercise electrocardiography has a higher false positive rate in women overall, however that improves when applied to women with a higher pre-test probability of disease (post-menopausal women, more typical angina, or with resting ECG abnormalities) and can provide similar estimates of prognosis compared to men (Osbakken, 1989; Mark et al, 1991). Other diagnostic techniques, such as thallium scans and echocardiography with exercise or pharmacologic stress, have shown higher specificity in women (Sawada et al, 1989; Hung et al, 1984).

Management and Outcomes

Women with established ischemic heart disease are more likely to be disabled and to have a poorer outcome, even when increased age and other concurrent risk factors are accounted for statistically (see: Ayanian & Epstein, 1991; Dittrich et al, 1988; Tofler et al, 1987). There are few data concerning specific medication treatment for ischemic heart disease in women. Fewer women are referred for coronary angiography than men, even with positive diagnostic tests, acute myocardial infarction, or greater functional disability due to angina. There is controversy as to whether or not this represents a gender bias (see: Ayanian & Epstein, 1991; Bickell et al, 1992; Mark et al, 1994; Steingart et al, 1991; Cowley et al, 1985).

Both coronary angioplasty (PTCA) and Coronary Artery Bypass (CAB) surgery have similar long term survival benefits for both men and women. Earlier reports of coronary angioplasty in women identified lower success rates, increased complications and procedural mortality, however, more recent studies show that this is no longer true (e.g., Cowley et al, 1985; Sawada et al, 1989). According to a Coronary Artery Surgery Study conducted in 1983, CAB surgery in women is associated with a higher operative mortality and a poorer clinical response. This operative mortality (approximately twice that of men) has been thought to be due to the smaller coronary artery size in women but may also be because of other variables such as age and status of the heart at surgery. To date, all research indicates that women are less likely to have any of the above mentioned invasive procedures (Ayanian & Epstein, 1991; Steingart et al, 1991; Jaglal, Goel & Naylor, 1994).

Non-anginal manifestations of ischemic heart disease are less common in women. Sudden death, in particular, accounts for only 7% of all coronary events in women compared to 10% in men. There is little data on silent ischemia in women, despite the greater frequency of unrecognized infarction: 35% in women versus 27% in men (Lerner & Kannel, 1986). Survival after the development of heart failure is better in women, and persists even when age and cause of heart failure are statistically controlled (Ho et al, 1993).

Acute heart attack is associated with a higher mortality rate in women across all age groups, with an overall case fatality rate of 32% versus 27% in the Framingham data (see: Lerner & Kannel, 1986). Women are more likely to have non-Q wave infarctions, reinfarctions, peri-infarction strokes and congestive heart failure. Since women overall have better left ventricular function as measured by systolic contractility, there seems to be a higher prevalence of diastolic dysfunction (see: Dittrich et al, 1988; Tofler et al, 1987; Greenland et al, 1991).

One year mortality after acute heart attack is higher in women, 29% versus 15% in men (GISSI, 1987). Thrombolytic therapy produces a comparable reduction in mortality for both men and women (see:

FTT, 1994; Weaver et al, 1993). However, women are more likely not to receive thrombolytic treatment. This may be due to delays in arriving at the emergency room, other concomitant conditions, or increased risk of bleeding complications, particularly haemorrhagic stroke (Ball et al, 1993; Maggioni et al, 1992). The use of beta blockers after acute heart attack has been shown to be beneficial in both women and men (Rodda, 1983). In women, ACE inhibitors used following myocardial infarction have been shown to reduce mortality (Pfeffer et al,1992; AIRE Study Investigators, 1993).

Stroke

Stroke mortality has been declining in Canada over several decades, however strokes are an especially significant cause of death and disability for elderly women. Of the various kinds of stroke, young women appear to have more subarachnoid haemorrhages, the least common type of stroke overall. Women are at increased risk of stroke because of exposure to unique risk factors such as toxaemia in pregnancy, oral contraceptive use, and conditions such as mitral valve prolapse and migraine headaches (Barnett, 1990).

High blood pressure is the most important risk factor for stroke in both genders. Women who smoke or have diabetes are at greater risk of stroke than men. A woman who smokes has almost twice the risk of stroke as a nonsmoker. The addition of hypertension places at even higher risk. Stopping smoking alone can reduce the risk by one third.

The long term effects of disability are greater in women than in men because women are more likely to survive. Furthermore, women account for the larger proportion of disabled stroke patients in nursing homes because more women survive into the latter decades of life. The treatment of stroke is the same for men and women , including endarterectomy and treatment of atrial fibrillation with aspirin or warfarin, however the effects of these treatments have been studied largely in men.

Environmental Factors

According to some studies working women are healthier overall, and have fewer risk factors for cardiovascular diseases than those not employed. The demands of the work, as well as the amount of personal control and social support, are factors that may be far more important than employment alone (Haynes & Czajkowski, 1993). Although women are usually better than men at both organizing and using social support, it would appear that lack of social support has more devastating effects for women. The risk of cardiovascular diseases in women is increased when they experience the stress of multiple roles, such working more than 20 hours per week and being a homemaker with little or no spousal support (Hall, 1989).

Anger and depression also increase the risk. It could be that the effect of social factors and how women respond to stresses changes according to age. Research is being done on these environmental factors to better understand the impact of stress and to develop effective preventive strategies (Johnson & Stewart, 1993).

Sudbury Breakfast Evaluation Results

Over 500 women attended the Breakfast Information Event that featured two speakers: a female cardiologist and a woman who told her personal story about experiencing a stroke. A questionnaire designed to evaluate the event was distributed to the women attending the breakfast, containing questions about the presentation and questions designed to gather information about respondents smoking, physical activity and nutrition behaviours. Data was also gathered about the types of information women want, and the format and timing of the presentation for any future events. Prochaska and DiClemente's Stages of Change (1982) provided the theoretical framework for the heart health behaviour questions.

A total of 383 respondents answered the evaluation questions. Of these respondents 98% were female; 57% were in the 45-64yrs age group; 33% were in the 25-44 yrs age group; 65% had completed college/university; and, 33% have completed grades 9-13. One hundred percent of the respondents indicated that they enjoyed the breakfast function, while 99% stated that they would attend another function, and 94% claimed to have learned something new. In terms of how the respondents learned about the breakfast, 31% stated that they heard about the breakfast from a friend, while 25% indicated they received the information from a committee member.

Results showed that 60% of the respondents did not know that the cardiovascular disease prevalence rates for women in Sudbury were higher than the provincial rate. The numbers for the risk factors for heart disease are dissimilar. The majority of those attending were non-smokers (89%), but only 54% of attendants indicated that they participated in regular physical activity sufficient to increase heart rate and cause perspiring. The majority of women indicated they ate low fat foods, while 87% said they enjoyed a wide variety of foods every day. Finally, 83% of the respondents indicated that they had their blood pressure checked during the previous 12 months.

In terms of future presentations, the respondents were interested in learning more about: heart healthy eating (46%), menopause (43%), handling stress (42%), risk for heart attack (37%), improving physical activity (32%), hypertension (27%), and smoking cessation (10%).

Discussion

In general the data gathered at the breakfast suggested that there was a lack of comprehensive understanding in the area of heart disease amongst these women. The Breakfast respondents said they wanted more education and information on all aspects of heart health promotion and cardiovascular disease prevention. In particular, this group of women wanted more information about eating a heart healthy diet and being physically active. Although respondents said they consumed a variety of foods every day, including lower fat foods, they also indicated that they would like to improve their eating habits. Furthermore, the data suggested that many of the respondents did not exercise regularly, a finding that is congruent with the national survey findings noted earlier in this paper. Since physical inactivity is a major risk factor, barriers and supports for regular physical activity need to be determined. Finally, the women who attended the breakfast were primarily highly educated professionals. Research has shown that there is a positive relationship between low socio-economic status (SES) and heart disease, therefore, future events should be targeted at these women as they did not attend the breakfast.

Summary

Although cardiovascular mortality continues to decline, for Canadian women there are causes for concern. An increasing number of women are beginning the post-menopausal phase of their lives, when their risk of cardiovascular diseases increases. The increasing impact of disease and disability, added to the effect of aging, will likely have economic demands on already over-taxed health care and social expenditures. Although cardiovascular diseases are being prevented and the prevalence of risk factors seems to be declining, the increase in smoking among young women is of tremendous concern.

The purpose of focussing on women and cardiovascular diseases is to create an awareness of this problem amongst women. In summarising the Canadian data that exist, it is important to note that there are gaps in knowledge and that there is a need to identify priorities for future research and health promotion activities. Future research and health promotion activities need to consider age, ethnicity (aboriginal women) and socioeconomic factors. Also, further clarification of hormone replacement therapy (HRT) is of critical importance, so that women can be advised of the latest relevant information to guide their decisions concerning HRT. Similarly, there is a need for more information on the effect of cardiovascular medications in women, as well as the differences according to gender in terms of access to diagnostic services, treatment and rehabilitation. We need to understand why this apparent difference occurs, so that strategies can be developed to ensure equity.

Beyond these research issues, there is the pressing need to understand how to disseminate relevant, scientific information to ordinary women in a user-friendly manner. We also need to better understand how to create community environments that promote and support heart healthy choices that are gender specific. Only by further discussion and research will we begin to ask and probe the right questions.

References

AIRE Study Investigators. (1993). Effect of ramipril on mortality and morbidity of survivors of acute myocardial infarction with clinical evidence of heart failure. (1993). *The Lancet, 342*, 821-828.

Abbott, R.D., Donahue, R.P., Kannel, W.B., & Wilson, R.W. (1988). The impact of diabetes on survival following myocardial infarction in men vs women: The Framingham study. *Journal of the American Medical Association, 260*, 3456-3460.

Ayanian, J.Z., & Epstein, M.A. (1991). Differences in the use of procedures between women and men hospitalized for coronary heart disease. *New England Journal of Medicine, 325*, 222-225.

Baird, D.T., & Glasier, A.F. (1993). Drug therapy: Hormonal contraception. *New England Journal of Medicine, 328*, 21, 1543-

1549.

Ball, S., Carrao, J., Gore, J. et al. (1993). *Patients ineligible for thrombolytic therapy: The GUSTO acute myocardial infarction census log.* Circulation, 88 (suppl.), abstract 0306.

Barnett, H.J.M. (1990). Stroke in women. *Canadian Journal of Cardiology, 6,* (suppl. B), 11B-17B.

Barrett-Conner, E., & Wingard, D.L. (1983). Sex differential in ischemic heart disease mortality in diabetics: A prospective population-based study. *American Journal of Epidemiology, 118,* 489-496.

Bickell, N.A., Pieper, K.S., Lee, K.L., Mark, D.B., Glower, D.D., Pryor, D.B., & Califf, R.M. (1992). Referral patterns for coronary artery disease treatment: Gender bias or good clinical judgement? *Annals of Internal Medicine, 116,* 791-797.

Connelly, P.W., MacLean, D.R., Holick,L., O'Connor, B., Petrasovits, A., & Little, J.A. (1992). Plasma lipids and lipoproteins and the prevalence of risk for coronary heart disease in Canadian adults. *Canadian Medical Association Journal, 146,*(11 suppl.), 1977-1987.

Coronary Artery Surgery Study (CASS). (1983). *A prospective randomized trial of coronary artery bypass surgery.* Circulation, 68, 939-950.

Cowley, M.J., Mullin, S.M., Kelsey, S.F., Kent, K.M., Gruentzig, A.R., Detre, K.M., & Passamani, E.R. (1985). Sex differences in the early and long term results of coronary angioplasty. In *NHLBI PTCA Registry.* Circulation, 71, 90-97.

Croft, P., & Hannaford, P.C. (1989). Risk factors for acute myocardial infarction in women: Evidence from the royal college of general practitioners' oral contraceptive study. *British   Medical Journal, 298,* 165-168.

Dittrich, H., Gilpin, E., Nicod, P., Cali, G., Henning, H., & Ross, J. (1988). Acute myocardial infarction in women: Influence of gender on mortality and prognostic variables. *American Journal of Cardiology, 62,* 1-7.

Eaker, E.D., Kronmal, R., Davis, K.B., & Kennedy, J.W. (1989). Comparison of the long-term, postsurgical survival of women and men in the coronary artery surgery study (CASS). *American Heart Journal, 117,* 71-81.

Eaker, E.D., Parkard, B., & Thom, T.J. (1989). Epidemiology and risk factors for coronary heart disease in women. Cardiovascular clinics 19(3). In F. Dans (Ed.), *Heart Diseases in Women*. Philadelphia, PA: Davis Co.

Fibrinolytic Therapy Trialists (FTT) Collaborative Group. (1994). Indications for fibrinolytic therapy in suspected acute myocardial infarction: Collaborative overview of early mortality and major morbidity results from all randomised trials of more than 1000 patients. *The Lancet, 343*, 311-322.

Greenland, P., Reicher-Reiss, H., Goldbourt, U., Behar, S., & the Israeli SPRINT Investigators. (1991). *In-hospital and one year mortality in 1,524 women after myocardial infarction*. Circulation, 83, 484-491.

Gruppo Italiano per lo Studio della Streptochinasi nell Infarto Miocardico (GISSI). (1987). Long term effects of intravenous thrombolytics in acute myocardial infarction: Final report of the GISSI study. *The Lancet, 2*, 871.

Hall, E.M. (1989). Gender, work control and stress: A theoretical discussion and an empirical test. *International Journal of Health Services, 19*, 725-745.

Haynes, S.G., & Czajkowski, S.M. (1993). Psychosocial and environmental correlates of heart disease. In P.S. Douglas (Ed.), *Cardiovascular Health and Disease in Women*. Philadelphia, PA: Saunders.

Health Canada. (1995). *Canadians and heart health: Reducing the risks*. Ottawa, ON: Author.

Health Canada. (1994). *Survey on smoking in Canada*. Ottawa, ON: Author.

Health and Welfare Canada. (1981). *The health of Canadians: Report of the Canadian health survey, 1978*. Ottawa, ON: Ministry of Supply and Services.

Ho, K.K., Anderson, K.M., Kannel, W.B. et al. (1993). *Survival after the onset of congestive heart failure in Framingham heart study subjects*. Circulation, 88, 107-115.

Hung, J., Chaitman, B.R., Lam, J., Lesperance, J., Dupras, G., Fines, P., & Bourassa, M.G. (1984). Noninvasive diagnostic choices for the evaluation of coronary artery disease in women: A multivariate comparison of cardiac fluoroscopy, exercise electrocardiography and exercise thallium myocardial perfusion scintigraphy. *Journal of the American College of Cardiology, 4*, 8-16.

Jaglal, S.B., Goel, V., & Naylor, C.D. (1994). Sex differences in the use of invasive coronary procedures in Ontario. *Canadian Journal of Cardiology, 10,* 239-244.

Joffres, M.R., Hamet, P., Rabkin, S.W., Gelskey, D., Hogan, K., & Fodor, G. (1992). Prevalence, control and awareness of high blood pressure among Canadian adults. *Canadian Medical Association Journal, 146,* (11 suppl.), 1997-2005.

Johnson, J.V., & Stewart, W. (1993). Measuring work organization exposure over the life course with a job exposure matrix. *Scandinavian Journal of Work Environment Health, 19,* 21-28.

Kennedy, J.W., Killip, T., Fisher, L.D., Alderman, E.L., Gillespie, M.J., & Mock, M.B. (1982). The clinical spectrum of coronary heart disease and its surgical and medical management: 1974-1979. *The Coronary Artery Surgery Study.* Circulation, 66(III suppl.), III16-III23.

La Rosa, J.C. (1988). The varying effects of progestins on lipid levels and cardiovascular disease. *American Journal of Obstetrics and Gynecology, 158,* 1621-1629.

Lerner, D.J., & Kannel, W.B. (1986). Patterns of coronary heart disease morbidity and mortality in the sexes: A 26 year follow-up of the Framingham population. *American Heart Journal, 111,* 383-390.

Lipid Research Clinics. *Lipid research clinics program follow-up study.* Circulation, 75, 1102-1109.

MacDonald, S., Joffres, M.P., Stachenko, S.J., Horlick, L., & Fodor, G. (1992). Multiple cardiovascular risk factors in Canadian adults. *Canadian Medical Association Journal, 146,* (11 suppl.), 2021-2029.

Maggioni, A.P., Franzoni, M.G., Santoro, A.P., et al. (1992). The risk of stroke in patients with acute myocardial infarction after thrombolytic and anti-thrombotic treatment. *New England Journal of Medicine, 327,* 1-6.

Mant, D., Villard-Mackintosh, L., Vessey, M.P., & Yeates, D. (1987). Myocardial infarction and angina pectoris in young women. *Journal of Epidemiology and Community Health, 41,* 215-219.

Mark, D.B., Shaw, L.K., Achong, E.R.,et al. (1994). Absence of sex bias in the referral of patients for cardiac catheterization. *New England Journal of Medicine, 330,* 1101-1106.

Mark, D.B., Shaw, L., Harrell, F.E., Hlatky, M.A., Lee, K.L., Bengston, J.R., McCants, C.B., Califf, R.M., & Pryor, D.B. (1991). Prognostic value of a treadmill exercise score in outpatients with suspected coronary artery disease. *New England Journal of Medicine, 325,* 849-853.

Ockene, I.S., & Ockene, J.K. (1992). *Prevention of coronary heart disease.* Boston, MA: Little, Brown & Company.

Osbakken, M.D. (1989). Exercise stress testing in women: Diagnostic dilemma. In P.S. Douglas (Ed.), *Heart Disease in Women* (pp.187-194). Philadelphia, PA: Davis Co.

Pfeffer, M.A., Braunwald, E., Moye, L.A., Basta, L., Brown, E.J., Cuddy, T.E., Davis, B.R., Geltman, E.M., Goldman, S., & Flaker, G.C. (1992). Effect of captopril on mortality and morbidity in patients with left ventricular dysfunction after myocardial infarction: Results of the survival and ventricular enlargement trial. *New England Journal of Medicine, 327,* 669-677.

Proschaska, J.O, & DiClemente, C.C. (1982). Transtheoretical therapy toward a more integrative model of change. *Psychotherapy, Theory, Research and Practice, 19,* 3, 276-287.

Rodda, B.E. (1983). *The timolol myocardial infarction study: An evaluation of selected variables.* Circulation, 677, 1101-1106.

Rosenberg, L., Palmer, J.R., Lesko, S.M., & Shapiro, S. (1990). Oral contraceptive use and the risk of myocardial infarction. *American Journal of Epidemiology, 131,* 6, 1009-1016.

Reeder, B.A., Angel, A., Ledoux, M., Rabkin S.W., Young, T.K., & Sweet, L.E. (1992). Obesity and its relation to cardiovascular disease: Risk factors in Canadian adults. *Canadian Medical Association Journal, 146,*(11 suppl.), 2009-2019.

Sawada, S.G., Ryan, T., Fineberg, N.S., Armstrong, W.F., Judson, W.E., McHenry, P.L., & Feigenbaum, H. (1989). Exercise echocardiographic detection of coronary artery disease in women. *Journal of the American College of Cardiology, 14,* 1440.

Shaw, L.J., Miller, D.D., Romais, J.C., et al. (1994). Gender differences in the noninvasive evaluation and management of patients with suspected coronary artery disease. *Annals of Internal Medicine, 120,* 559-566.

Stampfer, M.J., Willett, W.C., Colditz, G.A., Speizer, F.E., & Hennekens, C.H. (1990). Past use of oral contraceptives and cardiovascular disease: A meta analysis in the context of the nurses' health study. *American Journal of Obstetrics and Gynecology, 163,* 285-291.

Steingart, R.M., Packer, M., Hamm, P., Coglianese, M.E., Gersh, B.,

Geltman, E.M., Sollano, J., Katz, S., Moye, L., & Basta, L.L. (1991). Sex differences in the management of coronary artery disease. *New England Journal of Medicine, 325*, 226-230.

Stephens, T. & Craig, C.L. (1990). *The Well-Being of Canadians: Highlights of the 1988 Campbell's Survey.* Ottawa, ON: Canadian Fitness and Lifestyle Research Institute.

Thorneycroft, I.H. (1990). Oral contraceptives and myocardial infarction. *American Journal of Obstetrics and Gynecology, 163*, 4, 1393-1397.

Thorogood, M., Mann, J., Murphy, M., & Vessey, M. (1991). Is oral contraceptive use still associated with an increased risk of fatal myocardial infarction? Report of a case-control study. *Obstetrical and Gynecological Survey, 46*, 512-514.

Tofler, G.H., Stone, P.H., Muller, J.E., Willich, S.N., Davis, V.G., & Poole, W.K. (1987). Effects of gender and race on prognosis after myocardial infarction: Adverse prognosis for women, particularly black women. *Journal of the American College of Cardiology, 9*, 473-482.

Vessey, M.P., Villarad-Mackintosh,L., McPherson, K., et al. (1989). Mortality among oral contraceptive users: 20 year follow-up of women in a cohort study. *British Medical Journal, 299*, 1487-1491.

Weaver, W.D., Wilcox, R.G., Morris, D., et al. (1993). Women in GUSTO: Baseline characteristics and effect of treatment regimen on mortality and complication rates. *Circulation,* 88 (suppl.), abstract 2738.

Wynn, V. (1991). Oral contraceptives and coronary heart disease. *Journal of Reproductive Medicine, 36*, (3 suppl..), 219-225.

Feminist Analysis of Employment Trends

S'éduquer et quitter les ghettos roses: des stratégies féministes efficaces?

Christiane Bernier et Simon Laflamme
Sudbury, Ontario

Résumé

En comparant les données de quatre recensements canadiens de 1971 à 1996 sur les revenus d'emploi selon le sexe, en fonction des variables de l'âge et de l'éducation (réparties en plusieurs catégories chacune), il est possible de voir sans équivoque où, depuis quand et dans quelle mesure il y a diminution de l'écart salarial entre les hommes et les femmes. Les données présentées ici portent principalement sur une comparison entre les femmes et les hommes ayant atteint le niveau des études supérieures. A, l'aide de (chartes) Bernier nous décrit de facon systématique les differences recueillies selon le sexe au cours des derniers 25 ans. (Représentations graphiques et de tableaux)

Introduction

Que le salaire moyen des femmes ne représente encore qu'une certaine proportion du salaire moyen masculin est une réalité largement admise au Canada, principalement parce que c'est un fait sans cesse dénoncé par les féministes, depuis une vingtaine d'années, dans le cadre de la lutte à l'équité salariale.

Rappelons que, bien que le principe de l'égalité des salaires entre hommes et femmes soit reconnu depuis longtemps chez nous[1], il a fallu les revendications des commissions des droits de la personne et les analyses féministes des années 1970 pour que la discrimination vécue par les femmes sur le marché du travail soit vue comme phénomène social grave. En fait ce n'est que lorsque les différentes recherches ont fait valoir que ce n'était pas tant la valeur du travail de l'homme qui était reconnue dans son salaire que l'homme lui-même, que la théorie féministe, qui dénonçait la construction économico-sexuelle de l'emploi, a pu être entendue. Cette théorie associait, comme chacun le sait, les bas salaires que gagnaient les femmes à leur infériorisation idéologique dans la symbolique sociale et à la division de la société en sphères publique/privée. Cette organisation sociale ne permet de voir le travail des femmes, en effet, que comme une extension de leur rôle de sexe, ce qui lui octroie une faible valeur d'échange. Cette conception ségréguée et sexiste des rôles sexuels a résulté en une ghettoïsation des femmes, tant dans certains *secteurs* d'emploi que dans des *types* d'emploi, dits féminins, démontrant par là la forme systémique de la discrimination (Connelly, 1978; Amstrong et Amstrong, 1978, 1990; David, 1986, 1988; Reskin, 1984; Gunderson, 1975; Wilson, 1991).

La dénonciation de cette construction idéologique et économique permit de passer de la revendication du *travail égal/salaire égal* à celle du *salaire égal pour un travail sensiblement identique* à, finalement, celle du *salaire égal pour un travail différent mais équivalent,* donnant lieu à la promulgation de différents programmes d'accès à l'égalité (PAE) et d'équité en matière d'emploi (PEE) tant au fédéral que dans la plupart des provinces canadiennes.

Suite à ces actions et à une transformation dans les attitudes et les mentalités à l'égard du travail féminin, on a pu constater un certain progrès: les femmes, pour l'ensemble des travailleuses à temps plein, au Canada, sont passées d'un salaire moyen de 0,59 en 1967, à 0,73 en 1997. C'est, sans contredit, une amélioration.

Mais cela ne semble-t-il pas bien peu, comme résultat, après vingt-cinq années de lutte? Après les efforts déployés et les stratégies utilisées?

Question à l'étude

Face à cette timidité dans la transformation générale des conditions salariales des femmes, on peut se poser la question suivante: si le salaire moyen des femmes, au Canada, ne s'est pas amélioré davantage, serait-ce que les stratégies déployées par les féministes depuis les années 70 n'auraient pas été efficaces? Il nous est apparu utile de regarder les changements survenus dans les rapports entre les revenus d'emploi des hommes et des femmes sur trois décennies, en fonction de ces stratégies. Quelles étaient-elles, ces stratégies, par rapport aux demandes salariales? Il y en a eu deux, principalement.

La première voulait que l'on encourage les filles à étudier le plus longtemps possible, afin qu'elles obtiennent des diplômes d'études supérieures: l'on croyait, en effet, les rendre ainsi concurrentielles sur un marché trop dominé par les compétences masculines.

La seconde, venue un peu plus tard, dans les années 80, était d'inciter les femmes à investir dans des secteurs de travail non traditionnels, pour y occuper les emplois dits masculins, lorsque ceux-ci étaient mieux rémunérés et avaient de meilleures conditions de travail que les emplois des femmes. En fait on voulait que les femmes quittent leurs ghettos roses pour se donner le droit d'accès à tous les secteurs d'emplois.

Où en sommes-nous à l'heure actuelle et dans quelle mesure ces stratégies ont-elles permis aux femmes, effectivement, d'obtenir des salaires équivalents à ceux des hommes, à scolarité égale, dans un même emploi?

À partir des données de recensements

Pour le savoir, nous avons fait une analyse exhaustive des revenus[2] provenant de la base des microdonnées des enquêtes sur les individus, pour les recensements canadiens de 1971, 1981, 1991 et 1996 (échantillon: 1 429 099 personnes)[3]. Nous avons procédé de la façon suivante: pour vérifier la question de l'écart salarial en fonction du *secteur* d'emploi ou du *type* d'emploi, nous avons réparti l'échantillon, selon le sexe, dans les catégories d'emplois identifiées par Statistique Canada (nous en avons retenu 14 sur 17)[4], ce qui nous donnait la répartition des hommes et des femmes dans chaque catégorie pour chaque recensement. Puis, pour vérifier la question de l'écart salarial selon le niveau de scolarité, nous avons comparé, dans chacune des catégories d'emploi retenues, pour chaque recensement, les salaires des hommes et des femmes en fonction de leur scolarité. Mais en plus, nous avons aussi ajouté l'âge comme variable, parce que, si l'on veut montrer l'amélioration des conditions salariales à un moment précis, dans le temps, il est impératif de faire voir l'écart existant, par rapport au salaire masculin, entre les femmes plus âgées et les femmes plus jeunes; les plus jeunes, en effet, non seulement sont, en moyenne, plus scolarisées, mais aussi, bénéficient généralement de l'amélioration des conditions à l'embauche. Ainsi, l'âge a été divisé en huit groupes, pour toute la population active de 15 ans à plus de 50 ans, et la scolarité, en cinq catégories d'éducation, de la fin du primaire aux études supérieures.

Cette analyse fournit donc une radioscopie intéressante des variations des moyennes salariales entre les hommes et les femmes, sur vingt-cinq ans, selon le type d'emploi, le niveau de scolarité et l'âge. Elle permet de voir, aussi, les variations salariales entre les femmes elles-mêmes.

Et qu'apprend-on? Voyons d'abord une synthèse des principaux résultats dans l'ensemble, puis, regardons de façon plus précise les données pour quatre catégories d'emploi—l'enseignement; l'administration; la vente; la fabrication—qui serviront de cas de figures.

Synthèse des résultats

De façon succincte, disons que l'âge et l'éducation font effectivement varier l'écart salarial entre les hommes et les femmes, sur une période de vingt-cinq ans. Mais dans le sens inverse pour chacune des variables. Et ajoutons, bonne nouvelle, qu'il y a, ce que nous nommerons un *effet 1996* de rattrapage sensible vers l'équité salariale dans certains secteurs lents.

Parlons d'abord de *l'âge*. La tendance est la suivante: plus une femme est âgée, plus elle est susceptible de vivre de la discrimination salariale. Ainsi, l'âge constitue presque toujours un facteur aggravant de discrimination. Pour les trois années de recensement 1971,1981,1991, et partiellement pour 1996, dans la plupart des secteurs d'emploi (sauf dans les *Arts* et dans les *Autres emplois du secteur primaire*, où le rapport à l'âge est plus complexe) l'écart salarial s'accroît avec l'âge. Donc, lors de chacune de ces années, les femmes plus jeunes obtenaient un salaire qui s'approchaient un peu plus du salaire moyen masculin que leurs aînées.

Cette tendance générale fait voir que la transformation se fait dans le sens d'une amélioration: en effet, lorsque les salaires des plus jeunes sont plus élevés, c'est une indication du fait que la condition salariale des femmes tend à s'améliorer dans l'ensemble de la société.

Pour l'éducation, les résultats sont différents. La première constatation est que, malgré nos espoirs et nos attentes, *l'éducation* n'a qu'un effet *partiellement* bénéfique sur le rétrécissement de l'écart salarial. Ainsi, on ne peut pas dire que plus une femme est scolarisée, plus son salaire s'approche de la moyenne salariale masculine, pour le même niveau de scolarité. Ici, ce sont les *secteurs d'emploi* et les *types d'emploi* qui représentent les variables les plus importantes.

Cela se passe de la manière suivante.

1. Dans les emplois où l'expertise et la compétence reposent sur des connaissances acquises à travers la scolarité, il y a un net recul de la discrimination salariale (par exemple,

dans l'*enseignement* et les *sciences sociales*).

2. Dans les secteurs qui représentent encore des secteurs non traditionnels d'emploi pour les femmes, le rétrécissement de l'écart salarial met du temps à se manifester, et ce, bien souvent malgré le niveau de scolarité atteint (par exemple dans l'*administration* et les *sciences naturelles*).

3. Cependant, dans les emplois qui n'exigent pas une compétence acquise à travers les études, on fait face aux pires scénarios de discrimination. Les améliorations y sont plus que timides, comparativement aux autres secteurs (ainsi, dans la *vente* et les *autres emplois du secteur primaire*).

4. *L'effet* 1996. Dans certains secteurs d'emploi — notamment dans les secteurs non traditionnels pour les femmes, quoique pas uniquement — entre 1991 et 1996, on assiste à un genre de rattrapage, à un phénomène de rétrécissement plus rapide de l'écart salarial, et ce, particulièrement pour les femmes de 35 ans et moins (*construction; transports; fabrication; personnel de bureau*).

Nous présentons un exemple pour chacune de ces quatre catégories.

Cas de figures

1. Le secteur de l'enseignement

En 1971, les femmes, dans ce secteur, n'obtenaient qu'entre 0,60 et 0,76 de la valeur du salaire masculin, selon les groupes d'âge et les niveaux de scolarité. En 1981, l'enseignante instruite travaillait déjà, de façon générale, dans un environnement plus équitable que dans la plupart des autres secteurs d'emploi. En 1991, la femme qui a fait des études supérieures bénéficiera très souvent de revenus semblables à ceux de ses collègues masculins. En fait, dès lors qu'elle a fait des études universitaires, il est peu probable, et même jusqu'à 50 ans, qu'elle gagne moins de 0,90 de ce qui est versé aux hommes; mais pour celles qui ont plus de 50 ans et qui ont fait des études supérieures le quotient se situe autour de 0,86.

En 1996, même si, dans l'ensemble de la profession, toutes catégories confondues, les femmes n'en sont encore qu'à 0,83 du salaire masculin, les quotients frôlent généralement les 0,90 pour toutes les femmes ayant un diplôme universitaire et *surpassent même les moyennes masculines* chez les 35 et moins ayant un niveau d'études supérieures. Le seul lieu remarquable de discrimination dans ce secteur se trouve chez les femmes diplômées des collèges, qui obtiennent autour de 0,75 du salaire masculin, pour toutes les femmes ayant entre 25 et 45 ans. C'est ici que l'influence positive de l'éducation a été le plus manifeste en vingt-cinq ans.

Le **tableau 1** (ci-dessous) résume la progression du secteur de l'enseignement vers l'équité salariale et les **graphiques 1** (en annexe) présentent, pour ce secteur, les polygones de fréquences en fonction de l'âge et de l'éducation, pour les quatre années de recensement.

Tableau 1: progression de l'équité salariale Secteur de l'*enseignement*	
1. Instauration du modèle de l'équité de 1971 à 1991	
en 1971	- pour les ♀ plus jeunes, aucun écart salarial - pour les 30 ans *et plus*: discrimination quelle que soit la scolarité (entre 0,60 et 0,76 du salaire masculin)
en 1981 et en 1991	- le niveau d'éducation est un facteur déterminant de rétrécissement de l'écart salarial - il y a atténuation de l'effet négatif de l'âge
2. Au seuil de l'équité en 1996	
en 1996	- les diplômées universitaires (tous les âges) obtiennent autour de 0,90 - les ♀ de 35 ans *et moins*: x̄ salaire annuel est supérieure au salaire ♂
3. Toutes catégories confondues	x̄ du salaire annuel ♀ est à 0,83 du salaire ♂ en 1996

2. Le secteur de l'administration

Dans les postes de direction et dans l'administration, les ratios tendent dans l'ensemble à augmenter de 1971 à 1996. En 1996, les femmes de moins de 45 ans connaissent moins de discrimination que leurs aînées et les plus instruites moins que celles qui ont fréquenté l'école sur une plus courte période, ce qui confirme les effets de l'âge et de la scolarité comme facteurs déterminants. Cependant, les quotients dans les 0,70 restent la norme bien que, chez les femmes de moins de 30 ans, on ne voit plus de moyennes inférieures à 0,80.

Et il ne s'agit pas là que d'une simple question de revenus: les femmes se sont nettement engagées dans ce secteur de travail. Prenons, à titre d'exemple, dans notre échantillon, le groupe des femmes de 25 à 29 ans qui ont fait des études de premier cycle: on n'en dénombrait que 0,13 (soit 20 femmes pour 132 hommes) en 1971, alors qu'en 1996, leur proportion grimpait à 0,44 (soit 779 femmes pour 991 hommes), preuve de leur présence nouvelle dans ce secteur.

Pour cette même catégorie, le ratio des salaires femme/homme, qui était de 0,64 en 1971, atteignait 0,86 en 1991 et 0,90 en 1996. Chez les femmes qui ont fait des études supérieures, on peut aussi voir une forte progression puisque les ratios passent de 0,78 en 1971 à 0,83 en 1991 et à 0,94 en 1996.

Le **tableau** 2 (ci-dessous) résume la progression du secteur de l'administration vers l'équité salariale et les **graphiques** 2 (en annexe) présentent, pour ce secteur, les polygones de fréquences en fonction de l'âge et de l'éducation, pour les quatre années de recensement.

Tableau 2: progression de l'équité salariale Secteur de l'*administration*		
1. Progrès mitigé de 1971 à 1991		
de 1971 à 1991	-	il y a de plus en plus de ♀ dans le secteur et dans les postes plus élevés
	-	la $\bar{x}$ du salaire annuel des ♀ est inférieure à 0,70

2. L'écart s'amoindrit en 1996	
en 1996	- amoindrissement de l'effet négatif de l'âge - la scolarité réduit l'écart salarial pour tous les âges - les ♀ ayant des études supérieures obtiennent de 0,76 à 0,94 du salaire ♂ (selon les âges) - chez les ♀ de moins de 30 ans: les x̄ sont supérieures à 0,80 quelle que soit la scolarité
3. Toutes catégories confondues	x̄ du salaire annuel ♀ est à 0,70 du salaire ♂ en 1996

3. Le secteur de la vente

La discrimination salariale a toujours été importante dans le secteur de la vente, du commerce de gros et de détail et on ne voit guère poindre à l'horizon de changements à court terme. En 1971, les femmes y étaient très mal rémunérées: elles ne parvenaient pas à gagner 0,45 du salaire des hommes. Et l'on n'observe qu'une légère amélioration au cours des vingt années qui ont suivi. Les ratios de 1991 restent faibles; au dessous de 0,70 pour les femmes de plus de 40 ans, ils n'atteignent qu'exceptionnellement 0,80 chez les plus jeunes. En 1996, les tendances se maintiennent en grande partie. On peut parler de stagnation même si l'éducation semble timidement jouer en faveur des femmes les plus jeunes.

On voit bien ici le modèle d'emploi où la scolarité, n'étant pas une condition à l'embauche, a peu à voir avec les caractéristiques salariales. Il est probable, aussi, que le peu de syndicalisation des femmes dans ce secteur constitue une condition aggravante de leur situation.

Le **tableau** 3 (ci-dessous) résume le peu de progression du secteur de la vente vers l'équité salariale et les **graphiques** 3 présentent (en annexe), pour ce secteur, les polygones de fréquences en fonction de l'âge et de l'éducation, pour les quatre années de recensement.

Tableau 3: progression de l'équité salariale
Secteur de la *vente*

1. Discrimination criante de 1971 à 1991	
en 1971 en 1991	- les ♀ ne font pas 0,45 du salaire ♂ - les ♀ de plus de 40 ans stagnent encore dans les 0,60, même si scolarisées
2. Toujours la discrimination en 1996	
en 1996	- l'âge est le principal facteur: moins la ♀ est jeune plus il y a discrimination - les ♀ de 35 ans *et plus* qui ont fait des études supérieures n'atteignent pas les 0,70 - timide effet de l'éducation sur les plus jeunes - pour les moins de 30 ans, la x̄ est à peine à 0,72
3. Toutes catégories confondues	x̄ du salaire annuel ♀ est à 0,68 du salaire ♂ en 1996

4. Le secteur de la fabrication

Dans le secteur de la fabrication, du montage et de la réparation, le progrès, là aussi, est d'une terrible lenteur jusqu'à 1991, les revenus des femmes demeurant nettement plus bas que ceux des hommes. En 1971, le salaire des femmes peu scolarisées (secondaire ou moins) se situait autour de 0,40 du salaire masculin. Peu de changement en 1981. En 1991, on peut voir une certaine transformation, passant de ratios qui se situent autour de 0,55 pour les personnes de 50 ans *et plus* à des moyennes se situant entre 0,65 et 0,70 chez les plus jeunes. L'éducation a aussi une légère influence: les universitaires s'en sortent un peu mieux. Cet aspect se confirme cependant en 1996 et on peut voir ici, tout spécialement, la tendance au rattrapage vers une plus grande équité entre les années 1991 et 1996. Ainsi, on peut prendre à titre d'exemple, le groupe des femmes qui ont fait des études de 1er cycle: elles peuvent désormais espérer obtenir autour de 0,80 du salaire de leurs collègues masculins si elles ont moins de 30 ans. Cela amène un peu d'espoir à plus ou moins long terme, surtout lorsque l'on réalise que le salaire moyen des femmes, dans ce secteur, en 1996, n'en est encore qu'à 0,61 du salaire moyen masculin. Ajoutons qu'il s'agit, là encore, d'un secteur où on dénombrait peu de femmes en 1971, mais que leur effectif n'a cessé de croître depuis 1981 et, qu'en 1996, elles forment une bonne proportion de la main-d'oeuvre.

Le **tableau 4** (ci-dessous) résume la progression du secteur de la fabrication vers l'équité salariale et les **graphiques 4** présentent (en annexe), pour ce secteur, les polygones de fréquences en fonction de l'âge et de l'éducation, pour les quatre années de recensement.

Tableau 4: progression de l'équité salariale Secteur de la *fabrication*	
1. Très peu de progrès de 1971 à 1991	
en 1971	- peu de ♀ ayant un niveau d'études universitaires - les ♀ peu scolarisées font autour de 0,40 du salaire masculin - peu d'effet d'éducation
en 1991	- encore peu d'effet d'éducation - mais effet d'âge: les ♀ plus jeunes font de 0,65 à 0,70 du salaire ♂
2. L'effet 1996: début de rattrapage	
en 1996	- accroissement sensible du nombre de femmes dans le secteur - effet combiné de l'âge et de l'éducation: - les ♀ de 35 ans *et moins* ayant un diplôme de 1er cycle font entre 0,75 et 0,80 - les ♀ de 35 ans *et moins* ayant un niveau d'études supérieures font plus de 0,80
3. Toutes catégories confondues	$\bar{x}$ du salaire annuel ♀ est à 0,61 du salaire ♂ en 1996

Des stratégies féministes efficaces?

Les quelques résultats présentés ici permettent de répondre à la question de départ: les deux stratégies — pousser les filles à poursuivre leurs études vers l'*éducation supérieure* et inciter les femmes à *quitter les ghettos roses* — ont-elles été efficaces?

On peut répondre à cette question par l'affirmative, avec un bémol, cependant, un genre de *oui mais*, un oui ambivalent. En fait, on peut reprendre les trois constats qui se dégagent de l'analyse:

1) que l'éducation joue effectivement un rôle positif, mais uniquement dans les emplois qui l'exigent comme condition d'embauche;

2) que, dans tous les autres cas, c'est-à-dire dans le milieu des emplois moins qualifiés, les traditions sexistes donnent peu de chance aux femmes. C'est souvent dans ces milieux que les femmes sont plus âgées, moins scolarisées et non syndiquées. Tous ces facteurs les rendent extrêmement vulnérables à la discrimination salariale;

3) que les avancées dans les secteurs d'emploi non traditionnels pour les femmes ont été nettement plus lentes qu'on ne l'aurait souhaité: le sexisme ambiant, là encore, ne s'y efface qu'avec beaucoup de résistance devant la compétence des femmes.

On peut, malgré tout, se réjouir des avancées salariales des femmes depuis vingt-cinq ans. Elles signifient que l'on vit dans une société où le principe de l'égalité entre les hommes et les femmes est reconnu et où des progrès sensibles se font en matière d'équité salariale.

Mais ces victoires progressives auraient un goût moins amer, semble-t-il, si l'on n'était pas obligés de reconnaître qu'elles sont quelque part fondées sur un principe sous-jacent — que nous avons nous-mêmes avalisé, en tant que féministe — à savoir que, pour une raison ou pour une autre, une femme *non instruite serait plus «discriminable».* Si l'on peut comprendre aisément, en effet, que l'âge soit une variable influente d'atténuation de l'écart entre les salaires moyens des hommes et des femmes, il est plus malaisé d'admettre l'effet et les variations attribuables à l'éducation. Parce que, enfin, pourquoi les femmes éduquées mériteraient-elles un salaire équitable et les autres non?

Aussi, il nous apparaît que c'est là, en tout premier lieu, qu'il faut désormais faire porter les luttes et les programmes d'équité en emploi, si l'on veut voir advenir, dans la société, un progrès autant transversal que longitudinal en regard de la discrimination salariale.

L'équité salariale, ce doit être pour toutes les femmes, quels que soient leur âge, leur niveau de scolarité, leur secteur d'emploi ou leur type d'occupation.

SECTEUR DE L'ENSEIGNEMENT

Enseignants et personnel assimilé; 1971, 1981, 1991
Service d'enseignement; 1996

Graphiques 1

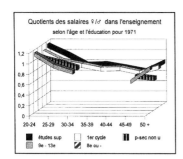

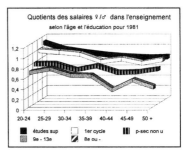

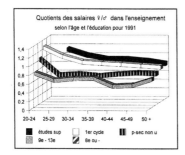

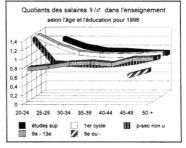

SECTEUR DE L'ADMINISTRATION

Directeurs, administrateurs et personnel assimilé; 1971, 1981, 1991
Cadres supérieurs & autres cadres & professionnels en gestion; 1996

Graphiques 2

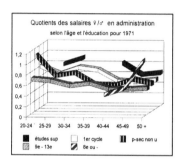

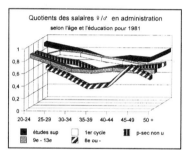

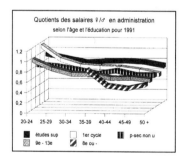

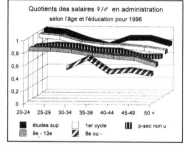

SECTEUR DE LA VENTE

Travailleurs spécialisés dans la vente; 1971, 1981, 1991
Commerce de gros & commerce de détail; 1996

Graphiques 3

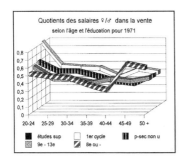

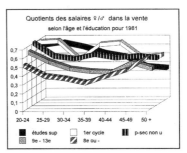

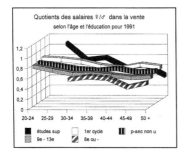

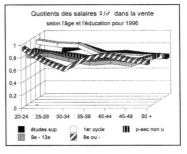

SECTEUR DE LA FABRICATION

Travailleurs spécialisés dans la fabrication, le montage et la
réparation de produits; 1971, 1981, 1991
Industries manufacturières; 1996

Graphiques 4

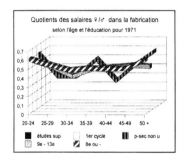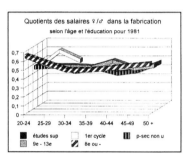

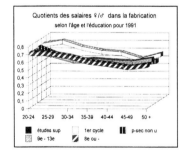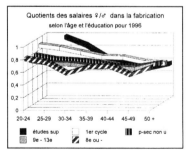

Notes

1. La question de l'équité salariale est évoquée, au Canada, depuis 1919, sans que cela change quoi que ce soit à la discrimination sexuelle dans l'emploi. Le Canada avait, en 1948, ratifié la politique de *travail égal/salaire égal* des Nations-Unies, mais n'a pas entériné la Convention 100 de l'Organisation internationale du travail de 1950, visant la reconnaissance d'une rémunération égale pour les travailleurs et les travailleuses accomplissant un travail d'égale valeur, avant les années 1970.

2. On trouvera une version détaillée de l'analyse dont il est question ici, une discussion méthodologique ainsi que la totalité des résultats obtenus dans *L'équité salariale: un progrès mitigé*, Christiane Bernier et Simon Laflamme, *à paraître.*

3. L'échantillon de 1971 compte 150 798 individus, soit 74 829 hommes et 75 969 femmes. Celui de 1981 comprend 377 234 individus dont 185 138 hommes et 192 096 femmes. L'échantillon de 1991 en comporte 420 088: 224 430 hommes et 195 658 femmes. Enfin, en 1996, on dénombre 480 979 cas parmi lesquels on trouve 254 093 hommes et 226 886 femmes.

4. Administration; sciences naturelles; sciences sociales; enseignement; santé; arts; employés de bureau; vente; servicesagriculture; autres travailleurs du secteur primaire; fabrication; construction (bâtiment); transports.

Bibliographie

Armstrong, P. et Armstrong, H. (1990a). *Theorizing women's work.* Toronto: Garamond Press.

Armstrong, P. et Armstrong, H. (1990b). Lessons from pay equity. *Studies in Political Economy*, n° 32, été.

Armstrong, P. et Armstrong, H. (1978). The double ghetto. Toronto: McClelland & Stewart.

Armstrong, P. et Armstrong, H. (1983). *Une majorité laborieuse. Les*

femmes qui gagnent leur vie, mais à quel prix. Ottawa: Le
Conseil consultatif canadien de la situation de la femme,
Ministre des Approvisionnements et Services Canada.

Bradley, H. (1989). *Men's work, women's work: A sociological
history of the sexual division of labour employment.*
Minneapolis: University of Minnesota Press.

Brayfield, A. A. (1990). *Gender, wage-labor characteristics, and the
allocation of household tasks.* Thèse de doctorat, Ann Arbor,
UMI, University of Maryland College Park.

Chaykowski, R. P. (dir.). (1989). *Pay equity legislation: Linking
economic issues and policy concerns.* Kingston: Industrial
Relations Centre, Queen's University, Research and Current
Issues, Series n° 59.

Chicha-Pontbriand, M-T. (1988). *Discrimination systémique,
fondement et méthodologie des programmes d'accès à l'égalité
en emploi,* Montréal, éd. Yvon Blais. Commission de l'équité
salariale (La) (1990). *Guide pour la comparaison des emplois et
l'équité salariale,* Toronto.

Connelly, P. (1978). *Last hired, first fired.* Toronto: Women's Press.

Cuneo, C. J. (1990). *Pay equity: The labour-feminist challenge.*
Toronto: Oxford University Press.

Davies, S., Mosher, C., et O'Grady, B. (1996). Educating women:
Gender ilequalities among Canadian university graduates.
Canadian Review of Sociology & Anthropology, vol. 33, n° 2,
mai, p.125-142.

David, H. (1987). *Les femmes et l'emploi, le défi de l'égalité.*
Montréal: P.U.Q..

David, H. (1988). La portée des luttes contre la discrimination
systémique et pour l'égalité professionnelle en emploi dans la
conjoncture actuelle. *Interventions économiques,* n°s 20-21,
p.191-204.

Day, T. (1987). *Equité salariale: questions à débattre.* Ottawa: Conseil
consultatif canadien sur la situation de la femme.

De Sève, M. (1988). Pour une mise à jour des caractéristiques de
l'emploi féminin de 1961 à 1986. *Interventions économiques,* n°
20, p. 59-101.

Dumas, M-C., et Mayer, F. (dir.) (1989). *L'équité salariale, un
pouvoir à gagner.* Montréal: Les Éditions du Remue-ménage.

Fudge, J., et McDermott, P. (dir.) (1991). *Just wages: A feminist
assessment of pay equity.* Toronto: University of Toronto Press.

Gunderson, M. (1994). *Comparable worth and gender discrimination: An international perspective.* Genève: International Labour Office.

Gunderson, M.(1975). Male-female wage differentials and the impact of equal pay legislation. *Review of Economics and Statistics,* vol. 57, n° 4, novembre, p. 462-469.

Gunderson, M., et Riddel, C. W. (1988). *Labour market economics: Theory, evidence and policy in Canada.* Toronto: McGraw-Hill Ryerson.

Huet, M. (1986). Déchiffrer le droit à l'emploi. *Nouvelles questions féministes,* n°ˢ 14-15, hiver, p. 13-29.

Humphrey, J. (1987). *Gender and work in the third world: Sexual divisions in Brazilian industry.* London and New York: Tavistock Publications.

Kelly, J. G. (1988). *Pay equity management.* Ottawa, CCH Canadian Limited.

Kempeneers, M. (1992). *Le travail au féminin: analyse démographique de la discontinuité professionnelle des femmes au Canada.* Montréal: Presses de l'Université de Montréal.

Krahn, H. (1991). Les régimes de travail "non standard". *L'emploi et le revenu en perspective,* Statistique Canada, catalogue 75-001F, hiver, p. 41-51.

Le Bourdais, C. (1989). L'impact des transformations familiales sur l'activité professionnelle des femmes au Canada. *Revue suisse de sociologie,* n° 1, p. 57-74.

Lewis, D. J. (1988). *Just give us the money: A discussion of wage discrimination and pay equity.* Vancouver: Women's Research Center.

Marcotte, M. (1987). *Equal pay for work of equal value.* Kingston: Industrial Relations Centre, Queen's University, Research Essay Series n°. 59.

McDermott, P. (1991). Employment equity and pay equity: And never the twain shall meet? *Canadian Woman Studies/Les Cahiers de la Femme,* vol. 12, n° 3, p. 24-27.

McDermott, P. (1990). Pay equity in Ontario: A critical legal analysis. *Osgoode Hall Law Journal,* vol. 28, n° 2, été, p. 38-407.

Morgan, N. (1988). *Jouer à l'égalité. Les femmes et la fonction publique fédérale (1908-1987).* Ottawa: Conseil consultatif canadien sur la situation de la femme.

Parr, J. (1990). *The gender of breadwinners: Women, men, and change in two industrial towns, 1880-1950.* Toronto: University of Toronto Press.

Reskin, B., et Roos, P. A.(1990). *Job queues, gender queues.* Philadelphia: Temple University Press.

Reskin, B. F. (dir.) (1984). *Sex segregation in the workplace: Trends, explanations, remedies.* Washington, DC: National Academy Press.

Reskin, B. et Padavic, I. (1994). *Women and men at work.* Thousand Oaks: Pine Forge Press, Sociology for a New Century.

Simard, M. (1989). L'équité salariale: un défi dans notre société, *in* Marie-Claire Dumas et Francine Mayer (dir.), *Les femmes et l'équité salariale: un pouvoir à gagner.* Montréal: Remue-ménage.

Sopher, C. (1985). *La division du travail entre hommes et femmes.* Paris: Economica.

Stiver, L., et O'Leary, S. (1990). *Storming the tower: Women in the academic world.* London: Kogan Page.

Terrell, K. (1992). Female-male earnings differentials and occupational structure. *International Labour Review,* vol. 131, n°s 4-5, p. 387-404.

Walby, S. (dir.). (1988). *Gender segregation at work.* Milton Keynes: Open University Press.

Weiner, N, et Gunderson, M. (1990). *Pay equity: Issues, options and experiences.* Toronto: Butterworths.

Wilson, S. J.(1991). *Women, families and work.* Toronto: McGraw-Hill Ryerson.

What Progress for Women in a Decade of Change?: An Overview of the Current Employment Situation for Women in the British Armed Forces.

Joan K. F. Heggie
York, England

Abstract

This paper gives an overview of the changes affecting women's employment status and the role within the British Armed Forces since the end of the Cold War, contrasting their experiences, where applicable, with those of women in the Canadian Armed Forces. Many modifications have taken place over the last decade including: the de-segregation of women's basic training; an increase in employment opportunities; the granting of maternity leave and benefits; the introduction of gender free fitness tests; and, increased deployment in conflict areas or as part of peace-keeping forces. The context within which women's employment conditions have changed radically during a relatively short period of time, includes the debate over the deployment of women in combat roles. Despite the progress made, the unwillingness to consider women as combat troops means there are still barriers to achieving a position of full integration and equity of employment.

Introduction

For over ten years, the British Armed Forces, like many other countries around the world, has been going through a period of restructuring, the outcome of which has had profound effect on the lives of women soldiers. These changes are the result of a combination of factors, which have been instrumental in fundamentally changing the role of women in the British military from that of passive observer to active participant, radically altering their role and level of participation. As the twentieth century draws to a close, this paper provides a timely opportunity to pause and examine in some detail how these changes have affected women soldiers and the military as an institution.

Traditionally, it has been understood that women's participation in the military has been that of an additional or reserve supply of labour, a means to supplement the core military force when the need arises — such as in times of national emergency or when there are shortages of qualified men. Once the crisis is over, or the shortage addressed, women's roles are again limited. Segal (1993) asserts that nations participate in a form of "...cultural amnesia regarding the contributions women made during emergency situations, until a new emergency arises and then history is rediscovered" (pp.82-83). In Britain, this can be verified by looking at the patterns of women's participation in the Armed Forces since the beginning of the twentieth century.

Women were first recruited during the First World War into severely restricted roles, such as nurses, cooks and drivers. Although most women were demobilised immediately after the war ended, a Nursing Corps was retained, thereby segregating military nursing into a task performed solely by women, a tradition only recently overturned. During the Second World War, all three branches of the Armed Forces, the Royal Navy, the Army and the Royal Air Force, established a formal Women's Auxiliary force. Women were recruited into the Branch of their choice and trained to carry out a variety of jobs. In 1941, as the war progressed and the demands for military women increased, conscription was introduced. As the situation worsened and all available men were sent to the front line, women were required to carry out more and more tasks that had previously been considered a 'male' domain. In 1945, however, the war ended and the crisis was over. Women were expected to return to their homes and families and to begin to rebuild the nation and so the Women's Services were again disbanded.

The long years of war service, however, had made a deep impression on both the country and the government. The capabilities of women had been tested under the most trying of conditions and had not been found wanting. As part of the restructuring of the Armed Forces in post-war Britain, the Women's Services were reformed in 1949, this time as a permanent, peacetime volunteer force. It could be argued that this initiative does not fit the model as mentioned above, however, I argue that it does. This occurred only four years after the end of the war, when the National Service was required to recruit sufficient men into the military. Many men of military age had either been killed in the war or were too sick or disabled to serve in uniform. The demands of the recovering economy also drew a potential pool of male labour away from the military and into the general workforce. Women, however, were not only available, but high numbers were already qualified from their war service. The policy to recruit women was economically viable, as best use was made of an available and trained resource; the wider society was accepting, having been used to seeing women in military uniforms carrying out this type of work; moreover, it solved a manpower crisis for the military.

The model for the peacetime volunteer force was similar to that used in wartime. Women were segregated into Women-Only Corps, separated by gender rather than by occupation. Their participation was limited: numerically via a quota system and by restricting their access to a high percentage of jobs, regardless of ability. Women were subject to different rates of pay and conditions of service than their male colleagues, thereby limiting their chances of career advancement. Given this trend, therefore, it would be expected that the latest restructuring programme within the Armed Forces would be highly disadvantageous to women soldiers. Yet, as this paper will show, the situation for women serving in the British military has not followed the traditional model at all, rather a new dynamic has been forged over the past decade with women's participation central to the overall effectiveness of the 'new' military institution.

Research into women's participation in the British Armed Forces since 1949 is practically non-existent – feminist-driven research even more so. All too often, feminist debate about women in the military centres around the United States of America. While interesting and informative, there are obvious limitations to the work of both British and Canadian researchers. The women soldiers being researched, the military institution being examined, the policies and laws being interpreted and the researchers themselves are often working within a different cultural and political system. By necessity, therefore, this paper is informative, in that it draws together snippets of information about women in the British military from a variety of different sources, many of them originating with the Ministry of Defence itself, in order to provide an overview of the last ten years. My aim is to focus on the British military model, using the information collated to draw conclusions as to the impetus for change behind the restructuring programme, to question the 'permanence' of the reforms, and to consider whether the impact on the lives of women soldiers can truly be considered to be 'progress'.

Historical Background

In order to set the scene historically, it is necessary to briefly outline the economic and political context within which these reforms took place. In 1985, there were 2,157 female officers and 14,244 other ranks in the British Armed Forces, representing only 5% of the total strength of nearly 327,000 regular (not reserve) troops. (Defence Analytical Services Agency (DASA), 1999, Table 2.19) Very little had changed within the Women's Services since the 1950s. Although equal pay had been introduced, men were still paid more to compensate them for their 'combat readiness', regardless of whether the male soldier was in the infantry or the catering corps. Women in the Royal Navy were not allowed to serve at sea, women in the Royal Air Force were not allowed to fly, and the limitations were even more severe in the Army. All infantry, artillery and armoured corps posts, as well as opportunities in any job considered to be 'combatant' were restricted to men only. There were no women above the rank of Brigadier, most basic training remained segregated by gender, and career opportunities for women were severely limited, both by their exclusion from 'combat' positions and the archaic regulations which had controlled their terms of service since the 1950s. (DASA, 1999, Table 2.19) Despite over a decade of service in Northern Ireland and limited involvement in the Falklands War, women were still very much regarded as 'Admin Annies',[1] certainly not as full participants in a larger military institution.

Although Britain, as a member of the European Community, had accepted various laws onto the statue books in the 1970s, intended to enhance equality of opportunity within employment for women, ethnic minorities and the disabled, the military had always claimed it was exempt. Stressing the special nature of military service, the Armed Forces were able to persuade the Government that these rules did not apply to the military. Women were, therefore, required to leave the military if pregnant, no maternity leave was available and mothers were not encouraged to re-enlist, even if they could provide evidence of adequate childcare arrangements. Upon marriage, women could request a Premature Voluntary Discharge (PVR) without penalty. In the mid 1980s, it was still considered strange if women wanted to remain in the Services after marriage, especially if their husbands were not in the military themselves. Women soldiers found it difficult to obtain married quarters in their own name and the military establishment, laden with centuries of tradition, had real problems accepting that any red-blooded British man would not only wish to be classed as a 'dependent', but be willing to follow his wife from posting to posting every two to three years. Homosexuality was not accepted, even though women could not be prosecuted under civil or military law. Women admitting to being lesbian, or being found to be lesbian after investigation by the Special Investigation Branch of the Military Police, were immediately discharged under administrative procedures, with no recourse to legal assistance.

The political high, generated by the success of the Falklands Campaign, was wearing thin for Margaret Thatcher's Conservative Government as Britain slumped into a major recession in the mid 1980s. Unemployment figures showed steep rises as traditional industries such as mining and shipbuilding were privatised. Mortgage rates soared and houses were repossessed as owners failed to keep up with payments. In this climate, the military was considered good, stable employment, especially for young men with few qualifications, who's only alternative would be the dole queue. The Armed Forces represented a legitimate chance for women to earn a decent income, even though the opportunities were less than for men. It was within this context that several crucial events occurred in the late 1980s.

First, the Government, partly in response to the recession, announced new management strategies for most government departments, including the Ministry of Defence (MoD). The intention was to force the military to be more efficient in the managing of the Defence Budget by getting better value for money, or by achieving the same results with a smaller budget. The savings target was to be in the region of £12 billion pounds a year (CAN$ 24 billion) and was implemented from April 1988. (MoD, 1989, para 507)

Second, demographic predictions forecasted progressive shortfalls in the numbers of young men available from which to recruit the soldiers of the 1990s. This problem had to be addressed urgently, before it started to affect the ability of the British Armed Forces to carry out their commitments.

Third, in 1989, the collapse of Communism in the Soviet Union and other Eastern Europe countries brought the Cold War to an end and thereby rewrote the geopolitical map of the world. The Berlin Wall was brought down, East and West Germany began the process towards reunification and the USSR's capabilities as a superpower was thrown into question. Almost overnight, Britain's military presence in West

Germany became untenable. A review of military requirements for the next decade was now vital. The role of the British Armed Forces in Europe and internationally had fundamentally changed, as had organisations such as the North Atlantic Treaty Organisation (NATO). Inevitably, as part of the review, it appeared that budgets would be cut and troop strengths lowered. There was no longer any justification for funding a military force of 317,700 and a civil service department employing 172,300 people. Things had to change.

Recruitment and Retention

Comments in the 1989 Statement of the Defence Estimates, published by the Ministry of Defence, provided the first inkling that the recruitment of new personnel and retention of trained staff was being considered as a long-term problem. The paper states that:
…recruiting was more difficult in 1988-89 than in earlier years, reflecting lower numbers of young people and more competition from other employers…the number of young people entering the employment market is set to fall further. This…so-called demographic trough affects almost all European countries. In Britain the number of men in the 16-19 age range, from which the Services now draw some 75% of their recruits, has fallen by 10% since 1983; by 1994 it will have fallen by 23% from current levels. And continued economic growth is likely to increase competition for labour, especially of highly educated and skilled people. (paras 513, 514)

By the end of the 1980s, the economy was starting to recover and many personnel were leaving the military voluntarily, either by submitting their notice to leave at the next re-enlist date or by requesting early release. The combination of the two factors led the MoD to admit that they were worried by these trends. Apart from an increase in the recruiting publicity budget and the provision of funds for research into what causes soldiers to leave before their service is completed, the MoD's answer to this problem was to extend the opportunities for women within the three Services.(MoD, 1989, paras 515, 516) This is borne out by Kate Muir who, in 1991, interviewed the officer appointed to carry out a six-month study at the end of the 1980s for the Navy into the viability of women serving at sea. Far from being an initiative to assess how opportunities for women could be enhanced, this study openly admitted naval fears that future recruiting targets could not be achieved. Captain West concluded that the Navy was wasting a vast amount of potential by restricting women to a narrow band of shore-based jobs. He said: "Those applying generally had higher IQs than the men we were taking on, but . . . there were not equal opportunities for women. Far fewer jobs were open for them" (Muir, 1992, p. 46). Concerns about the physical abilities of women to do particular tasks, especially heavy lifting, as well as how their presence at sea might disturb the 'fraternity', or affect the combat status of a warship, were all addressed during the study. Captain West's report reflected that the Navy was not getting the best value for their money from this "...high-grade commodity" (p. 46). Consequently, in 1990, the Navy opened sea-going posts to women.

There are, of course, other ways to deal with demographic troughs and high outflow rates but, as has been highlighted previously in this paper, the British Armed Forces have used the traditional 'Segal' model successfully throughout the twentieth century. The other potential options were considered too risky. Rates of pay could have been increased to tempt personnel to stay, but this was in opposition to the Government's policy of budget cuts. Under-represented communities, such as ethnic minority groups, could have been targeted for recruitment campaigns, but previous attempts had not been successful enough to generate the shortfall needed. Lastly, the Government could have introduced a limited form of conscription or National Service as a temporary measure, a common practice among other European countries, but this was politically risky at a time when a general election was imminent. (pp.46-47) The answer was already there—politically acceptable, economically viable and in agreement with society's increasing acceptance of women's expanding role in the paid workforce. Retain the women already serving by providing more opportunities, better conditions of service, promotion and equal pay. Retrain those women willing to transfer to new jobs and recruit more women into all branches of the military by abolishing quotas and disbanding the separate Women's Services.

So far, this scenario is depressingly similar to the ones examined in the introduction to this paper. Problem – Shortage of manpower. Solution – Recruit more women. No longer a shortage? – Restrict women's participation again to make way for the men. Surely it could be argued in this case that any shortage caused by demographic trends was going to turn into a surplus with the end of the Cold War? Yet, women's participation has increased in all three branches of the Armed Forces over the last decade. What makes *this* situation different?

One influencing factor, I would argue, has been the integration of women into the 'malestream' and the subsequent disbanding of the separate Women's Services, completed by 1993. By doing this, the military *itself* removed the means by which servicewomen had been previously targeted as an identifiable, auxiliary body of labour, surplus to the main fighting force. The integration process provided women with pay, pension and conditions of service on par with their male colleagues. Competition for promotion and opportunities for career advancement became less restrictive. Also, at the time, the demographic trend predicted shortages for most of the 1990s. The end of the Cold War and the subsequent reduction in manpower levels could not have been predicted. By the time these events unfolded, the machinery of reform had already swung into action and it was, therefore, much more difficult to target women alone to bear the brunt of the redundancies.

Ironically, I consider the very fact that women had *not* been integrated before that date to be the basis of their protection against the cutbacks. In Table 2.1 ("Regular Service and Civilian Personnel Strength"), it can be seen that, between 1990 and 1999, the total strength of the British Armed Forces fell from 314,700 to 212,600 personnel. Between 1992 and 1995, 60,000 personnel or 20% of the regular forces left the military, the majority through redundancies directly attributable to the changing international political order and the resulting budget cuts. (DASA, 1999) This three-year period, therefore, saw a reduction in personnel strength the equivalent of the total Canadian Defence Force.[2] Closer scrutiny of the breakdown of these figures, however, shows that the vast majority of the cutbacks were borne by the Army, numerically the largest force, but also the Branch most affected by the changing deployment situation in the former West Germany. (DASA, 1999, Table 2.11) In other words, it was ground troops, infantry, artillery and armoured corps posts which were the most vulnerable at this time – posts not available to women.

Another contributing factor was Britain's participation in the Gulf War, followed by a period of international peace-keeping. This changing role for the British military provided women with immediate opportunities to demonstrate their capabilities in the newly integrated posts. Their presence was necessary and without them, the missions would not have been successful.

Throughout the 1990s, the Ministry of Defence commissioned studies, introduced reforms and reviewed procedures, processes which are ongoing. Some changes were particular to one branch of the Services or another, such as the percentage of jobs open to women, but other changes were more inclusive, such as reforms to rates of pay. As previously mentioned, the Navy decided in 1990 to allow women to serve at sea. This was followed by the Royal Air Force's announcement that women would be recruited as pilots and navigators for the first time. The Army completed its study on the future role of women and proposed that they: "…should be allowed to fill all posts except those that would normally be expected to deploy to forward areas in war and that they should be more closely integrated with the regiments and corps employing them" (MoD, 1990, p.27).

Further reforms to the pay and conditions of servicewomen meant the level of 'X-factor' pay, previously referred to in this paper as that element paid to reflect 'combat-readiness', was brought in line with male colleagues. New opportunities were made available for women to serve as aircrew in the Navy and twenty women were deployed to the Gulf in 1991 as part of the crew of *HMS Brilliant*. (MoD, 1991, paras 508-509) Women Army soldiers were also deployed to the Gulf as part of *Desert Storm* in their capacity as doctors, nurses, drivers and signallers and in various other specialties. By 1992, the Ministry was able to report that virtually all trades within the Navy were available to women and that conversion of surface vessels to accommodate mixed crews was continuing. A study was ongoing into the viability of women serving on submarines and the changeover to Royal Navy ranks and decoration was complete. The integration of female Army personnel into their employing Corps was achieved in April of 1992 and the Women's Royal Army Corps passed into history. Opportunities for women aircrew expanded yet again to cover all aircraft, including combat jet aircraft and operational helicopters. (MoD, 1992, p.45) Female musicians were accepted into the Royal Marines band for the first time in late 1992 and a similar entry in the history books was written by the young girls who were successful in gaining a place at Welbeck College, the Army's Sixth Form Technical College, previously only open to boys. (MoD, 1993, para 754)

Equal opportunity policies, while not being universally applied within the military, were beginning to show real results by 1993. The Ministry of Defence Statement of the Defence Estimates (1993) reported that over 700 women were serving at sea all over the world, 2 female pilots and 9 female navigators were deployed in the RAF, with a further 28 pilots and 14 navigators undergoing training. The report also announced the intention of the Army to develop plans to introduce "…gender-free physical testing so that in future physical capacity rather than sex will determine an individual's eligibility for a particular specialisation" (para 754). At the height of the cutbacks, in 1994, recruiting was 'significantly reduced' across all the Armed Forces, but this did not appear to affect female recruiting figures. Ironically, the concerns raised about high levels of Premature Voluntary Release (PVR) in the late 1980s had turned to despair that not enough soldiers were voluntarily leaving the Services. The military's phased redundancy measures were therefore necessary to achieve the reductions in personnel strength required. The Women's Royal Air Force (WRAF) formally ceased to exist in April of 1994 and the first woman accepted as a naval pilot entered training at the Britannia Royal Naval College. (MoD, 1994, paras 506-510, 522)

In 1995, the restructuring plan, as laid out in the late 1980s, and the redundancy programme had been completed. However, two subsequent defence studies showed that more reductions were going to be necessary if economic targets were to be achieved. In late 1995, announcements were made as to future redundancies. These included targets of 80 posts at Colonel and Brigadier level and up to 17 posts at Major-General level in the Army, up to 2400 personnel in the Royal Navy and a further 8600 in the Royal Air Force. However, opportunities continued to open up for women who were, for the first time, able to apply to train as Ammunition Technical Officers, leading to the possibility of qualifying as Improvised Explosive Device Disposal officers (bomb disposal). Due to the greater diversity of employment opportunities, women were also able to participate, in higher numbers than ever before, on United Nations missions. In 1995, women were deployed in peacekeeping roles in Cyprus, the former Yugoslavia and as part of the naval patrolling of the Adriatic Sea. (MoD, 1995, paras 506, 524)

In 1996, changes were made to the way in which the Armed Forces advertised for recruits, by placing recruiting literature and details of vacancies within local and national Job Centres. Amendments were also made to the Armed Forces Bill as part of it's five yearly reviews, acknowledging in law for the first time that European legislation regarding employment conditions was also to be adhered to. These amendments provided Service personnel with access to some formal Industrial Tribunal complaints system for the first time. (MoD, 1996, paras 506, 536) As can be seen in the following section on legal challenges, women played a large part in bringing these changes about.

In 1997, the Ministry of Defence at last announced that the study undertaken in 1990 was complete and that the Army was increasing posts available to women from 43% to 70 %. (MoD, Oct.27, 1997) Women remained barred from Infantry and Armoured Corps posts but were now able to enter the Royal Artillery, the Royal Engineers and the Royal Electrical and Mechanical Engineers. Continuous reviews of job requirements, together with the introduction of the new 'gender-free' physical selection tests in 1998, have extended that figure even further. (Soldier, April 1998, pp. 21, 67) In February 1998, the Royal Navy announced that the first women to command warships would be taking up their posts later in the year. The reaction from both the Equal Opportunities Commission (EOC) and the Ministry of Defence reflected the changes to recruitment policies over the decade. In an article in *The Times*, Karmlesh Bahl, head of the EOC stated: "These appointments send a great message to all young people with aspirations to join the Armed Forces" ("Women to command,"1998, p.7) The Armed Forces Minister at that time, Dr. John Reid, said: "Appointments such as these clearly demonstrate the Royal Navy's commitment to full integration of women" (p.7). A year later, a review of the possibility of women serving on submarines was announced, as well as the intention of the Royal Marines, the infantry wing of the Royal Navy, to allow women into the commando-training course. (See: "Navy to Order,"1999, pp.1-2; "Women Soldiers,"1999, p.8). Women gaining command experience and the possibility that the last few areas of segregated employment may disappear over the next few years are important steps leading to the full deployment of women within the Forces and demonstrates very clearly the changes taking place within the military institution.

All of the changes mentioned above have played their own part in the process of reducing the barriers for women serving in the Armed Forces. However, having examined the impact of the cutbacks and restructuring on the military over all, it is hard to believe that women's representation maintained the status quo, or managed to increase. The DASA Table 2.25 ("Intake to the UK regular forces: By Gender and Service"), however, demonstrates quite clearly that, since 1993, female recruitment has increased every year, both at officer and other rank levels. In percentage terms, the numbers of women entering the Services has doubled from 6.9% in 1985/86 to 13.2% in 1998/99. (DASA, 1999) The fluctuation in women's representation as a 'percentage of the total' is understandable when considering how unpredictable recruiting was throughout the decade, as the military struggled to achieve the balance between recruitment and redundancies. A more meaningful comparison is that between the 1993/94 and 1998/99 figures for other rank recruitment. Across all three Services, the recruitment figures more than tripled from 1085 in 1993/94, to 3135 in 1998/99. (DASA, 1999) I would argue that, because more opportunities of job choice have been available to young women and substantial improvements have been made to pay and conditions, the Armed Forces are viewed more favourably as an employer by women. I would also argue that the recruitment increases are also due to the fact that women entrants are, in general, better qualified than male recruits (Muir, 1992, p.46) and have been able to take advantage of the opportunities available in more highly skilled technical trades. Women have grasped the opportunities offered and have been instrumental in challenging any obstacles in their path on the road to full equality.

Legal Challenges

This past decade has been unique in the history of the British Armed Forces. Never before have there been so many challenges to the authority of the military regarding employment terms and conditions of service. Although the original injustice may have been directed at an individual, most of the legal rulings, achieved by taking the Ministry of Defence to court, have had a 'knock-on effect' on the wider public and the military institution itself. The other interesting aspect of these legal challenges to military policy is that, when the British legal system has been unable to help, complainants have been prepared to take their cases to the European Court of Human Rights to achieve justice. A ruling from such a court has legal weight in Britain and supersedes the appropriate British law, rendering it illegal.

The first legal battle of note was one brought in 1990 to challenge the military policy of discharging pregnant soldiers and the failure to provide maternity benefits. The Ministry of Defence, in the 1994 Statement of the Defence Estimates, admitted that it was unaware that this European law applied to military, but accepted that the High Court in London had ruled that: "...the policy of compulsorily discharging Servicewomen on grounds of pregnancy was discriminatory and a breach of European Community Directive 76/207 on the equal treatment of men and women in their conditions of employment" (para 511). The Ministry of Defence was ordered to financially compensate all women that had been discharged from the Forces in this way between 1978, when the Directive came into force, and 1990, when the policy was abandoned. It was an expensive mistake. By the end of 1996, 98% of all claims submitted had been paid and the final cost to the taxpayer was circa £55 million (CAN$ 110 million). (para 519)

Due to this case, military policy was overturned and the Armed Forces had to introduce proper maternity conditions for women soldiers into military regulations. This ruling, together with the up to date conditions regarding marriage, has caused an appreciable difference in the retention rates of women. As can be seen in Table 2.12 ("Outflow of UK Trained Regular Forces: By Category"), the number of female trained other ranks leaving the Services on the grounds of marriage reduced from 545 in 1990/91 to nil in 1998/99. (DASA, 1999) There is no longer any need to leave the Services, whether on marriage or when pregnant, unless it is the individual's wish to do so. This is indeed an example of 'women-power' in the face of adversity!

The other landmark ruling, as far as the British Armed Forces is concerned, has been the recent decision by the European Court of Human Rights to declare unlawful the ban on allowing homosexuals to serve in the military. It took several years of legal wrangling for four, individual ex-service personnel, three men and one woman, to have their cases heard in the European court system, after exhausting every legal possibility in Britain. The case was heard in May 1999, where the Ministry of Defence found it hard to provide evidence to support its claim that homosexuality was contrary to the good order and discipline of the Forces and would have a negative effect on morale and good conduct if the ban was overturned. Their only 'evidence' was an internally generated report entitled, "Report of the Homosexuality Policy Assessment Team," compiled in February, 1996. The court judged this report to be "…founded solely upon the negative attitudes of heterosexual personnel towards those of homosexual orientation" ("Historic Ruling," 1999, p.3). The military was deemed to have breached Article 8 of the European Human Rights Convention, covering the right to respect for private life. In addition, the applicants were also able to claim that the British legal system had been in breach of Article 13, because it had failed to provide an effective solution. The third challenge was to the conduct of the military's investigation into the lives of the four applicants, which the court ruled to be 'exceptionally intrusive'. There was no doubt that the inquiries had been carried out in a manner intended to cause distress and had, in two of the cases, resulted in what amounted to 'inhuman and degrading treatment', contrary to Article 3. ("Historic Ruling,"1999, p.3)

Upon receipt of the ruling on the 27th September 1999, the Ministry of Defence immediately suspended action on the 60 cases against alleged homosexual service personnel that were in the investigative pipeline and prepared for another lengthy battle for compensation, from those soldiers discharged purely on the basis of their homosexuality. This is an important case for several reasons. First, there is growing evidence that, despite being less that 10% of total military strength, women soldiers have been disproportionately the victims of this method of discrimination. Perhaps it *is* an employment which attracts a higher proportion of gay women than some civilian occupations, but that point has never been the subject of research as far as I know. However, research has been done on how women are viewed by male colleagues within the military and this certainly suggests that, if women do not show an interest in men in general, or display characteristics thought to be masculine, such as physical strength, assertiveness or leadership qualities, they are often thought to be lesbians. Figures suggest that women are up to twelve times more likely to have been discharged from the British Armed Forces on grounds of homosexuality and, since they are administratively discharged, they have no recourse to legal support as they are not being charged with an offence contrary to either civil or military law. (See Muir, 1992, pp.155-175; Herbert, 1998; Harries-Jenkins & Dandeker, 1994, pp.191-204)

Second, it is an important ruling because, with the overturning of the ban, the British military has become, through no desire of its own making, one of the most progressive employers in Britain – certainly one of very few employers that has in place legislation protecting employees against discrimination on the basis of homosexuality. Since women are still one of the groups most likely to be subjected to harassment and discrimination, *any* legislation which contributes towards a fairer workplace can only be a good thing.

Conclusion

The purpose of this paper was to provide an overview of the

current employment situation for women serving in the British Armed Forces and to trace how those changes have come about over the last decade. I have argued that the restructuring programme, instigated by the military itself in response to a predicted demographic shortfall of young male recruits, forged a very different and dynamic model than that of previous years. Using information culled from primary and secondary sources, I have shown that this 'British model' is truly unique. Undertaken at a time other than the 1990s, within a different political and economic climate or without the committed individuals willing to challenge the military institution in their search for justice, the outcome would have been unrecognisable. The combination of timing and the military's own economic and political agenda, was overtaken, some would say hi-jacked, by world events, international power struggles and changing defence policy. Add to that, women soldiers' own ability to grasp the opportunities available, regardless of the reason behind them, and to reinforce, by legal means, their rights to those opportunities and it becomes clear why I am convinced that the past decade truly represents a unique period in the history of British military women.

The other aims of the paper included drawing conclusions as to the permanence of these reforms and considering whether the impact on women soldiers' lives can be considered to be progress. While carrying out the research for this paper, I have become increasingly convinced that these changes represent real and permanent reform for both women soldiers and the military as an institution. As I have shown, the disbanding of the separate Women's Services and the integration of women into the main military force has been of vital importance. The more women are integrated, the more difficult it becomes to segregate them again. The opening up of increasing numbers of jobs to women means that their participation is now central to the overall effectiveness of the 'new' British military institution. Women function at almost every level throughout the command structure, they are deployed at home and abroad, on land, in the air and at sea. The jobs they do are an integral part of the effective running of a unit and without them, the military could not function. Gone are the days when the only women who go to war are nurses. Another vital aspect to this image of permanence is the legal reinforcement that has been provided to women under European law. Future British governments may wish to retract opportunities offered but they are now all too aware of the financial and political penalties of doing so.

Like many other countries, Britain's military role within the international community has also changed since the end of the Cold War. This has meant women soldiers being deployed into situations never experienced before. Since 1989, women have been mobilised to the Gulf twice and have been deployed in peace keeping roles to Cyprus, Bosnia-Herzegovina, Kosovo and Indonesia. The Gulf War happened soon after the initial reforms were put in place and I would argue that this fact, together with the number of deployments throughout the decade, has been instrumental in helping women establish their permanent place within the modern military. In their own way, whether women soldiers personally identify as feminists or not, they are providing a different image of women in conflict situations than that normally seen. Usually it is women as 'refugee', 'victim', 'homeless' or 'sexual object'. These women are 'capable', 'skilled', 'professional', 'responsible' and 'in charge'.

Economically, I would have to argue that women have made real progress in the past decade. Achieving parity of pay rates and conditions of service have long-term economic benefits. The average pay for a Private after all basic and trade training has been completed is over £12,500 per annum (CAN$ 25,000). A seventeen year old, with basic academic qualifications and no specific skills, would find it hard to match that salary in civilian life, remembering that accommodation, food, uniforms, four weeks holiday per year plus bank holidays and medical/dental cover are all provided by the employer. The average starting salary for the first grade of officer is £15,739 (CAN$ 31,500), again with all facilities being provided by the employer. (DASA, 1999, Table 2.15) There are implications for pensions and gratuities too. The military pension and the lump sum gratuity are based upon the salary being earned at the point a soldier retires. The higher the salary, the higher the pension and the bigger the lump sum. Since women are living longer than men, yet tend to have fewer years in full-time paid employment throughout their lifetime due to raising their children, they have limited options for earning high enough wages to provide an adequate pension for their retirement. It is important, therefore, that women in the military have achieved parity with their male colleagues in this area.

I feel more progress has still to be made in certain areas. Conditions of service regarding age and disability are still out of synch with wider society. There is no consistency across the Services so an enlisted woman in the Army must leave when she reaches the age of forty, while a colleague in the Royal Air Force can serve on until fifty-five. There are very real concerns as to how this disadvantages Army personnel financially. There are also age restrictions at recruitment, again with no parity across the Services. In 1976, a woman could join the Army if she was aged between 17 and 33, the upper age limit is now 26 (28 for graduate nurses). This obviously discriminates against a large proportion of potential recruits who may fulfil all other criteria and could be an asset to the Services. In regard to disability, the military has always been particularly rigid concerning the employment of disabled personnel. Even personnel disabled whilst on active service are discharged on medical grounds. Both of these areas are now under review by the military, partly because of the lack of consensus across the Services and partly because of pressure from the Equal Opportunities Commission and European law. The military actively promotes itself as an 'Equal Opportunities Employer' but still restricts access by age, disability and gender (combat posts).

My final concern has to do with the impact of these reforms on the military institution itself and how that may impact upon women. The military culture is a very traditional one and often attitudes take a long time to change. As women have progressed in this past decade, male roles and male space, previously sacrosanct, have been invaded and forever altered. Inevitably, there has been friction as people get used to the new ways of working together. However, the number of sexual harassment cases going to a tribunal are increasing. Although the military has taken certain steps to address this growing problem, such as by introducing training for staff and setting up a 24-hour confidential helpline, there is still a perception by many male officers that sexual harassment doesn't exist. ("Private Parade," 1999) Those personnel alleging harassment are offered an avenue to take a grievance procedure through the Industrial Tribunal system, unavailable until 1996. These measures are therefore in their infancy and a lot more time and effort will need to be spent on this area.

Although there are still barriers to women's full and equal deployment within the British Armed Forces, this paper has shown how much can be achieved in a relatively short period of time. The changes made have been far-reaching and permanent, affecting not just the women soldiers themselves but also the wider military institution. The benefits have been economic, legal and political in nature and do, I believe, constitute real and effective progress for women.

Endnotes

1. Kate Muir, *Arms And The Woman* (London: Sinclair-Stevenson Ltd., 1992), p. 50. Captain West's term used to explain how women in the Women's Royal Naval Service (WRNS) were regarded as " . . . a sort of protected species, cosseted, charming and delightful."

2. The strength of the Canadian Defence Force was expected to be circa 60,000 according to information published on the Department of National Defence website.

References

Defence Analytical Services Agency (DASA), Ministry of Defence, United Kingdom. (1999). Chapter 2: Personnel - Table 2.1: Regular service and civilian personnel strength. *UK Defence Statistics 1999* [On-line]. Available: <http://www.mod.uk/dasa/Products/UKDS/1999/chapter2.pdf>

Defence Analytical Services Agency (DASA), Ministry of Defence, United Kingdom. (1999). Chapter 2: Personnel - Table 2.11: Outflow of UK regular forces: By service. *UK Defence Statistics 1999* [On-line]. Available: <http://www.mod.uk/dasa/Products/UKDS/1999/chapter2.pdf>

Defence Analytical Services Agency (DASA), Ministry of Defence, United Kingdom. (1999). Chapter 2: Personnel - Table 2.12: Outflow of UK trained regular forces: By category. *UK Defence Statistics 1999* [On-line]. Available: <http://www.mod.uk/dasa/Products/UKDS/1999/chapter2.pdf>

Defence Analytical Services Agency (DASA), Ministry of Defence, United Kingdom. (1999). Chapter 2: Personnel-Table 2.19: Strengths of UK regular forces: By gender and rank. *UK Defence Statistics 1999* [On-line]. Available: <http://www.mod.uk/dasa/Products/UKDS/1999/

chapter2.pdf>

Defence Analytical Services Agency (DASA), Ministry of Defence, United Kingdom. (1999). Chapter 2: Personnel - Table 2.25: Intake to the UK regular forces: By gender and service. *UK Defence Statistics 1999* [On-line]. Available: <http://www.mod.uk/dasa/Products/UKDS/1999/chapter2.pdf>

Department of National Defence, Canada. (1999). Defence statistics. *Department of National Defence* [On-line]. Available: http://www.dnd.ca

Harries-Jenkins, G., & Dandeker, C. (1994). Sexual orientation and military service: The British case. In W.J. Scott, & S.C. Stanley (Eds.), *Gays and lesbians in the military: Issues, Concerns and Contrasts*. New York: Aldine de Gruyter.

Herbert, M. S. (1998). *Camouflage isn't only for combat: Gender, sexuality and women in the military.* New York: New York University Press.

Historic ruling ends services gay ban. (1999, September 28). *The Guardian*, p.3.

Howes, R., & Stevenson, M. (1993). *Women and the use of military force.* London: Lynne Rienner Publishers Inc.

Ministry of Defence (MoD), United Kingdom. (1989). *Statement on the Defence Estimates 1989 (Vol. 1).* London: HMSO.

Ministry of Defence (MoD), United Kingdom. (1990). *Statement on the Defence Estimates 1990.* London: HMSO.

Ministry of Defence (MoD), United Kingdom. (1991). *Statement on the Defence Estimates 1991.* London: HMSO.

Ministry of Defence (MoD), United Kingdom. (1992). *Statement on the Defence Estimates 1992.* London: HMSO.

Ministry of Defence (MoD), United Kingdom. (1993). *Statement on the Defence Estimates 1993.* London: HMSO.

Ministry of Defence (MoD), United Kingdom. (1994). *Statement on the Defence Estimates 1994.* London: HMSO.

Ministry of Defence (MoD), United Kingdom.(1995). *Statement on the Defence Estimates 1995.* London: HMSO.

Ministry of Defence (MoD), United Kingdom.(1996). *Statement on the Defence Estimates 1996.* London: HMSO.

Ministry of Defence (MoD), United Kingdom.(1997, October 27). Greater opportunities for women in the army. *Press Release 152,* 97.

Muir, K. (1992). *Arms and the woman.* London: Sinclair-Stevenson Ltd.

Navy to order women on subs. (1999, March 5). *The Express,* pp.1-2.

Private lives on parade. (1999, March 23). *The Scotsman,* p.11.

Scott, W. J., & Stanley, S.C. (1994). *Gays and Lesbians in the Military: Issues, Concerns and Contrasts.* New York: Aldine de Gruyter.

Segal, M.W. (1993). Women in the armed forces. In R. Howes, & M.R. Stevenson, *Women and the use of military force.* London: Lynne Rienner Publishers Inc.

Women soldiers set to join the marines. (1999, May 23). *The Sunday Times,* p.8.

La cinquantaine de l'an 2000: apogée ou cul-de-sac?

Lise Jacquot et Clémence Lambert
Montréal, Québec

Résumé

A cinquante ans la femme est encore pleine d'énergie, a de belles experiences de vie et ne veut pas être mise de côté, abandonnée par la société. Le projet 'Transition 50 a pour but d'aider les femmes' à se valoriser tout en mettant l'accent sur leurs compétences, et aussi en encourageant les groupes communautaires a developper pour ces femmes des services a partir d'une approche holistique.

Qui est Nouveau Départ?

Un organisme d'éducation populaire travaillant auprès des femmes du Québec et des communautés francophones des provinces et territoires du Canada depuis 1977. Depuis 22 ans Nouveau Départ diffuse son programme éponyme dans 9 provinces et au Yukon.

Les objectifs

Les objectifs poursuivis visent la réorientation, le maintien de l'insertion sociale et la revalorisation personnelle. Nouveau Départ favorise une approche globale des problématiques qui touchent les femmes. Ses interventions proposent des informations éclairées et adaptées sur l'ensemble des options qui leur sont offertes en tenant compte du contexte et des besoins. L'accompagnement dans le processus de choix est à la fois collectif et personnalisé.

Émergence d'une nouvelle problématique

Les changements rapides des technologies de l'informatique et de la robotique ont évacué ces dernières années des milliers de travailleurs et travailleuses du marché de l'emploi, qui s'est graduellement restructuré autour des nouveaux techniciens et techniciennes spécialisés, moins nombreux et capables de produire une multitude de tâches en moins de temps. En conséquence, nous avons accusé une demande accrue d'aide à la réinsertion de femmes de plus en plus âgées soit de 45 ans jusqu'à 60 ans, riches d'une expérience de vie et de travail sans pour autant détenir les diplômes nécessaires au maintien de leur emploi. Les employeurs ne sont pas disposés à assumer les frais de formation et de mise à jour qui leur permettraient de rester compétitives.

Environ 50% d'entre elles séparées et ont dû rejoindre les rangs des assistées sociales à 500$ par mois, soit bien en deçà du seuil de pauvreté; voilà l'espoir des babyboomers les plus démunies. D'autre part, les femmes du baby-boom entrées massivement, dans les années 60-70, dans les postes syndiqués de l'État, telles les infirmières, les enseignantes, les fonctionnaires, sont subitement devenues un poids physique et financier pour ce dernier dans sa course au déficit zéro. La solution de l'État: la retraite. Les babyboomers, riches ou pauvres, doivent faire de la place coûte que coûte.

Le projet transition 50

En 1997, Nouveau Départ entreprend une recherche-action sur cette problématique. Notre hypothèse était que nous assistions à un début de crise induite par les nouvelles technologies et leurs répercussions sur le marché du travail et l'ensemble des rapports économiques, sociaux et politiques. Un changement qui remet en question la valeur du travail et la redistribution de la richesse, plus particulièrement chez les femmes, et qui creuse un «espace inoccupé» entre l'âge adulte et l'âge d'or, c'est-à-dire entre 50 et 65 ans, espace proportionnel à l'accroissement de l'espérance de vie.

Nous étions fort préoccupées de vérifier auprès des ressources du milieu leur analyse et leur implication face à cette problématique grandissante. Nous avons donc ciblé les secteurs de la formation, de l'orientation et de la préparation à l'emploi, de même que les groupes de services et de support aux femmes dans des domaines variés comme la santé, les loisirs, l'engagement social, le vieillissement. La recherche a d'abord rejoint les intervenantes de différents milieux francophones du Canada, via nos groupes collaborateurs dans chacune des villes et provinces.

Analyse des données

Toutes les données recueillies auprès des ressources contactées permettent de conclure que ni les femmes ni les intervenantes ne réalisent l'ampleur de ce virage déjà irréversible. Certains groupes offrent des services aux femmes de la cinquantaine des services surtout axés sur la santé, notamment la ménopause et la prévention du cancer, le bénévolat, la retraite, et beaucoup d'ateliers sur l'estime de soi. Les femmes ne demandent pas plus qu'elles ne reçoivent.

En effet, jamais aucun de ces services n'aborde le fait que l'entrée dans la cinquantaine implique une réflexion globale sur sa vie, ses acquis, son devenir et le sens de sa vie en général. Aucune réflexion non plus face à l'impact d'une perte d'emploi et du statut social que procure le travail sur les travailleuses de 50 ans. Comment les femmes peuvent-elles continuer à donner un sens à leur vie dès lors qu'on leur signifie qu'elles «ont fait leur temps»? Autre observation, si l'on aborde abondamment le thème de la santé physique, plus rarement il est question de santé mentale. Pourtant, les statistiques en santé et nos résultats internes dans l'expérimentation révèlent que près de la moitié des participantes ont recours à des médications diverses pour le système nerveux, le sommeil, la dépression. Plusieurs participantes en phase de transition à la ménopause disent avoir eu peur de devenir folles à l'un ou l'autre moment.

Transition de la cinquantaine

Cinquante ans est l'âge de toutes les transitions cumulées. C'est encore un âge tabou hanté par nos images collectives de la perte de la féminité et du spectre du vieillissement et de la souffrance. Pour la première fois on songe sérieusement à sa mort.

Première transition, les changements physiologiques

Entre 45 et 50 ans, l'appareil hormonal cesse graduellement de fonctionner, ce qui entraîne une multitude de changements dans tout l'organisme. L'impact psychologique est tout aussi réel. De femme adulte, reproductrice et désirable, on devient soudainement incertaine, sans âge, pour ne pas le nommer «retour d'âge» comme du temps de nos grands-mères. Tous les questionnements sur soi, sur son image, ses émotions et ses certitudes se fragilisent. Une mauvaise blague ou une simple remarque peut parfois suffire à semer le désarroi et la perte de confiance en soi.

Deuxième transition, l'apparition du vieillissement

La santé en général commence à donner des signes de fatigue. Il faut ajouter à son emploi du temps de l'exercice physique pour le cardio, la souplesse, la bonne forme. Pour les sédentaires, c'est la catastrophe. Il faut aussi arrêter de fumer pour éviter le cancer, changer l'alimentation, ajouter à son horaire une multitude d'examens et de rendez-vous médicaux. Tout un programme!

Troisième transition, les changements de rôles

Il est parfois très difficile d'apprendre à transformer son rôle de mère nourricière en mère d'adultes et en grand-mère. Le syndrome du nid vide, ainsi nommé et décrit par les chercheurs, démontre les difficultés d'effectuer le passage d'un statut très valorisant d'une mère occupée à répondre aux besoins des enfants et du mari à celui d'une femme occupée à ses intérêts personnels: «une mère mature». C'est aussi à cet âge que les femmes deviennent les mères de leurs parents âgés. Les nouvelles femmes, celles du babyboom, ajoutent à ces changements de rôles celui du passage du statut de travailleuse à celui de chômeuse ou de retraitée: un retour au foyer, au bénévolat. Un retour au privé, après tant d'efforts collectifs et personnels pour accéder à cette fameuse autonomie sociale et financière.

Quatrième transition, les masques tombent

C'est l'épreuve de la maturité. C'est le moment ou jamais de trouver le sens, l'essentiel de sa vie. C'est l'heure des bilans: on additionne ses acquis, on pleure ses pertes, on fait les deuils nécessaires, on sort de ses illusions, on transforme ses échecs en expérience. On se retire progressivement des apparences pour faire place au vrai SOI.

On a connu d'autres transitions dans sa vie, celles de l'enfance, de l'adolescence et de l'âge adulte. Le premier défi que pose cette nouvelle transition, c'est de la considérer, aussi comme une étape de croissance normale. Il faut résister à l'idée de déclin, de fatalité, au conformisme, aux préjugés de l'âgisme. Le deuxième, c'est d'intégrer et de vivre sa maturité sans cesser de rêver sa vie jusqu'à la dernière goutte. Le mythe de la jeunesse permanente est une tromperie qui risque de se transformer en infantilisme. Il risque de nous priver d'une partie parmi les plus riches de notre vie. Une personne mature est une personne ouverte, souple, donc jeune. La plénitude de la vie n'est pas à 30 ans, même si la publicité et les modèles de femme enfant et de super-femme imprègnent une image fascinante de vie active. Le cumul des quatre transitions décrites plus haut se transforme en crise: « …je ne sais plus par quel bout commencer, il y a trop de problèmes» nous disait une participante.

Il y a cinquante ans à peine, on passait de l'âge de la production et de la reproduction à la vieillesse, l'espérance de vie étant de 66 ans chez les femmes. Nous du babyboom, nées avec tous les espoirs et les changements du vingtième siècle, **il nous appartient encore de définir cette nouvelle étape de vie adulte** tout comme nous avons été les premières à vivre une adolescence alors que nos aînées, elles, étaient passées de l'enfance au mariage.

Un modèle d'intervention: le programme transition 50

Nous proposons de répondre à quatre questions fondamentales. Qui suis-je? Que sais-je? Que puis-je faire? En quoi puis-je espérer?

●   Qui suis-je?

Il importe de connaître la nouvelle personne que je suis devenue. Généralement, même préparées, les changements nous tombent dessus en ce sens que la réalité du vécu apporte toujours quelques surprises. Il faut donc du temps de réflexion, du temps et de l'espace pour accepter le dérangement et le questionnement. Il faut aussi trouver les bonnes questions, se les poser individuellement mais aussi collectivement.

●   Que sais-je?

Faire la liste de ses expériences est en soi une révélation sur l'ampleur de ses acquis. C'est un capital personnel et il faut trouver l'art de le mettre à profit. C'est de ce capital que va surgir le projet de sa vie personnelle, une deuxième ou une troisième carrière. C'est une démarche d'intégration que nous proposons, la demande des femmes est unanime: elles veulent être utiles, se réaliser dans une fonction qui fait appel à l'ensemble de leurs expériences tout en tenant compte des nouveaux besoins de l'étape de vie.

●   Que puis-je faire?

Tout est permis. Tout dépend de la largeur et de la profondeur de vue. Tout dépend aussi de sa créativité. C'est le moment de puiser dans ses ressources et son réseau de relations. Quelqu'un qui n'a pas fait de réserves passe difficilement cette étape. C'est aussi le moment de faire un choix: ou bien des victimes du contexte qui se révoltent et se réfugient dans un temps ancien, idéalisé, ou bien des personnes autonomes capables d'affronter lucidement la crise et de la transformer positivement. Cette démarche exige de réévaluer les croyances et les modèles et de les confronter à la réalité.

- En quoi puis-je espérer?

Le temps qui reste en espérance de vie, c'est-à-dire 25-30 ans, c'est beaucoup de temps. Il vaut donc la peine de s'y préparer et d'explorer toutes les options. D'abord le temps, ce temps donné, il faut bien le gérer et surtout l'habiter. On n'a pas le droit de le gaspiller. Ce temps est précieux pour l'intégration et l'émergence de son projet et cela ne se fait pas dans l'éparpillement.

Se sentir utile et appréciée, avoir une place dans la société, c'est ce qu'apportent le travail et la juste rémunération. La crise actuelle affecte donc l'individu dans ses valeurs fondamentales. L'appauvrissement entraîné par le taux élevé de chômage est une profonde injustice sociale dans un pays nanti qui ne réussit pas à réorganiser la répartition de la richesse. Évacuer systématiquement les 50 ans du marché de l'emploi risque aussi, à long terme, de coûter très cher socialement car même si la viabilité financière assure la survie, l'être humain n'est heureux que lorsqu'il se réalise pleinement.

Les acquis des luttes féministes

Le gain le plus important est certainement celui de la possibilité de choisir. Non pas dans le sens de la liberté, mais dans l'accès à toutes les avenues. L'exercice du choix commande cependant un incontournable: l'information. L'isolement, l'ignorance mènent à tous les préjugés: sexisme, âgisme, racisme….Ils sont persistants, ils traversent les générations et résistent aux changements.

Durant les cinquante dernières années, les femmes ont investi toutes les sphères du social, du politique et de l'économique. L'équité n'est cependant pas encore acquise et le chemin à parcourir encore long. Voilà un but, une cause à poursuivre, un héritage à sauvegarder et à léguer.

Conclusion

La recherche sur la problématique émergeante qui touche les femmes de la cinquantaine soulève plusieurs questions. Il faut redéfinir des notions jusqu'alors prises pour acquis:

- Par exemple la retraite qui appartenait aux hommes du temps où les femmes demeuraient au foyer. Une femme n'est jamais à la retraite... Au fait, qu'est ce que la retraite pour une femme de 50 ans?
- L'âge d'or et ses nombreuses associations qui recrutent maintenant leurs membres chez les 50 ans, faute d'alternative, avec le résultat que les 50-60 ans ne se reconnaissent pas dans les activités privilégiées par les 70-80 ans qui, eux, se sentent envahis par les «plus jeunes». Au fait, qu'est-ce que l'âge d'or?
- Le passage à la retraite, au «repos», qui se faisait auparavant ipso facto, dès qu'on quittait le marché de l'emploi. Une nouvelle tranche d'âge émerge, qu'il faut nommer pour mieux la comprendre, mieux l'utiliser, mieux la vivre... Âge de production non compétitive? Deuxième âge de maturité? Au fait, comment faut-il la nommer?
- Et bien d'autres encore...

Transition 50 veut créer ce lieu et cet espace de questionnement qui permettra aux femmes et aux organisations une recherche personnelle et collective de solutions.

Actuellement, le programme, d'une durée de 50 heures, est disponible et déjà diffusé auprès de la population à Montréal ainsi qu'à Sudbury.

La prochaine étape consistera en un colloque prévu pour mars 2001 à Montréal:

«JE SUIS TOUJOURS LÀ... ou l'émergence de la cinquantaine».
C'est un rendez-vous!

Strategies for Overcoming Barriers to Women Entrepreneurs With Disabilities

Colleen Watters
Winnipeg, Manitoba

Abstract

Self-employment can be seen as a realistic option for women with disabilities but for various reasons few women choose this option. Watters will describe how little material is available to help disabled women entrepreneurs become self-employed. Findings from a recent national study titled "Urban Business Development and Disability: Models and Strategies" will be shared. The paper will conclude with an identification of key elements that should be included as a mechanism for entrepreneurs with disabilities, as well as recommendations for development of a Canada-wide strategy to meet the needs of these women.

Introduction

Self-employment is a realistic option for women with disabilities, but few of these women choose this option. The presence of disability is not always the main issue: government policies, societal attitudes and barriers, and financial constraints are much larger obstacles. This paper will describe what we know from the sparse literature that exists about women with disabilities who are now self employed.

Various approaches to providing services and supports to women entrepreneurs with disabilities will then be outlined from three sources. First, services and approaches from findings of research into women's employment will be summarized. Second, findings from a very recent national study titled *Urban Business Development and Disability: Models and Strategies* (1999) will be shared. Third, an identification of the key elements which should be included in urban delivery mechanisms for entrepreneurs with disabilities will be delineated. Recommendations for the development of a Canada-Wide strategy to meet the needs of entrepreneurs (including women with disabilities) will also be outlined.

The paper will conclude with a description of this author's own experience as a woman with a disability carrying out contract research to provide one example of what can keep women with disabilities out of, or bring them into self employment.

Summary of Research on Women With Disabilities

Research by the Women Business Owners of Manitoba (1994) indicates that 60 percent of new businesses are being started by women. To assist them in dealing with some of the barriers to establishing their own businesses, services such as enterprise centres have been developed to provide business-related services and supports and to help women gain an established credit rating, etc. The reasons for the growth of specialized population approaches can be largely attributable to the difficulty people with disabilities and other specialized groups that have encountered marginalization, have experienced in accessing generic resources. This type of marginalization contributed to a lack of understanding of their particular needs and inaccessible generic resources. For example, a number of studies have demonstrated that women had difficulty getting bank loans for businesses, even when they had sound business ideas. Other barriers to self-employment also existed for women. (See: Women Business Owners of Manitoba, 1990; Women's World Banking, 1992; Western Diversification, 1994). Armed with such evidence, and with persistent advocacy, a number of Women's Enterprise Centres have been developed in Canada.

While the federal government has been instrumental in setting up these Centres, a number of provincial governments encouraged development of self-employment by women both before and after these Centres began. For example, the Government of Manitoba's Department of Industry, Trade and Tourism operates a Women Entrepreneurial Initiatives program. In Saskatchewan, the Loans Cooperatives Program has been set up for a broad range of individuals who have been disadvantaged in accessing loans, including women. Similar initiatives have been developed in other provinces.

Also noteworthy is that women business owners associations have emerged throughout Canada, some more formal than others. These organizations typically have regular meetings to allow for information exchange, mutual support and to address barriers encountered by women entrepreneurs. While generic resources are, no doubt, of considerable importance to the growing number of self-employed women, the specialized resources seem to have met a significant need. Many of the above-mentioned resources are inaccessible to women with disabilities or are just beginning to address the needs of this population in developing service programming.

However, there is little research on women with disabilities and the barriers to self-employment. In a recent study entitled: *Urban Business Development and Disabilities: Models and Strategies*, (Neufeldt, Enns, Watters and Sannuto, 1999), only one study on women with disabilities and self-employment was uncovered.

In May 1996, Employment Action (a non-profit society) undertook research on women entrepreneurs with disabilities for the Women's Enterprise Society of British Columbia, entitled: *Self-Employment As An Option For Women With Disabilities: A Report For the Women's Enterprise Society of British Columbia*. The main objectives of the project were to raise awareness among women with disabilities and generic business supports and services of the feasibility of self-employment as a viable option for women with disabilities and to develop strategies to support these entrepreneurs.

The BC study demonstrated that self-employment is a realistic and appropriate option for many women with disabilities. In practice though, few Canadian women with disabilities choose self employment. Our research indicates that the disability itself is not always the main issue preventing women with disabilities from starting their own businesses. Government policies, social and attitudinal barriers and financial constraints were much bigger obstacles for the women with disabilities who participated in the research.

Although the BC project initially focussed on women with disabilities, much of the information applies equally to men with disabilities. The blueprint made the following recommendations as a means to promote self-employment among women with disabilities:

1. Prepare case studies of women entrepreneurs to serve as role models;
2. Design an information package on specific disabilities for entrepreneurial trainers and lenders to help them understand and work with clients;
3. Propose the use of information workshops to educate business support professionals;
4. Develop specialized entrepreneurial training and support

programs for people with disabilities and others who are outside the labour market;

5. Develop directories of lending institutions, entrepreneurial trainers and community support services;

6. Form a community advisory committee composed of representatives from the disability community, economic development agencies, businesses, educators, banks, advocacy organizations, etc. that is linked to an existing community development agency to spearhead and support programs to assist the entrepreneur;

7. Perform an asset inventory to determine the specific skills and interests of people with disabilities that can be used as the foundation for business development;

8. Examine existing programs and identifying working models on which to build;

9. Conduct a feasibility study into specific for profit ventures that could provide self-directed employment for workers with disabilities.

To the knowledge of researchers at the Canadian Centre on Disability Studies, no follow-up has been done by the Women's Enterprise Society of British Columbia on this research.

In May, 1997, the Network for Entrepreneurs with Disabilities (NEWD) undertook a study of its membership of 171 persons to update their information on the barriers experienced by entrepreneurs with disabilities and to make recommendations for overcoming these barriers (NEWD, 1998). Of the 61 responses received, 31 percent were women with disabilities. Respondents expressed a desire for independence, understanding and respect, the removal of disincentives to pursuing self-employment especially on a part time basis and help to level the playing field with non-disabled entrepreneurs. Recommendations are offered to help address these issues including:

1. The need for organizations like NEWD to support entrepreneurs with disabilities.

2. Continued support of training for disabled entrepreneurs.

3. Establish a special loan fund for disabled entrepreneurs.

4. Establish a sensitivity training program for business development professionals.

5. Establish clearly defined supportive policies regarding people with disabilities developing self-employment.

6. Eliminate the financial disincentives to pursuing self-

employment.

Based on the foregoing information, it is clear that additional research on women with disabilities and self-employment needs to be carried out to further examine the barriers confronting this population with respect to obtaining accessible self-employment services and supports, to identify the parallels between women with disabilities and people with disabilities, to promote awareness among women with disabilities that they can be entrepreneurs and how to access services and supports, to promote awareness among the business community about how to address the needs of women with disabilities and to further develop resources for women with disabilities.

Urban Business Development and Disability

The *Urban Business Development and Disability* report demonstrated that many of the findings common to women with disabilities are applicable to people with disabilities in general. This research was jointly facilitated by the Canadian Centre on Disability Studies (CCDS), The University of Calgary and the University of Manitoba. The project began in October, 1997, and the final report was published in January, 1999. The purpose of the project, funded by Human Resources Development Canada, Western Economic Diversification and the Manitoba Government, had two purposes:

1. To review economic structures that exist across Canada for their overall suitability and accessibility for promoting entrepreneurship for persons with disabilities.
2. To develop delivery mechanisms for urban Centres in Western Canada.

The research identified existing self-employment support initiatives and analyzed them for their relevance to developing urban delivery mechanisms for entrepreneurs with disabilities. Of particular interest were those programs that focussed on the provision of self-employment supports to disadvantaged populations: Aboriginal people, those on low incomes, women, youth and people with disabilities. General business services were also examined in terms of their accessibility to people with disabilities.

Types of Programs Found

Researchers found general business programs (those that can be utilized by anyone) and services designed for specific populations, such as those on low incomes, Aboriginal people, women, youth and persons with disabilities. With respect to people with disabilities, the majority of initiatives had emerged relatively recently. Some initiatives offered pre-employment support, while others provided assistance in developing business skills and business start-up support, and monitored businesses once they were up and running. Some programs also provided loans to people with disabilities.

The difficulty with short-term, specialized initiatives is that, once these programs end, entrepreneurs with disabilities are without sustainable sources of support to facilitate the development of their businesses. Many general business services are inaccessible to people with disabilities and lack awareness of the needs of entrepreneurs with disabilities and how to address them.

Issues in the Removal of Barriers to Self-Employment for People with Disabilities

The research identified a number of issues which must be addressed in the removal of barriers to self-employment for persons with disabilities. These include the following:

1. Limited business sector understanding of disability.
2. Insufficient support by disability organizations providing employment services.
3. Disincentives of public policies, including income security and policies concerning part time work.
4. Inaccessibility of business resources.
5. Lack of access to technology.
6. Need to enhance self-confidence.
7. Need for role models.
8. Difficulty in accessing capital. Specialized loan programs, peer lending approaches and obtaining loans from alternate sources of financing (such as Credit Unions) have been utilized successfully to deal with this issue.

Key Elements of Urban Self-Employment Development Mechanisms for People with Disabilities

The study identified a number of key elements which should be included in urban delivery mechanisms for entrepreneurs with disabilities. These include:

- Awareness Raising and Confidence Building:

Information should be disseminated about self-employment

possibilities for people with disabilities, and pre-entrepreneurship training made available.

- Acquiring Knowledge and Business Skill:

Accessible training resources that enable people with disabilities to acquire skills, appropriate to their businesses, should be developed. These include not only learning about the most optimal way to organize one's production or service processes, but also development of business and market plans, funding, personnel management, etc. One to one mentoring for individuals requiring more intensive support in getting their businesses under way should be included, as well as, voluntary business advisory committees to assist with decision-making.

- Ensuring Funding is Available and Accessible:

The development of micro-loan funds for people who are ineligible for the normal asset requirements of lending agencies should be instigated. This measure would assist entrepreneurs with disabilities to gain business experience with small businesses and a credit worthiness track record. Larger specialized loans should also be available for individuals with some experience, a sound business plan, but whose credit rating may not as yet be sufficient for loans from generic lending sources. In these instances, the level of loan support should be determined by participants' business plans and the business requirements for capital.

- Building a Supportive Environment:

The allocation of resources to increase the accessibility of the business development service sector for people with disabilities should be addressed. Such resources would be allocated to awareness raising about accessibility and facilitate service improvements. Moreover, federal and provincial governments need to re-examine and revise policies that currently serve as barriers to self-employment. These include the eligibility requirements for various types of education and training programs and the policies, regulations and practices governing income, personal and health support programs for people with disabilities.

Conscious effort must be given to building linkages between specialized business start-up initiatives and the business community, as specialized programs will fail without connections to the business community, and generic programs will not succeed without linkages to the disability community and supports for entrepreneurs with disabilities. Also, efforts should be given to linking existing disability services and supports to self-employment programs.

- Sustainability:

While the many short-term business start-up initiatives raised awareness, and demonstrated that self-employment was a reasonable option for people with disabilities, most did not last long enough to allow for any reasonable number of individuals to start their own businesses. The possibility no longer needs to be demonstrated. Urban delivery mechanisms should take steps to become sustainable over the long-term, in order to increase the likelihood of success, and be developed through consultation with and linkages to business, government and disability sectors.

- Cross-Disability Approach to Urban Initiatives:

The needs of entrepreneurs with disabilities belonging to more than one target group must be addressed. While the specific kinds of accessibility issues faced may be unique to different forms of impairment, the reality is that even within one type of disability there are ranges of accessibility. Furthermore, there are a broad variety of common needs across disabilities which can best be addressed through a cross-disability approach.

- Mutual Support of Specialized Initiatives:

Understanding of what it takes to enable people with disabilities to become full participants in Canada's economic fabric still is at an early phase. Much can be learned from the experience of various initiatives established across the country. To enhance learning across localities, urban delivery mechanisms should examine the possibility of establishing a network of disability enterprise initiatives across Canada.

- Need for Evaluation:

The lack of sound evaluations of all kinds of self-employment initiatives was most noticeable. Ongoing evaluative components to measure both short and long term success indicators rather than only self-sufficiency would address this deficit.

- Bringing Various Stakeholders to the Table:

In order to build effective urban delivery mechanisms for entrepreneurs with disabilities, various stakeholders must be brought to the table. These include representatives from government, the business and disability sectors and entrepreneurs with disabilities.

The companion volume to the *Urban Business Development and Disability* report contains detailed descriptions of entrepreneurial programs across Canada. This volume, entitled: Canadian Initiatives In Supporting Self-Employment will be published in November, 1999.

The process of developing and implementing models of entrepreneurship for persons with disabilities will vary with the location and community context and needs. The research will be useful to entrepreneurs with disabilities, disability organizations, the business service sector and governmental organizations seeking an overview of entrepreneurial programs across Canada. They will be able to utilize the services listed or to work in concert with others towards the development of viable and sustainable urban delivery mechanisms for persons with disabilities.

Recommendations From the Round Table on Entrepreneurship

Following the publication of *Urban Business Development and Disability*, the Federal Government conducted a round table on entrepreneurship and people with disabilities in March, 1999. Participants at the round table sessions made the following recommendations:

1. That existing social support systems and services, available to Canadians with disabilities, accommodate entrepreneurial aspirations by removing the punitive aspects that act as a disincentive to entrepreneurship.

2. That strategic processes for the provision of business support services and products for entrepreneurs with disabilities be developed in partnership with entrepreneurs with disabilities, private and public sectors including:
    -   a repertoire of fully accessible business support services and products available to entrepreneurs with disabilities, developed and maintained as subsets of existing business services now delivered by Industry Canada and other organizations.

- all new business resources developed and made available in alternate format and that existing resources be made available on demand in an accessible format.
- a communication strategy implemented to ensure potential and existing entrepreneurs with disabilities know what accessible resources and services are available.
- assurance of the continuity of the Western Economic Diversification's Entrepreneurs with Disabilities Program (EDP) and, that this program be extended to all of Canada. An evaluation should be undertaken after five years with a view to evolve to a more comprehensive program.

3. That business service providers and other partners actively seek to employ people with disabilities in the delivery of their services and contract with entrepreneurs with disabilities where possible.

4. That a venture capital fund be established to assist Canadians with disabilities fulfil their entrepreneurial aspirations.

5. That a national awareness campaign be launched to promote entrepreneurship as an option for Canadians with disabilities, and to educate other Canadians on the important economic contribution these entrepreneurs make to society.

Since that time, the Network for Entrepreneurs with Disabilities (a self-help support group for entrepreneurs with disabilities in Halifax, Nova Scotia), has received funding from Human Resources Development Canada, Western Economic Diversification and the Atlantic Canada Opportunities Agency to develop chapters across Canada to provide networking and support to entrepreneurs with disabilities. This initiative will further address the needs of entrepreneurs with disabilities across the country, including women with disabilities.

Experience as a Contract Researcher

To provide one example of what can keep women with disabilities out of, or bring them into self-employment, I will conclude with a description of my own experience as a woman with a disability carrying out contract research.

Over the past several years, I have worked as a contract researcher on a variety of projects for several disability-related organizations. In some cases, this has meant working beyond the contract deadline to complete project tasks when activities took longer than expected, or working without remuneration to prepare project proposals that could possibly result in future employment.

I appreciate the flexibility inherent in this type of work and have gained a wealth of knowledge as a consequence of the variety of positions I have held. In fact, one employer recently stated that I was very versatile and could fill in anywhere. In addition, I can work at home in quiet surroundings with computer equipment which is accessible. However, this type of work offers little security, part time hours and lower pay than full time employment, with a living situation that can move from feast to famine.

In my research on self-employment, I have encountered people with disabilities who live in much worse circumstances than my own, including individuals who were selling crafts and other products for virtually no wages. Situations, such as the above, or my own current one, could discourage many women with disabilities from embarking on contract work or self-employment.

There are no easy solutions to this dilemma. It behoves organizations who employ people on contract to recognize the value of these employees with appropriate wages and working conditions. We, as workers in these situations, need to recognize the value of our skills and abilities and advocate for conditions, including wages, which are in line with those skills. Within a societal context, greater value should be placed on contract work and self-employment, and the appropriate supports provided to encourage a greater number of individuals to embark on this type of work.

References

Cohen, G. L. (1998). Aspects on self-employment. In labour and household analysis division. *Work arrangements in the 1990s: An analytical report.* Ottawa, Ontario: Minister of Industry.

Gray, L. (1996). *Self-employment as an option for women with disabilities: A report for the Women's Enterprise Society of British Columbia.* Prince George, B.C.: Women's Enterprise

Society of British Columbia.

Network for Entrepreneurs with Disabilities. (1998). *Entrepreneur survey* (Final Report). Halifax, Nova Scotia: Network for Entrepreneurs with Disabilities.

Neufeldt, A.H., Enns, H., Watters, C., & Sannuto, V. (1999). *Urban business development and disability: Models and strategies.* Winnipeg, Manitoba: Canadian Centre on Disability Studies.

Watters, C., Sannuto, V., Neufeldt, A.H., & Enns, H. (1999). *Canadian initiatives in supporting self-employment.* Winnipeg, Manitoba: Canadian Centre on Disability Studies (in press).

M. Jones Consulting. (1999). *Agenda for change: Entrepreneurs with disabilities.* Winnipeg, Manitoba: M. Jones Consulting.

Women Business Owners of Manitoba. (1990). *Enterprise centre.* Winnipeg, Manitoba: Women Business Owners of Manitoba.

Community Awareness

Parenting Classes for Women Who Have Been Abused or Who are Recovering From Addictions

Jane Fox
Ottawa, Ontario

Abstract

Organizations in Ottawa have collaborated in offering a variety of self-help programs for women dealing with abuse or addiction issues. Each is very much about helping women on the periphery of society get back their power, and at the same time encourage healing, bonding and strengthening. Fox is involved in two special projects, that help women learn how to become better parents as they are trying to get their power back and another helps women deal with their recovery from addictions. Both projects benefit women who welcome their healing as well as act as support to those experiencing similar pain and later similar joy, independence and self-confidence. What makes this project unique is that it involves the children as well as the mothers, and both groups benefit from these parenting sessions. This paper will describe the meeting process, the format and the information sources for the projects.

Introduction

In 1995 I was asked to participate in a project which was a collaborative effort of the counselling department of the YW-YMCA and the Family Service Centre of Ottawa-Carleton. Project coordinator, Chitra Sekar was interested in providing a twelve week play therapy program for children aged 3 to 6 who had witnessed violence against their mothers, as there was no such program in the city at that time. The mothers were in a similar group at the same time as the children; this was felt to be an important part of the children's healing process. These meetings were (at time of writing), an hour and a half long with a half-hour snack/relaxing time before-hand. As part of the program, drinks, daycare, and transportation costs were provided for the women as well as any supplies. This paper will focus on the two very special groups of mothers that I work with in Ottawa.

The Program's Beginnings

There were a number of volunteer co-facilitators with varying backgrounds, however I found that the two most successful had previous counselling experience. Also included in the group, was a volunteer "graduate" mother from an earlier group. For the first time an art therapist was working with both groups, which added a wonderful dimension to them.

These meetings were and continue to be a work in progress, constantly changing with the people involved. We are justifiably proud of what we have achieved with these meetings, in terms of helping the women and children move forward in their healing and building their self-esteem.

One Story

Ann[1] illustrates the process that mothers go through in these meetings. During the first few meetings, Ann did not speak unless spoken to, instead she sat in a corner very quietly, didn't smile, didn't look up. After about the third or fourth sessions, she began to share some of her experiences, not so much about her addiction but about her shame at "losing" her children, first to the Children's Aid Society (CAS) and then to her abusive ex-husband. At the time she had her daughters only every other weekend. She was filled with remorse and grief at this loss, and was still verbally abused by her ex-husband and his new wife whenever they met.

She had been through the court system twice and felt let down by the judges, lawyers and social workers who were supposed to protect her and her children. Ann had done everything she could within the system and had gotten nowhere, so you can imagine how strong her trust level was when she came to the group. When she had fled to the shelter to save her life, there was no room for her daughters. Once they were in the care of CAS, she had no more control over what happened to them and her husband could afford a better lawyer. The rest is history. This story is all too familiar, heard too many times from too many women to doubt it's validity.

When I met Ann, she came to the group at the Amethyst Women's Addiction Centre, where she saw an addiction counsellor on a weekly basis. Her addiction, incidentally, was to prescription drugs, prescribed to help her deal with her depression and anxiety disorder, resulting from the physical and sexual abuse she experienced in childhood.

As the weeks of our meetings went by, Ann opened up more and more. She devoured all the written material, asked questions, read books. She participated at a high level and was changing weekly! By the end of the twelve weeks she was smiling and trusting. She also attended our "Y" group for women who have experienced abuse. Even though she told us she went around the block six times before she could enter the building the first night, she offered support to the other women. She told us that the group was just what she needed and we watched her grow stronger and more assertive as the weeks went on.

The Participants

Both groups had between eight and ten women, and one or two either did not show up or they dropped out. A fairly high drop out-rate with these high risk groups is not a surprising result. The "Y" group had a careful screening process for the children. If it was felt that the child was not ready for a group experience, or if the father still had visitation rights and was seen as a potential problem for the child in regard to the group, other recommendations, such as individual counselling, were made. This being said, both groups were open to any woman who fit the criteria and who wanted to come.

We found, through trial and error, that a group of fewer than six did not work well because the same richness of support and experience was missing. The women were often extremely lacking in self-confidence because of what they had been through, and had experienced a lot of isolation, some of them were even bullied by their children. We found that there was often, but not always, a history of violence and / or sexual abuse in their own childhood. Overall, the women needed to get some support from women who have been in similar situations, they needed some parenting skills, and they needed to start healing.

The women sometimes overcompensated for the violence by being too lenient in their homes and needed to learn how to set up some structure. They also needed to make friends, have fun and feel some hope. Some had been moved to shelters a long way from home, one group held women from British Columbia and Nova Scotia. Although most of the women were Canadian born and Caucasian, most groups had at least one woman from another country of origin.

The First Program: Women and Children in Violence

These meetings can be considered unique for a number of reasons. First, we tried to follow the same structure that the children's group was following, a structure which has been developed by Chitra Sekar and Jan Christenson, a counsellor from Family Service Centre. For example, when the children's theme was feelings, the parent group's was as well. The purpose of this was to connect the mother-child experience as much as possible, in order to aid understanding of how the violence witnessed affected the child and how the mother could help the child to deal with it. The mothers were repeatedly told to expect changes in their child's behaviour with the possibility of it becoming worse during this process.

Second, Jean Illsley Clarke's (1998) models found in *Self-esteem: A Family Affair* and *Growing Up Again, Parenting Ourselves, Parenting Our Children* were adapted to fit the program and the mothers. I trained with Jean in 1994 in Minneapolis and then worked with her to train others in Ottawa in 1995, so I relied on a lot of her techniques for these groups. One of our favourites was the "Suggestion Circle". This has been a very empowering tool to use in our groups as it depends very much on group wisdom.

Another feature of these meetings was the safety we provided within the group by having "Ground Rules." We started with the following formula and asked for any additions:

- Personal Responsibility: I will attend all meetings, be on time and be attentive.
- Right to Pass: I will listen but do not have to speak if I don't wish to.
- All Beliefs are Honoured: We come from different backgrounds, religions, even cultures.
- Mutual Respect: No side conversations, we are all entitled to our say.
- Confidentiality: This is a safe place.
- Abstinence (for the Amethyst groups).

These Ground Rules were posted at every meeting and pointed to by any member of the group if necessary.

The Second Program: Women and Children in Addictions

In 1997, we began a similar program at Amethyst Women's Addiction Centre which has evolved in quite a different way due to the different needs and experience of the group members. To describe this organisation to you I'll quote from the Addiction Centre's publication, *Here's to you Sister*.

> Amethyst Women's Addiction Centre was founded in 1979 in Ottawa-Carleton to provide alternative addiction services to women. Working from a feminist perspective, Amethyst makes direct links between the unequal position of women in society, the forms of violence against women and their substance use. (Amethyst Women's Addiction Centre, 1999)

Amethyst had a program for six to twelve year olds for several years and was interested in meeting the needs of the preschool age group. They believe that a consistent group for both the mothers and their children, could really help to lower stress for both and enhance the prevention effort.

Consisting of women who were at various stages of drug or alcohol addiction recovery, this group had an addiction counsellor as co-facilitator. She was able to address any addiction issues which came up, and they did come up. These women had often lost their children to CAS and, even if they still have their children, were dealing with a tremendous amount of guilt because of past behaviour. Most were also solo parenting, were dealing with the struggle that brings, as well as dealing with the very hard work of recovery.

The women and children had pizza and drinks during their meetings; a nice touch, since they met from 4:30 to 5:45 and everyone was usually hungry. There was no play part to this program for the mothers; it was a full seventy-five minute session. Many of these women were already familiar with group process so they could talk about their issues more easily. In fact, my biggest challenge with this group was sometimes the talking, talking, and more talking!

Program Funding

In both organizations money came from the United Way, therefore an evaluation process was essential. The "Y" also asked for volunteers from the groups to speak to United Way sponsors when they applied for funding. Needless to say, ongoing funding for these programs was and remains a challenge.

Program Structure

During the first meeting we learn "Suggestion Circles" and use them throughout the duration of the program, twelve weeks. There are very few weeks where there are not requests for them, so you can see why they are built right into the schedule.

We allow time at the beginning for a kind of debriefing of participants' week. This can be problematic for staying on track when someone is very upset but since this is one of the purposes of the group, we adapt.

The parent education part of the meeting is next, and this is where time is cut if necessary, so I provide them with a lot of good handouts and reading lists. If there have been specific requests for a topic, I'll be sure to include it.

The final fifteen to twenty minutes we sometimes use as "play time." Other years we read stories, did relaxation exercises, listened to music and perhaps made something. But as I mentioned, this year we were privileged to have had an art therapist who had some wonderful ideas that we incorporated into the meetings.

Humour is also an integral part of our groups and I often pass around some cartoons that relate to the evening's topic. Some of the women have forgotten how to play, but they all remembered how to laugh. It's quite a revelation for all of us when I pose the question, "What do you do for fun?" And they can't come up with an answer. Since Jean-Illsley Clarke's (1998) work on self-esteem is based on the premise that "A child's needs are best met by a grown-up who's needs are met," that is our intent as well.

What makes these parenting classes unique in the Ottawa-Carleton area is the link created between mother and child through shared themes; the flexibility in meeting the needs of the parents during the sessions; and the progress participants made because of the valuable resource, group wisdom.

Closure is an important part of any group and our last meeting is dedicated to it. There is some necessary written work as we give them evaluation forms to complete, but mainly we have a small ceremony in the mothers' group when they are given an angel which has been made by a women's cooperative in Bangladesh. I tell them a story about how it was made and why, using it as a metaphor for their own lives. Then in the "Y" group, we join the children for a party.

In Closing

The women in these groups are building cathedrals to themselves. But we who are privileged to be working with these very special women are building cathedrals ourselves.

Endnotes

1. The names of all of the participants have been changed to protect their identities.

References

Amethyst Women's Addiction Centre. (1999). Here's to you sister [on-line]. Available:
    http://infoweb.magi.com/~amethyst/here.htm

Illsley-Clarke, J. (1998). Growing up again: Parenting ourselves, parenting our children (2nd Ed.). Minnesota: Hazelden Press.

Illsley-Clarke, J. (1998). Self-esteem: A family affair. Minnesota: Hazelden Press.

Self-Help Groups and Women as Primary Family Caregivers of the Chronically Mentally Ill

Lisa Hanna
Ottawa, Ontario

Abstract

This paper is based on a qualitative, in-depth and semi-structured interview study that uses a political economy framework and Foucault's (1991) notion of 'governance' to examine the use of self-help groups by seven of fifteen female primary family care givers of chronically mentally ill family members to manage problems, issues and tensions. These women reported that self-help groups give them a place to: 1) disclose, share and relate experiences with one another without social stigma 2) assist one another with information on how to recognize and manage the manic and depressive episodes of their chronic manic depressive and schizoaffective family members, which helps women deal with crisis and uncertainties and indirectly help family members with chronic mental illness 3) obtain support and encourage one another, and 4) have access to educational material on mental illness. Self-help groups were not accessible to all women because of overburden, location, culture and language. Some implications of this discussion for mental health care and the expansion of self-help groups are presented.

Introduction

Deinstitutionalisation and the shift to community care in Canada began as early as the 1960s and 1970s in several provinces with the stated objective of placing as many psychiatric patients as possible in the community. (Grier, 1992) The government's increased efforts at deinstitutionalisation have intensified the trend of decreasing mental hospital populations. Although more of the mentally ill are remaining in the community, the question increasingly becomes, "[u]nder what conditions?" (Conrad & Schneider, 1992, p.68)

Overall, the process of deinstitutionalisation has had mixed results. According to researchers Conrad and Schneider (1992) and Armstrong and Armstrong (1996) the process, to date, has had both positive and negative outcomes. More of the mentally ill are receiving treatment in outpatient facilities, fewer are becoming "institutionalized," a few previously unserved populations are being served, and some reforms have taken hold in mental hospitals. Hospitalization of the mentally ill is shorter, and the team approach has included more non-psychiatrists, such as occupational therapists, in treatment programs.

However, there has been no apparent success in preventing mental illness; difficulties have been encountered in the continuity of care of the chronically mentally ill in communities; patients have been "dumped" from mental hospitals without the availability of appropriate alternatives; and, rehabilitation has been minimal. (Conrad & Schneider, 1992; Armstrong & Armstrong, 1996) Consequently, the care giving needs of the chronically mentally ill have been neglected. The conditions that ensue impose personal and financial costs on family caregivers, more than likely to be women (Armstrong & Armstrong, 1994), the state's mental health and legislative systems to which they turn to for assistance, and ultimately on society as a whole.

This paper is based on a larger case-study involving in-depth, semi-structured individual interviews with a purposive sample of fifteen female family[1] caregivers of chronic[2] manic depressives and schizoaffectives.[3] The larger case-study was designed to examine: 1) the problems, issues and tensions created for fifteen women as primary family caregivers of seventeen chronically mentally ill family members 2) governance of these women of their family members, and 3) resistance of their family members. This paper examines the use of self-help groups by seven of fifteen female primary family caregivers to manage problems, issues and tensions. For the purposes of this study, governance is defined in a broad sense according to Foucault (1991) as "the institutions, procedures, analyses, and reflections, the calculations and tactics that allow the exercise of this very specific albeit complex form of power" (p.102).

This paper argues that deinstitutionalisation; cutbacks to mental health services; expectations of the health promotion framework; and, mental health policy on a macro level, or what I term the "macro care giving context," have created problems, issues and tensions on a micro level for female family caregivers. Through the regular attendance in a self-help group by these women, they try to manage these problems, issues and tensions.

In this study, I assert that women are the primary caregivers of mentally ill adults or children. Their experiences have not yet been previously examined as case studies of in-depth qualitative interviews in sociological research. However, indirect evidence supports the assertion that women are the primary caregivers of the mentally ill. According to Ascher-Svanum and Sobel (1989) in surveys of the needs of family members of psychiatric patients, up to 86 percent of the responses have been from women and similarly, when patients were asked in interviews about the family caregiver most likely to be affected by their returning home, the great majority of caregivers were women. All research material in this study was collected and analysed through a feminist political economy perspective with the use of Foucault`s notion of governance.

Methodology

At the time of the interview, six of the fifteen caregivers reported that they regularly attended a monthly self-help group for family members of the mentally ill. One of the fifteen caregivers with manic depression reported she regularly attended a monthly self-help group for family members with mental illness[4] as a consumer/survivor and caregiver. All fifteen women self-identified as primary family caregivers of their chronically mentally ill family members.

All subjects have identified their family member as having been professionally diagnosed according to the official nomenclature of the American Psychiatric Association's Diagnostic and Statistical Manual of Mental Disorders (1994) (currently termed DSM-IV), as manic depressive or schizoaffective. The subjects ranged in age from twenty to sixty-nine years with a mean of thirty-eight years of age. Two subjects identified themselves as having been professionally diagnosed according to the official nomenclature of the DSM-IV with manic depression.

Interview Data and Analysis

The semi-structured interview data with the women in the study produced rich and eloquent descriptions of the use of self-help groups. The data suggest that the self-help groups gave them a place to: 1) disclose, share and relate experiences with one another without social stigma 2) assist one another with information on how to recognize and manage the manic and depressive episodes of their chronic manic depressive and schizoaffective family members, which helps women deal with crisis and uncertainties and indirectly help family members with chronic mental illness 3) obtain support and encourage one another, and 4) have access to educational material on mental illness.

At the time of the interview, *Anne*[5] was in her 40s. She is a primary caregiver for her two manic depressive sons, both in their 20s. *Anne* reported that the group provided her with a place to share and relate experiences with other caregivers, and obtain information on how to recognize and manage the manic and depressive episodes of her chronic manic depressive family members to help her deal with crisis and uncertainties, and indirectly help her family members:

> I could talk to other people [in the group] and sometimes you'd get little tips on how to handle the situation. Mostly everybody had a sense of humour which really helped. It made a very big difference because you feel so alone and so helpless… frightened… and I think a family must go through a lot of the same feelings as the patients themselves do. They [the patients] must be frightened, they [the patients] must be very frightened.…even if…as the minister said 'I don't have a magic wand to say that everything's fine again' …that's not a reality. But even if nobody had any answers, you have somebody to talk to, and somebody who understands makes all the difference in the world to the caregivers of the patients themselves.

Similarly, *Brenda*, who is in her 50s and a primary caregiver for her schizoaffective daughter who is in her 20s, stated that the group provided her with a trusted place to disclose, share and relate experiences with other caregivers without social stigma, and obtain information on how to recognize and manage the episodes of her family member:

> Oh, I have found the group very useful, very wonderful. You disclose in a way you do not disclose at work. I don't want to spill my guts out at work. These people have been down this road and they have tips, and if they don't have tips they have friendship and encouragement.

Carolyn is in her 60s and is a primary caregiver for her schizoaffective daughter who is in her 40s. She also reported that the group provided her with a place where she could share and relate experiences and obtain support:

> Well certainly it [the group] was a great help for me meeting other people with the same kind of thing…having to cope with the same problems. Really before I went to the group I just felt that I was alone in the world. I don't know if I did know other people like this. It seems so common now, but it didn't then.

It's a great support . . . and very nice families. To just talk with people, that's a great thing. It's somewhere you can talk to people. That's what you want so desperately to do, is talk.

Dorothy is in her 40s. She is a primary caregiver for her schizoaffective mother, in her 60s, and her manic depressive brother, in his 40s. *Dorothy* reported that she found that although the group was quite good she needed to meet more than once a month. She stated, "I find it [the group] quite good. But I find that meeting once a month isn't sufficient for my own needs. I find that I need more than once a month."

Esther is in her 30s and has chronic manic depression, and is a primary caregiver for her manic depressive husband who is in his 40s. She reported that she regularly attended a self-help group for manic depressives and schizoaffectives as a consumer/survivor and caregiver, and that the group made her feel like part of a community who could share and relate experiences and support one another:

I think it [the group] helped both of us…and it was the first opportunity I had to meet a number of people who had manic depression, and not feel so isolated. I mean a few people, but not too many at that time. Going to meetings and hearing about other people's experiences…helps you to feel that…I wasn't going through something on my own. It was comforting to know for example, that you've done that stupid thing, that other people have done things equally as stupid. So it kind of… it helps you become more self-expressive. I think I would say also, an important part is almost a spiritual aspect that when I met people who were in worse shape than I was, I felt grateful, and when I meet people who were in better shape than I was…it made me hopeful. For my husband…I think that he found it useful in the same way and he felt… you know . . . we both found the presentations interesting from an information point of view. Again I think it's just that part of being part of a community of people…

Gayle is in her 50s, a primary caregiver for her schizoaffective husband who is also in his 50s, stated: "It helped me [the group] because I got all the information [about schizoaffective disorder] from the pamphlets and papers. It taught me about the illness and how to deal with it. I could bring this information to educate the family. As a result, they better understand the illness." However, she also complained about having to travel to the city on a monthly basis from a rural town to attend the self-help group because "[t]here is nothing in Manou" [in rural Quebec] in terms of a self-help group.

Two women in the study, *Sophie* and *Laura*, never attended a self-help group but expressed their desire to regularly attend a group. However, *Sophie*, living in rural Quebec stated that "[t]here was nothing in Laduc" and without transportation she remains unable to attend a self-help group in Ottawa or Quebec. Meanwhile, *Laura* stated that "there's no organization set up within the East Indian community" that has a self-help group for family members of the mentally ill.

Women who regularly attended a self-help group in the study suggest a beneficial role for the expansion of self- help groups to assist them in exercising power over the crisis-like conditions and tensions emerging from social, political and economic forms of their oppression as primary family caregivers and state designated mental 'health promoters'. The groups are not accessible to all women for reasons that include: overburden, location, culture and language. It is important that self-help groups for family caregivers and their chronically mentally ill family members continue to expand in both rural and urban communities to better serve these marginalised individuals beyond participants who are typically white, married, better educated and more financially advantaged. (Jones & Jones, 1994) Self-help groups need to expand to many rural areas where women as primary family caregivers are without support and resources. They also are needed to represent the needs of diverse cultures where women as primary family caregivers are also without support and resources. These groups, that exist in the present and future, need to consider bi-monthly meetings and car pools for women who as primary family caregivers are without adequate support and resources.

Conclusion

Increasingly, women will be expected by the state to take on more of the additional caring work of family members with chronic mental illness during the ongoing deinstitutionalisation process, growing fiscal crisis of the state, and ensuing cutbacks to health and mental health care. Self-help groups can provide women with an opportunity to learn how others cope with issues similar to their own and give the sense that they are not alone with problems dealing with mental illness. Self-help groups can, as well, give these women a place, not only where they can vent their frustrations and other reactions, but where they can receive assurances that their reactions are normal. Many women find this particularly valuable after finding themselves misunderstood for so long. Self-help groups also provide a forum for the exchange of vital information about the nature of chronic mental illness and the availability of treatments, formal psychiatric rehabilitation programs, and other resources. (Lafond, 1994)

Essential is that the state strengthen services for women by expanding much needed community services such as self-help groups, respite care, twenty-four hour crisis hotlines, community health and mental health centre counselling, education, crisis intervention and self-help groups.

Finally, more extensive research is required to further develop the theoretical and practical understanding of female family care giving and the governance of chronically mentally ill family members and to build on the findings of this study. Feminist political economy and Foucault's notion of governance have proven useful for revealing not only the reality of community care but how women manage the private troubles and public/macro changes. As the macro-context changes we need to remain concerned first with the consequences for women and second with focussing on organising support systems for primary family caregivers.

Endnotes

1. All subjects and their chronically mentally ill family members are members of different kinds of families that include: nuclear, extended, blended, childless, lone-parent and Common Law marriages.

2. The term 'chronic' is defined in this study according to Rosen (1990) as "mental disorders that reoccur periodically or exist over a long period"(p.2).

3. Approximately one percent of the population suffers from manic depression, a severe long-term mental illness (American Psychiatric Association, 1994b; Thompson et al., 1984). Although lay people ordinarily use the term 'manic depressive illness', psychiatric professionals are increasingly using the term 'bipolar disorder' as is demanded by current diagnostic manuals. Manic depression or

'bipolar disorder' is a disturbance of a person's mood characterized by alternating episodes of depression and mania. Bipolar refers to the 'two poles' of the continuum of moods with depression or feeling down at one end and mania or feeling high at the other end. Switching from depression to mania is referred to as an episode. Episodes are classified as mild, moderate or severe and these mood swings are accompanied by changes in thinking and behaviour. (American Psychiatric Association, 1994a; Hilliard, 1992)

The essential feature of manic depression with schizophrenic tendencies or 'schizoaffective disorder' is a continual period of illness during which at some time, there is a major depressive, manic or mixed episode concurrent with two or more of the following symptoms of schizophrenia: delusions, hallucinations, disorganized speech (such as frequent derailment or incoherence), grossly disorganized or catatonic behaviour, negative symptoms such as affective flattening, and alogia or avolition each present for a significant portion of time during a one month period, or less time if successfully treated. In addition, during the same period of illness, delusions or hallucinations are present for at least two weeks in the absence of prominent mood symptoms. Mood symptoms are present for a substantial portion of a total duration of schizoaffective disorder. (American Psychiatric Association, 1994a) There are two subtypes of schizoaffective disorder based on the mood component of the disorder: bipolar type applies if a manic episode or mixed episode is part of the presentation and major depressive episodes may also occur, and the depressive type applies if only major depressive episodes are part of the presentation.

4. Self-help group participants in this study do not charge for participation in the group and retain ownership and control over the workings of the group. As Lavoie et al. (1994) note "[m]any [self-help groups] believe the empowerment inherent in the self-help ethos of (1) giving as well as getting help, and (2) retaining control over the functioning, goals and ultimate destiny of the group, is central to the successful functioning of these groups"(p.280).

5. In this study, all subjects are assigned a pseudonym to protect anonymity.

References

American Psychiatric Association.(1994a). *The diagnostic and statistical manual of mental disorders.* Washington: The American Psychiatric Association.

American Psychiatric Association.(1994b). The practice guideline for the treatment of patients with bipolar disorder. *Supplement to the American Journal of Psychiatry* 151, 12, pp. 1-36.

Armstrong, P., & Armstrong, H. (1996). *Wasting away: The undermining of Canadian health care.* Toronto: Oxford University Press.

Armstrong, P. (1994). Closer to home: More work for women. In P. Armstrong, H. Armstrong, J. Choiniere, G. Feldberg & J. White (Eds.), *Take care: Warning signals for Canada's health system* (pp.95-110). Toronto: Garamond Press.

Ascher-Svanum, H., & Sobel, T. (1989). Care giving of mentally ill adults: A women's agenda. *Hospital and Community Psychiatry* 40,8, 843-845.

Conrad, P., & Schneider, J. (1992). *Deviance and medicalization: From badness to sickness.* Philadelphia: Temple University Press.

Foucault, M. (1991). Governmentality. In G. Burchell, C. Gordon, & P. Miller (Eds.), *The Foucault effect: Studies in governmentality,* pp. 87-104. Great Britain: Harvester Wheatsheaf.

Grier, R. (1993). *Putting people first: The reform of mental health services in Ontario.* Toronto: Ministry of Health.

Hilliard, E. (1992). *Manic-depressive illness: An information booklet for patients, their families and friends.* New Westminster: Royal Colombian Hospital.

Jones, S., & Jones, P. (1994). Caregiver burden: Who the caregivers are, how they give care, and what bothers them. *Journal of Health and Social Policy* 6,2 , 71-89.

Lavoie, F, Borkman, T., & Gidron, B. (1994). *Self-help and mutual aid groups.* New York: Haworth Press.

Lafond, V. (1994). *Grieving mental illness: A guide for patients and their caregivers.* Toronto: University of Toronto Press.

Rosen, D. (1990). *Stress and the family of manic depressives: A guide for families.* St.Louis: Malcolm Bliss Mental Medical Center.

Thompson, R., Stancer, H., & Persad, E. (1984). *Manic-depressive illness : A guide for patients and families*. Toronto: Clarke Institute of Psychiatry.

Building Healthy Communities for Lesbians Through Safe and Accessible Services

Kia Rainbow
Ottawa, Ontario

Abstract

In 1994, the Women's Action Centre Against Violence in Ottawa-Carleton initiated the Quincy Project. The objective of the project was to bring together different groups of abused women to gain an insight into how the criminal justice system responded to their experiences of violence. The issue of lesbian partner abuse emerged from these discussions. If a lesbian was experiencing violence in her life, accessing essential and appropriate services in mainstream organizations was difficult at best and often impossible, due to a lack of understanding and willingness to address the unique barriers faced by lesbians. The Lesbian Issues Subcommittee (LISC) of the Regional Coordinating Committee to End Violence Against Women (RCCEVAW) provides an important forum for lesbians to articulate their collective needs, concerns and desires in achieving accessibility. The following is a brief synopsis of the purpose and objectives of the committee as well as the audit tool used in creating their report.

Introduction

In June of 1998, the Ad Hoc Committee of Accessibility and Lesbian Issues was formed to bring together representatives of the Regional Coordinating Committee to End Violence Against Women (RCCEVAW). The purpose of this committee was to develop a project that would provide assistance and support to mainstream services with the Ottawa-Carleton region in order that they become more accessible and responsive to the needs of women with disabilities and lesbians.

Purpose

The purpose of the ad hoc committee was to:
- Improve the quality of life for women with disabilities and lesbians.
- Improve services and access to services for women with

disabilities and lesbians.
* Broaden awareness of the reality of abuse in relationships for women with disabilities and lesbians.

Rationale

In the early to mid 1990s, lesbians and disabled women began to speak of their frustration with accessing appropriate services within the network of social service agencies in Ottawa-Carleton. Specifically, violence against women with disabilities and lesbian partner abuse were identified by members of each group as issues that had long been ignored or misrepresented in mainstream services.

In 1992, the Ottawa-Carleton Independent Living Centre, with funding from the Ministry of Community and Social Services, embarked on a project that would spotlight the issue of violence against women with disabilities. The Women with Disabilities and Abuse Project served to improve access to services for women with disabilities who were in abusive relationships; and in the process of doing so, allowed these same women the opportunity to speak of the violence they were experiencing in their lives.

In 1994, the Women's Action Centre Against Violence initiated the Quincy Project. The objective of the project was to bring together different groups of abused women to gain an insight into how the criminal justice system responded to their experiences of violence. The issue of lesbian partner abuse emerged from these discussions. If a lesbian was experiencing violence in her life, accessing essential and appropriate services in mainstream organizations was difficult at best and often impossible due to a lack of understanding and willingness to address the issue of lesbian partner abuse. Lesbians also spoke of the prevalence of homophobia within these same agencies, which compounded the difficulties they experienced in their pursuit of services.

Today, women from both communities continue the struggle for safe, appropriate and accessible services. The Lesbian Issues Subcommittee and the Accessibility Subcommittee have both become strategic inclusions in the structure of the RCCEVAW.

Project Objectives

The project, *Working Toward Accessibility: Eliminating Barriers to Women With Disabilities and Lesbians*[1] is a unique approach to identifying gaps in services within an agency. It combines the use of a self-auditing tool alongside a participatory workshop. The design allows the participating agency the opportunity to make changes to areas of their organization, which they themselves have identified as lacking in accessibility to either or both groups of women.

A grant from the Status of Women Canada along with working within the Framework For Services For Abused Women, the first three objectives of the project were to:

1. Develop an audit tool that would allow participants an opportunity to self-audit their respective agencies. This audit tool will assess the agencies' human resources, operational policies and procedures, attitudinal barriers and the physical environment of the social service agencies.

2. Develop and conduct a workshop designed to assist participating agencies in completing the audit tool. The workshop would also provide the opportunity for agencies to develop a work plan to set out short and long term goals for their agencies.

3. Conduct a follow-up meeting with any interested agencies to offer staff, management and board members the opportunity to re-examine the goals set for their agency.

Design of the Audit Tool

The audit which was utilized in the project was the initiative of the Lesbian Issues Subcommittee, had been developed by members of LISC as an educational and proactive tool. The objective in developing this audit was for it to be used to assess the appropriateness of services offered by social service agencies when servicing lesbians and the level of commitment to promoting awareness of lesbian issues. In collaboration with the Accessibility Subcommittee, members of both committees worked to amend the content of the audit in order that women with disabilities be reflected in its content.

Conclusion

The assessment of an agency's human resources, operational policies and procedures, attitudinal barriers and physical environment, through a self-evaluation, was the primary focus of the audit. This tool would be required to lay the groundwork for building a work plan that could be incorporated into an agency's strategic plan.

Endnote

1. A complete copy of the audit tool can be found in the report *Working Toward Accessibility: Eliminating Barriers to Women With Disabilities and Lesbians*. The report is available in English, French, braille and audiocassette through the Community Resource Centre of Goulbourn, Kanata and West Carleton, phone (613) 591-3686, fax (613) 591-2501.

Child Care Workers as a Source of Parenting Education for Japanese Mothers

Sumiko Tachinami
Nagano, Japan

Abstract

This paper presents the results of a survey of the perceived effects on parenting abilities associated with the attendance of preschoolers at regulated child care centres. The survey was based on samples of more than a hundred parents of young children in Shinminato Toyama Prefecture Japan. The importance of the availability of regulated child care facilities has been a recurrent theme in Canadian feminist policy analysis, even taking into account cross-cultural differences, this report provides rich information which will benefit Canadian feminists and child policy makers.

Introduction

The Japanese child care system was set up in 1947 and currently comprises 22,000 centres, 2 million childcare spaces, 200 thousand childcare workers and over 300 training schools including universities and colleges. Preschool-age Japanese children are usually three to five years old. Of all five year old Japanese children, 31.5 percent are in the childcare system and 62.5 percent are in kindergarten. The children who go to childcare centres, also get regulated kindergarten education under the Japanese kindergarten course of study.

At the present time, there is an increasing number of working mothers who take their babies or toddlers to childcare centres and therefore, many children are staying for longer hours and more years in the centres. The Japanese birthrate is also decreasing from year to year (e.g., 1.57 in 1989 and only 1.39 in 1998), therefore many young parents have only one or two children. I think that this is why many young parents do not gain enough experience in caring for their children and require much more specific experience and help. I also believe that childcare workers are the best partners and helpers for young parents who are isolated or inexperienced, requiring an especially good relationship to get the benefits from the partnership. This paper presents the research I completed, based on a questionnaire for the mothers and the childcare staff in a Japanese Childcare Centre in 1998.

The Survey Group

From the hundred surveys distributed, 67 responses were received, including 56 from mothers, 9 from the staff and 2 from unknown persons, which accounts for a 44.7 percent response rate. The mean age of the mothers was 29.4, with 1.55 children per household. Of the mothers, 23.2 percent were working full time and 60.7 percent of the households were based on the nuclear family.

The Questionnaire

The questionnaire that was presented to the childcare workers and parents asked the participants to check one of the following: strongly agree, slightly agree, don't know, don't really agree, don't agree at all, unknown, in regards to the following questions and issues:

1. While mothers are at work, they are able to work with a certain peace of mind, if their child is in a safe and lively environment.
2. Mothers learn how to relate to their children by seeing childcare staff at work.
3. I am very happy that I can follow my child's progress through the mother/caregiver contact notebook.
4. When asking questions regarding such things as the care of my child, toilet training, bedtime, and relations to other persons, the daycare staff members provide good advice.
5. If I worry about the upbringing of my child, that my child is developing slowly, that I do not have enough experience, energy or time to bring up a healthy child, I can comfortably approach the daycare centre staff for advice.
6. If a mother receives positive evaluation of her own child raising skills from members of staff, she will feel encouraged and have her confidence boosted.
7. If staff members encourage fathers to drop off and pick up their children at daycare, and to become more involved in centre events and meetings, mothers are helped by the positive

evaluation of their husbands.

8. When working mothers are feeling self-critical about their own ability to properly care for their children, centre staff can boost their self-confidence through a number of means. For example, the centre staff can remind them that child raising is not the sole responsibility of the mother, but one shared with other family members and society as a whole.

9. I feel that mothers and staff members are always cooperating and learning about child care from one another. At times when I do not receive much support from my husband or other family members, I can share the burden of child raising with others and not feel that I am the only one taking responsibility for raising my child.

10. By meeting, talking and making friends with other young mothers at, daycare, mothers can receive hints and ideas on how to handle a busy life, filled with work, housework, and child raising.

11. By positively participating in daycare centre events and meetings, even though it can be difficult at times, parents can benefit. They benefit by sharing useful information and having an enjoyable time.

12. In recent, times there has been a tendency for small children to live separated from their grandparents. I am very happy that my child has the chance to associate with all generations and learn from many different people at daycare.

13. If both the parents and grandparents of daycare children are involved in their upbringing, the two generations will have a lot more in common. Although there will inevitably be differences, by sharing opinions and experience, parents and grandparents are able to lessen the burden of raising a child.

14. If daycare centres cooperate with public welfare committees, city associations and local neighbourhood groups in exchanging information and ideas, the lives of children and young families will become easier, and local residents will gain a better understanding of the lifestyles of young families.

Survey Response

Generally speaking, the survey showed that our hypothesis was correct. There was a great deal of agreement in all questionnaire responses, indicating that mothers have an especially strong need to know the state and the condition of their children in the centre, which is why they hope eagerly that childcare workers make contact with them frequently. One way in which childcare workers can do this is by making written comments in the mother/caregiver contact notebook every day. This notebook can be exchanged daily by parents and caregivers, in which the child's health condition, meals, sleeping hours, and playthings can be noted.

Participant Quotations

"I am very interested in my child's daycare lifestyle. As a parent, if I can find out just one thing regarding that lifestyle then I am very happy. If I read something about some progress that my child has made, then I am really happy at my child's growth."

"I really appreciate having even the smallest of questions answered. However, although I have a lot of questions regarding small children and childcare, the teachers are too busy and it is difficult to find the time to ask anything. Often, when a teacher is in the middle of answering one of my questions, a child will interrupt us and I will be put off asking anything else. Therefore, whenever I go to daycare I am always full of unanswered questions."

"Because I don't know how my child is spending their time at daycare, I would like to know both the good and the bad. I want to know everything to do with his progress."

Unfortunately, the mothers know that Japanese childcare workers cannot meet the expectation that they record the daily activities in the notebook every day for all of the children for whom they are responsible, nor can they speak often with each mother. Japanese government regulations require a caregiver to take care of three babies, or six toddlers, or twenty children of three years of age, or thirty children of four and five years of age in each class. Therefore, they are too busy to write in the notebook every day for each child.

Participant Quotations

"If filled out every day, I think that it's useful to find out what my child is doing at daycare. I know that the teachers are busy, and that writing a comment for every child is tough, but as a parent I would like the book to be filled in every day."

In the cases of infants and toddlers, Japanese daycare centres and parents often use this kind of notebook for communicating and getting information to each other, but it is not done every day for older children. Nevertheless, in spite of too much work and too little time for the caregivers, many parents and caregivers have a good relationship.

Participant Quotations

"When I was already thinking about toilet training, I asked the advice of the centre staff and they thought that it might be a little early. After that, when I did actually start toilet training the process ran very smoothly. I owe a lot to the centre staff."

"I have been depressed by the many demands of both working and raising a child, early mornings and overtime, but was inspired after receiving some encouraging words from the centre staff."

"While I am doing housework at home and my child asks me to listen, I tell her to wait until later because I am busy and don't listen to her. However, daycare teachers are always sensitive to the children's needs and have the time to relate to them properly."

"I consulted centre staff when I was worried about my child not eating dinner properly. They advised that I stop giving my child sweets and drinks before dinner and that I start having it earlier in the evening."

The second response seems to reflect the dissatisfaction that the mothers feel because they expect their husbands to be the most reliable partners for raising their children. I think it is their ideal and not a real expectation. They often say their husbands do not have enough time for raising their children. I think it is one of the biggest problems for Japanese families. But they don't say clearly that they need other people's help more in order to decrease their everyday anxiety or worry about caring for their children.

Participant Quotations

"I would like to be of the same opinion as my husband, in front of my child's grandparents. For example, even if my child starts crying, for various reasons, I don't give my child sweets before bedtime. My husband's idea, however, is to give the child something because they are crying. I don't believe that this in for the child's best interest. I also think my child is cute but this seems to be all that my husband thinks."

Many Japanese parents seem to be very isolated in raising their children. I think that this is because they are often too busy at work, or worried and/or ashamed that their child-rearing practices are inadequate. Historically in Japan, three generations of the family usually lived in the same house and shared everything. Young mothers used to learn how to raise children from their own mother or mother-in-law and their neighbours. Today, many young families tend to live independently, especially in urban areas. Many of them are trying hard to be good parents and they would like to be able to see good models of parenting in their neighbourhoods. However, some of them hardly associate with their neighbours and have few opportunities to see or hear about the other people's ways of bringing up their children.

Participant Quotations

"I haven't made any close friends at the centre. However, I do talk and exchange ideas with old friends and acquaintances."

Many parents have given up or totally lost their confidence as responsible parents, many after suffering some form of criticism. For example, they are often criticized about not knowing how to discipline their children. Sometimes, they are tired and are therefore criticized for not being eager enough. But my survey suggests that deep-down, parents hope to have good and helpful communication with each other, with their neighbours and their children's caregivers.

Participant Quotations

"Because my child is an only child, I think it is good that they have a chance to be involved in a group with lots of different people."

"I believe that by associating with children of different ages, my child has become much kinder to younger children. Because she is an only child, she had no experience in relating to small children but by belonging to a group has gradually become a kind big sister."

"Because my parents do not live near by, the only people I can consult about problems are the centre teachers. I find this very easy and helpful."

I think that caregivers should encourage parents to be confident and happy. But my survey also suggests that at the present time, not all parents think of caregivers as being reliable enough. I think this is the biggest problem creating distance between parents and caregivers. Sometimes the two have different opinions, emotions, skills and so on. They need to learn and teach each other to have a good partnership.

Conclusion

How do we get the best partnership among parents, communities, caregivers and the relevant authorities? I think this is the most important problem for us. Some parents suggest the following:

Participant Quotations

"I believe that, the daycare staff members are looking after the children very well, but that there are too many children per teacher. I would like for the number of teachers to be increased so that, the child/teacher ratio could be decreased."

"I would like to work but still have a small child at home, so cannot find the chance. The centre says that they will look after the child once I have found work, but not beforehand. I find myself in a bit of a dilemma."

"Because I believe that, a father's role and presence in the home is important, a husband who doesn't cooperate with childcare will cause stress."

Perceptions of the Body

The Healing Journal

Ellen Jaffe
Woodstock, Ontario

Abstract

This paper is based on a writing workshop presented at the Conference. It stems from her belief that creativity and "finding one's voice" are major steps toward healing, and that many women have experienced being silenced and/or self-censorship in their relationships with others and with themselves. Through the writing exercise workshops, she encourages women to write as a means of self expression, find their personal voice, become empowered as they share their inner feelings and allow themselves to write about things they might not be able to speak about.

Introduction

This paper will describe the process of a workshop that we experienced at the CRIAW Conference in October, 1999, and is based on a program developed for Ingamo Family Homes, a second-stage housing development for women in Woodstock, Ontario.[1] The roots for the program stem from many years of working with women, children, and adolescents in writing groups and programs, both as a facilitator and as a participant. Elements of the program include visualization exercises, music, meditation and of course writing. After a brief introduction and outline of the workshop, the attendees did several writing exercises together as described below. My aim for the session, was to make the space as safe as possible, so that participants could feel free to write, and perhaps share, their own words.

Program Foundations

These programs are based on the premise that, while some people have a gift of writing that would flourish anywhere, even on the proverbial desert island, many other people — with encouragement — can use writing as a tool of self-expression and as a way of finding their own voice and knowing the things they want to say.

That is, the tools and the practise can sometimes stimulate

someone's ability and desire to express herself, rather than the other way around. Writing one's own feelings and hearing the words of other women in similar situations can be a source of empowerment for anyone, especially people who are feeling marginalised (a good image from the field of writing itself!) and helpless. In my workshops, I try to help people develop their own inner language, their memories and personal stories — the images that shape their lives. We can look for new, perhaps more creative or empowering images, and we can try to write new versions of the old stories and scripts, so that women will literally, "write their lives," as in the title of Carolyn Heilbron's (1989) book about biography.

Interestingly, the word "write" is a homonym for three other words with the same pronunciation: right (r-I-g-h-t), rite (r-I-t-e), and wright (w-r-I-g-h-t). These words are also relevant to our purpose: to right something means to make it better, to correct, to straighten — for example to right a wrong, to right a table that has been turned upside down. Sometimes "righting" a situation means creating new forms, not simply returning to the old. A rite is a ceremony, a ritual, relating back to myth, celebration, belief. Ritual can become empty, sterile, and meaningless, or even cruel and abusive, or it can also be endowed with new forms and beliefs to make it truly spiritual, linking the individual with her Self and the world around her.

Wright means "maker" — as in wheelwright, wainwright, cartwright, playwright. It derives from the word "work" (middle and old English, Anglo-Saxon, old High German), and is related to a word which means "skilled worker." Thus, when we write a poem, story, or a journal entry, we are making and shaping something important, with skill and caring. We are working — not being frivolous, or indulging "idle fantasies" that are "all in our heads" — though we are, in fact, often working with our imaginations, fears, and hopes, as well as with our five senses. The words "poem" and "poetry" also mean to make, to shape, and "story" means to tell.

To complete our detour into word origins, the word "voice" comes from a basic Sanskrit word that means "spoken word," and relates to words that mean "noise" and "war-cry." We have derivatives such as advocate, invocation, vociferous, vouchsafe, invoke, avow, and revoke. Voice does give a sense of power. The word "silence," a much shorter entry in the dictionary, means literally to say nothing, to keep quiet, and might relate to still or quietly flowing water. A friend of mine who is a therapist recently had laryngitis and she wrote on her pad, as she couldn't speak, "I normally have a big voice—it feels very odd not being able to speak—disempowering—like being invisible."

This reminds me of Berthold Brecht's play about the Czech good soldier Schweik.[2] During the Second World War, a Nazi soldier came into Schweik's home and ordered this man to serve him, cook for him, clean his boots, do whatever he wanted. Schweik did this all for seven years, but never said anything. Finally, the war was over and the Nazi soldier left, or was killed or imprisoned and Schweik opened his mouth and said "NO!"

Too often, we do suffer in silence, acting in ways we do not believe or agree with to save our lives, keep the peace, stay in "our place." Sometimes, this is essential for self-preservation; the silence, the still place, can actually keep our voices alive. In addition, meditation, day-dreaming, and taking time to pause in the chatter of our lives and minds can actually create a space in which we discover what we think and feel, what we want to say. We need to dip into that well of silence and stillness to find our words.

The Workshop Discovered

Writing—or any art—can then help draw these things out, into the light and the outside world. The late American Black poet and feminist Audre Lorde (1984) wrote a famous and inspiring essay, "The Transformation of Silence into Language and Action." Lourde delivered the paper at the Modern Language Association's Lesbian and Literature Panel in 1977, which was first published in *The Cancer Journals* (1980), and reprinted in *Sister Outsider* (1984) a collection of her essays and speeches. In this essay, she writes, "I have come to believe over and over again that what is most important to me must be spoken, made verbal and shared, even at the risk of having it bruised or misunderstood. That the speaking profits me, beyond any other effect." During a time when she was told she needed surgery and might have cancer, she re-evaluated her life and noted:

> What I most regretted were my silences . . . Death on the other hand, is the final silence . . . I was going to die, if not sooner then later, whether or not I had ever spoken myself. My silences had not protected me. Your silence will not protect you. But for every real word spoken, for every attempt I had ever made to speak those truths for which I am still seeking, I had made contact with other women . . . bridging our

differences . . . What are the words you do not yet have? What do you need to say? (1984, pp. 40-41)

Lourde goes on to make a statement which had a great impact on me, and which I often use to open a writing workshop. In fact, this statement was printed on the memorial service leaflet for my friend Yvonne, who died in 1996 and is the statement we used for our first piece of writing during the workshop: "I AM NOT ONLY A CASUALTY, I AM ALSO A WARRIOR."(p.42). In this statement, being a casualty, a "victim," is accepted — we do not have to deny it — on the other hand that is not all that we are. Being a warrior is also possible — at the same time. How does this apply to your life, your situation, to someone you know?

I described techniques to overcome fear of writing and the "inner critic," such as those suggested by Natalie Goldberg (1986) in her book *Writing Down the Bones*. Goldberg suggests that when writing to keep your hand moving all the time, write whatever comes into your mind, even if it sounds "silly". She says to turn off the voice of censor or inner critic. To this I added the thoughts that even if you write, "I don't understand this, I'm not a warrior, this is a stupid exercise," that's fine, just keep going and something will emerge. If it doesn't, that's okay too because this is a workshop (or, at home, one can use this technique in journal writing). It's okay to be less than "perfect".

We wrote on this for about ten minutes, and then several women shared their work. One woman felt that she was not, in fact, a "casualty," and I noted that this sentence, like any writing exercise, is intended only as a starting-point. It is entirely up to the individual whether it is something you can agree, or disagree with, or elaborate on in your own way.

Audre Lorde once wrote that her daughter, commenting on the fear that may go with speaking out, said,

> Tell them about how you're never really a whole person if you remain silent, because there's always that one little piece inside you that wants to be spoken out, and if you keep ignoring it, it gets madder and madder and hotter and hotter, and if you don't speak it out one day it will just up and punch you in the mouth from the inside. (1984, p.42)

This may be a cause of many of our physical as well as emotional ills — headaches, depression, upset stomach, backache, panic and eating disorders, addictions.

Many women are not in a good relationship with their bodies. This may be because of memories—stored in our bodies, as well as our minds and hearts—of sexual and physical abuse. Or it may be because of the barrage of (mis)information from the media on the "right" way to look, the emphasis on the "perfect"—slim—figure, the perfect style and colour of hair and make-up, the right clothes, the best way to exercise, and so on. Women of colour and women who are physically challenged have an especially hard time seeing images of themselves in the media. Experiences of our mothers, grandmothers, and great-grandmothers may also influence our feelings about our bodies – residential schools, slavery, and other experiences of colonization and mistreatment. Women who have had illnesses and physical challenges may have had their bodies poked, prodded, and "objectified" by the medical system—even though this was for "their own good." We may have chosen to cope through eating disorders or other addictions. We need help in reclaiming our own beauty, as we would reclaim land for a garden that has lain in waste for a long time.

For the next exercise, I played the song "I Am A Beauty" by Laura Smith. The singer looks at parts of her body—her eyes, her hands—and realizes that "there's a surprise there." Each woman in the workshop wrote as if she were speaking as a part of her body. We wrote for about fifteen minutes, and the women then shared their work. These were deeply felt pieces, writing about their feet, their hands, their hair, even their wombs.

The other exercises that we did not have the time to include in the workshop involved writing about a safe place and about our grandmothers. We concluded our session with a brief exercise of choosing a colour we wanted to be—these included "the blue of a peacock's tail" and "the colour of the sky at midnight."

After the workshop, several women spoke to me about forming writing circles in their home communities. One woman said that she began writing a piece about her grandmother, that she had always wanted to do.

Conclusion

We are learning that the area in the brain call the Bronca's Centre, which affects speech and language, is severely inhibited by trauma. This can "freeze" us into a state of anxiety. Writing about traumatic and other important experiences can help us understand and deal cognitively as well as emotionally with these experiences, and move on with the flow of our lives.

Endnotes

1. Ellen Jaffe is the originator of the Healing Workshop program. She is both a writer and psychotherapist who has done extensive work with women and youth. She is currently working on a book, developing ideas and journalling exercises from the workshop presented at the CRIAW Conference.

2. The story is from a Berthold Brecht play *Scweyk in the Second World War*, published 1956 and based on Jaroslav Hašek's novel *The Good Soldier Schweik* from 1920-23.

References

Goldberg, N. (1986). *Writing down the bones: Freeing the writer within*. Boston, MA: Shambhala Publications.

Heilbron, C. (1989). *Writing a woman's life*. New York, NY: Ballantine Books.

Lourde, A. (1980). *The Cancer Journals*. San Fransisco, CA: Aunt Lute Books.

Lourde, A. (1984). *Sister Outsider: Essays and Speeches*. Freedom, CA: Crossing Press.

Smith, L. (1998). I am a beauty. *It's A Personal Thing* [CD]. Universal Music, USMD 81033.

YM Magazine 1998: A Content Analysis of the Messages Projected to Young Women

Karen Thistle
Sudbury, Ontario

Abstract

This paper explores the contribution YM Magazine makes to the education of young girls in cultivating their healthy lifestyles. Young girls are influenced by the media when developing their sense of self-worth and making lifestyle choices. YM Magazine, after Seventeen, has the second largest circulation in North America. While there has been research completed on Seventeen there is a lack of content analysis, from an academic perspective, regarding the lifestyle choices presented in YM Magazine. While this paper does not suggest that the media is the only influence on young girls, Thistle argues that though the media is not the only influence on this group, they play an influential role through the limited behavioural options they offer the readers and may in fact help reinforce stereotypes.

> You've outgrown all that young stuff. You're coming into your own as a woman. It's the most important, exciting, most confusing time of your life. If you want to make the most of it, you'll want to check out YM. And now you can— absolutely free!
>
> Ask yourself: Could your love life be better? Your social life more fun? Your school life more rewarding? Would you like straight advice you can trust? Real opinions from real guys? Fashion and beauty that brings out the best you? The latest on your favorite celebs? Plus all kinds of pull-out guides, pages of guys and contests every month.
>
> *YM* No Risk Offer

Introduction

In a study conducted by Lisa L. Duke and Peggy J. Kreshel (1998), concerning young women's interaction with the magazine media, they concluded that while "girls were aware of the 'beauty equals success' message inherent in these magazines," they were not willing to give "this medium carte blanche access to their value systems"(p.67). At a 1992 symposium, young women delegates attending a media workshop expressed the opinion that "magazines should be more realistic. We don't have to be like the person on the magazine cover; magazines should show all varieties of people and appreciate people for how they are; and media images are affecting young women's self-esteem"(Symposium Report, p.26). Evidently, there are young women who are well aware of the messages being sold by the various 'teen' magazines, however these magazines are continuing to sell in large numbers.

In 1997, *Seventeen*, a magazine for young women, reported a circulation of 1,950,000 and *YM* (*Young and Modern*), another magazine targeting the same audience, reported a circulation of 1,829,515. Both magazines are published in New York and sold across North America. There are those who are concerned not with the distribution size of these magazines but with the messages the magazines are selling.

Several studies have been conducted on the magazine *Seventeen* including those by Kate Peirce and Jennifer A. Schlenker (1990), Sandra L. Caron and William A. Haltman (1998). These content analyses were conducted to determine the feminist content of *Seventeen* throughout their publication history, and involved a thorough examination of the magazine (which started in 1944) until the mid 1990's.

To date, no studies are available conducted on *YM*, or *Young and Modern* which was first published in 1953. Ulrick's International Periodicals Directory describes *YM* as a magazine: "for young women between the ages of 14-20. Covers [sic] relationships, self-discovery, entertainment, fitness and careers, with emphasis on beauty and fashion." As the second largest North American teen magazine, *YM* has had little feminist based content analysis, so this study was designed to better comprehend what messages this magazine offers young women.

METHODOLOGY
Sample
This study was modeled after the content analysis study of *Seventeen* conducted by Kate Peirce (1990) and the study by Jennifer

A. Schlenker et al (1998) which expanded Peirce's original work. The 1998 year was selected for availability and relevance of the media messages sent to youths today. A one year subscription consists of 10 issues, with June and July a combination issue as well as December and January. Throughout 1998, Lesley Jane Seymour was the Editor-In-Chief; however, she left the magazine in February 1999. Currently, *YM* holds registered trademarks on *YM* Young & Modern, including specific article titles "Get Gorgeous," "Babe Watch," and "Say Anything" (*YM*, Oct 6).

Procedure

Each month of the 1998 publishing year was analyzed to determine which pages were advertisements, and which were editorial pages. The editorial pages were divided into eight categories including a category for advertising. Each magazine was first read through in its entirety, then scanned page-by-page, maintaining a count of the number of pages that were devoted to each article. Each article was given a code (1-8) for the appropriate category it belonged to, and was coded only once, never being used in more than one category. The number of editorial pages were added and combined with the pages that were advertising to determine the percentage of each category, per month. The page totals were also added to determine the percentages for the year (10 issues). There is a 0.01 to 0.25-margin of error due to the nature of the magazine. For example, one page would contain a column ad, another column would be the continuation of an article, and the third column would be a new article, making the page difficult to categorize.

Definition of Categories

The eight categories for article coding were based on the study by Schlenker et al (1998), including: appearance, male/female relations, home, self-development, career development and political/world issues. In their study the first three categories were considered traditional messages and the last three were considered feminist messages. (Schlenker, p.140) In their study, they did not include "Letters to the Editor," "Horoscopes," or "Star Talk," which are all regular features of *YM* Magazine and included in the category of "Other." The following gives a breakdown of each of the eight categories:

- *Appearance*: latest fashion trends, fashion info, beauty info, makeup, hairstyles, beauty products, and how you look to others.
- *Male-Female Relations*: advice columns about relationships/dating, and feature articles on male actors/models ("Babe Watch," "Guy Talk").
- Home: decorating, sewing, crafts, cooking, and preparing to move to another school.
- *Self-Development*: health, how to take care of yourself, personality quizzes, relationships with friends and family (excluding boys), readers personal stories, and hobbies.
- *Career Development*: going to college or university, spotlight on famous women and their careers, and what it is like to work in a certain career area.
- *Political/World Issues*: environment, international issues, volunteering, and political articles.
- *Other*: horoscopes, numerology, "Say Anything," "Letters From the Editor," "Letters From Readers," "Fanclub," and "Entertainment" (not related to "Male Watching" or "Babe Watching").
- *Advertising*: "Where to Shop," ads for *YM* events and subscriptions, full page and page sections that were not editorial pages including ad pages which look like the rest of the editorial pages, but are set apart with message at top of the page ("Special Advertising Section").

Content Analysis Results and Discussion

If one were to look only at *YM* Magazine to define what young women are interested in, the answer would overwhelmingly be: their appearance and having boyfriends. While other magazines may offer young women an alternative to these stereotypical messages, *YM* continues to sell the message that being beautiful and having a boyfriend is the main goal of young women. The results from the content analysis contribute to the growing numbers of studies that are being conducted on teen magazines. As other researchers have noted, "in order to understand the impact of these magazines, we need to first understand their content"(Schlenker et al, p. 146). Content analysis is also important because "teenage publications and their roles as socialization forces have been largely overlooked. However, this does not diminish the importance of such publications"(p.146). By understanding the content of the magazine, the messages that are being heard by young women become clear. While some young women may be able to say "this is not for me," or "I don't believe this," there are those who are influenced by the messages. (Duke and Kreshel, p. 57). The following section will examine the categories and the messages in them in more depth.

- ## Appearance

The percentage of pages dedicated to telling young women how they should look, aside from the advertising, represented 20 percent of the magazine, and the largest percentage after advertising (See Appendix 1). Throughout the year, the percentage for the Appearance Category was never below 17 percent (*YM* September, 1998) and at its highest, was 22 percent (YM February,1998; YM April, 1998). It is interesting to note that when the total pages dedicated to appearance was at its lowest, advertising was at its highest (50 percent).

What kind of beauty is being promoted? Beauty is divided into categories within the magazine, with regular page features entitled: "Fashion Info," "Beauty Info,"and "Hair Info." Other editorial pages are dedicated to fashion spreads where a particular theme is identifiable and young women are shown the latest fashion styles, or ways to wear makeup. Not once within the eleven issues, does it suggest that young women look beautiful without makeup, moreover it assumes that young women want to wear the clothes presented, with no thought to a personal sense of style.

At some points in the magazine it is hard to tell if it is really an article or another page of advertisements. For example, the "Beauty Info" page in the October issue of *YM* (1998) was titled "Tricks and Treats - Get Into the Swing of the Spooky Season With These Terror-ific Black and Orange Scores. You'll Be So Sexy It'll Be Scary!"(p.19). On the left side of the page, nine products that are either black or orange were arranged in order of number, while the right side of the page consisted of a legend with the name of the company that makes the product and the American price. The "Hair Info" page is similar to the "Beauty Info" page in that it offers small articles, usually four to a page, which give tips on what products are best for different types of hair or face shapes and where to buy them.

While these pages are set up as editorial pages meant to offer young women advice on how to look, they also represent what the ad world coined, and Gloria Steinem (1990) called "supportive editorial atmosphere" or "complementary copy"(p.108); editorial pages that complement or support ads for the same products. For instance, an add for makeup would be placed beside an article like "Tricks and Treats," which endorses the advertisers products and the use of them.

What is most disturbing is the number of products that are praised by the magazine in order to entice company sponsorships, such as Cover Girl Makeup which endorsed the "Cover Girl Model Search" in the October issue. Not only did Cover Girl have nine full pages of advertising, they were placed between editorial pages where the contestants in the model search were all wearing Cover Girl Makeup. The contestants were telling the readers what colours they chose to help with their various problems, such as thin lips. While the young women reading the magazine are told how to fix their small eyes or play up cheekbone, they are also being told that Cover Girl is the product that will make it happen. As Gloria Steinem notes, when "women's magazines from *Seventeen* to *Lear's* praise beauty products in general and credit Revlon in particular to get ads, it's just business as usual"(p.108). When this becomes the practice, the pages that are left for editorial pages that are not complementary text are still far below the journalist and ethical standards of news and no longer able to adequately cover general interest articles.(Steinem, 1990)

Along with the complementary texts are the fashion spreads, which are approximately four to six pages, with at least two per month, often having a theme such as "Sweater to Fall For," or "Generation Next." These spreads included page by page information for the readers to know who is making the clothing, the cost, and a "Where to Shop" page so they can "Go and Get the Look." These spreads are placed within other clothing ads and often look very similar in layout.

An even more disturbing element in the fashion spreads is the models chosen to show the clothing. These girls are thin and young, yet wearing makeup to look older, and are often pictured with other young women or young men. Certainly, *YM* is not the only influence or measure young girls use to determine their self worth, but it is part of a media culture. This culture is sending out the message that tells young women that in order to be considered beautiful it is not enough to have great hair, or properly applied makeup, but you must be thin to wear these in-style clothes.

According to Akande (1993), the fashion spreads like those in *YM* have contributed to "a shift in the idealized female shape from a voluptuous curved figure to an angular, lean look. The impact of this changing idealized female shape is exemplified by the pervasiveness of dieting among women"(p. 250). This media shift and society's focus on the need to be thin have been linked to the increase of eating disorders among young women as they try to conform to the images presented to them. Furthermore, there is a need to address "the acquiescence to social prejudice implied by a life chronic hunger and the pursuit of thinness"(p. 256). This is not to suggest that a young woman will read one issue of *YM* and start to devalue herself, however it is suggesting that *YM* contributes to a media culture where the overwhelming messages at every turn are of young women who not only need to be beautiful, but want to be beautiful using makeup and the latest fashions.

- ## Male Female Relations

In 1998, the Male-Female Relations Category was the third largest category in the content analysis at 17 percent of the total magazine (See Appendix 1). The largest percentage of this category was in February at 25 percent, not surprising given that Valentine's Day was the focus. The lowest percentage, at 9 percent, was in September where the ads and the Appearance Category were more prevalent.

YM like other teen magazines is in the unique position to influence the ways in which young women understand young men. For many young women this is one of the only forums where they can learn about boys with information that is tailored to answer their uncertainties and concerns, yet they do not have the skills to evaluate the information given. (Duke & Kreshel, 1998) *YM* has several standard pages that appear every issue, which include; "Guy Talk," "Love Crisis," "Boys & Love," "Romance," and "Babe Watch." Aside from these standard pages there are also photo spreads of young men meant to be gazed upon, entitled "Guy Watching." These young men can be entertainers (actors or musicians) or models.

The pages entitled "Guy Talk" and "Guy Watching" offer advice to young women, not from editors or professionals, but from young men who are interviewed and polled by *YM.* "Guy Talk" is a standard feature where one page is devoted to five or six responses from young men about a question, and one "Celeb Sweetie of the Month" who answers the question or is quoted on a similar topic. Some of the questions posed included: "Can you be friends with your ex?"(November), "How can a girl get your attention?"(March), and "How do you make a long-distance love work?" (June/July). Accompanying the five quotes and pictures is the poll result based on the 100 young men that were also asked the question.

The advice columns are the monthly pages that offer alternatives and solutions to those young women who are already in a relationship. The column "Love Crisis" by Lisa Sussman was changed in the April issue to "Boys & Love." Aside from the name change, this advice page now features one question that is answered by a panel of guys, as opposed to the previous format where letters were answered by various authorities, like authors and psychologists. According to the editors, the format was changed to include more answers from young men to add to the authenticity of the answers. Apparently, young women would rather know what boys their age are thinking and not adult doctors.

According to Duke and Kreshel (1998), the role that these advice columns take is to present the boys' voices as authorities. Young men dictate how a girl should act to please boys, what to wear, say, and how girls can get what they want from boys. (p. 58) In the June/July issue of *YM* there is an article entitled "500 Guys Spill How to Get His Attention Now," which suggest that guys are attracted to girls that walk tall, look at the guy, play with their own hair and dress nicely whatever the style (i.e. preppy, vintage, sporty). In this article, guys also reveal that they are not attracted to girls who act dumb, over do the glamourous look, smoke, drink, or swear. (p. 48) While these overt messages may seem to be positive, empowering messages for young girls, they continue to reinforce a passive posture. (Duke & Kreshel, p. 59) The message is that young women need to know how to act and please guys to have the approval of or attain a boyfriend. It is not the smart girl who gets the boyfriend and wins the popularity, but the young woman who knows how to act and please a boyfriend who wins the popularity. The teenage girl is encouraged to spend her energy not in developing herself, but creating the right image and attitude to "snag" a boyfriend. She then uses the advice columns to keep that boyfriend. (Schlenker et al, 1998, p. 147)

These messages are also reinforced on the "Romance" page where girls can write in and praise their boyfriends under titles like "The Time He Was There For You" (January, p.54) or "How Can You Ever

Forget the First Time He Said 'I Love You'" (August, p. 59). As well, there is a "Boyfriend of the Year" contest where readers can vote for their boyfriends based on his actions (May). While these features may be rewarding to those readers who are looking for approval, they also affect the self-esteem of those girls who are not in a relationship, in that they are excluded from participating. The quizzes and stories circulate around those readers who are in a relationship, and if she is not, then there is a negative reenforcement that boyfriends equal status or popularity.

However, *YM* offers young women who are not in a relationship, a different incentive to read the magazine in the form of "Guy Watching." Every month has pages dedicated to photo spreads of young men, not for fashion, but for gazing upon and reading about what they want in relationships. Each month has the "Fox File: Babe Watch," where a popular male actor or singer is interviewed and a full page picture is included for young women to admire.

The focus in this category is on what makes a desirable boyfriend, which is followed up with advice on how to get into a relationship. No matter what stage a young woman's relationship is at, there is advice and reinforcement of how to attract, become part of, or find a new relationship. There is only one article in the entire year, "101 Cool Reasons to Stay Single", to offset the male female relationship focus of the magazine. (April, p. 62)

- Home

In the studies conducted by Kate Peirce (1990) and Jennifer A. Schlenker et. al (1998), the Home Category was more relevant to earlier issues of *Seventeen*, since there was a large drop in percentage after the 1980's. The results from Peirce's work show that in 1985, the Home Category made up 11 percent of editorial pages. (p. 498) Jennifer A. Schlenker et al results indicated that in 1985, 10 percent of the editorial pages were part of the Home Category. This percent had been reduced to less than 1 percent in 1995, where only one article was written about decorating a dorm room. (Schlenker et al, pp. 143-44)

In 1998, the *YM* percentage for this category was 0 percent (See Appendix 1). The decline of articles which would have been featured under the Home Category may be attributed to the magazine's recognition of the feminist movement, in not stereotyping young women in the role of homemaker. Yet there is also a lack of articles talking about how young women can prepare for leaving home and living on their own, whether it is to attend school or start a career.

- ## Self-Development

The Self-Development Category makes up 11 percent of the total year of magazines (See Appendix 1). The lowest percentage is found in the August issue where it is only 4 percent and the highest is found in April where the content is 16 percent.

Each issue contains a health page entitled "Ask Anything" where readers can ask questions about their bodies, ask for information about sex, and are answered by authorities in the medical field. There is also a regular page in each issue called "Fitness Info," which includes small articles on a variety of topics such as "Sneaker-Fit Secrets" and "5 Fitness Fibs Busted" (April, p. 30). These sections offer readers information about safe ways of caring for themselves. There are also articles found on the health page which are not only health related but appearance related.

Following the standard pages in each issue there are also articles devoted to informing readers of different workouts they can do in the comfort of their own homes. While these exercise articles are informative, the way they are presented is troubling. A two page exercise article in the January issue was named "Hot Bod on a Budget" and told readers to "Just Sweat it Out With Our Serious Sculpting Sesh (sic) Three Times a Week For One Month and You'll Be On Your Way to Sleekdom [sic]" (p. 90). There is a mixed message in these articles. On one hand it could be considered a positive message to help young women take care of themselves through proper diet and exercise, however, the reasons to do so are not for health but to look good. The articles do not talk about exercise and fitness in relation to young women's long-term health or self-esteem, instead they stress how these physical activities will give you the sexy body needed to attract boys. As a whole these magazines present a clear example of the hostility the Western culture holds for those who are even mildly obese. The underlying messages are that only those who are totally fit and sleek can be seen as beautiful, or desirable. (Akande, p. 251)

YM also has monthly stories where one reader's personal experience is told with the help of a *YM* staff writer. The titles of these stories include: "Adopted: Personal Story" (January), "We Were Sexually Harassed on Our School Bus" (April), "I Didn't Know I was

Pregnant" (May), "I Drove too Fast and Killed a Pregnant Mom and Her Child"(June/July), "Shoplifting Nearly Trashed My Life" (August), "My Loving Stepfather Molested Me" (September), "I've Been to Hell and Back and I'm Only 17" (October), "Highschool Bloodbath"(November), and "My 40EEE Breasts Made Me the School Freak" (December).

These stories were coded as the Self-Development Category due to the way they were written. While each story has political implications, the writers focus on the one young woman's account of what happened. For readers who are in similar situations, no resources are offered other than the sources of help that the particular young women received. The readers may live in a different state or province where the resources are different. Also, these stories are placed in this category because the focus is on how the girl overcame the adversity with the help of family and friends. There is no connection to the larger implications, namely that these girls' experiences are not isolated accounts.

With such a large focus on male-female relations, it is not surprising that the advice column or articles would reflect discussions on sex. Aside from the monthly advice columns advocating the use of condoms, *YM* also has features on topics like September's "Safe Sex Essentials" (p. 90) or the eight page section in the May issue, which includes information on the different types of contraceptives, 21 alternatives to sex, and questions to help determine if the reader is really ready to have sex .(p. 67)

Teenage sexuality continues to be a large area of study in which many surveys find that young people are having sex in their early teens and cite this age as too young for sex. (McLean, 1998, p. 37) There are those who believe that it is important to get the information to young women so they can make informed decision, unfortunately, "the editors do not examine whether their influential magazine, among many others, that unabashedly use sex to sell their publications to juveniles, are partly responsible for the contradictions" (p.37). Magazine editors will often take the stance that they are only giving out information so that young women who decide to have sex are informed; however, they do not discuss the large content of articles discussing relationships or the implied pressure for intimacy between couples.

- Career Development

    The Career Development Category accounted for only 2 percent of the magazine content in 1998 (See Appendix 1). There are several months that contained no such articles. The largest percentage of articles devoted to this category was in June/July and August, 4 percent, where the spotlight was on an actress' or singer's career.

    Of the 2 percent for the total year, there are no articles pertaining to highschool or college. There are no articles which discuss the vast possibilities for different careers. There was one article discussing a reader's suitability for a summer job based on answers given from a personality quiz, however this article did not include how to find a summer job, just the types of jobs your personality type would prefer. (May, p.120) What is coded as Career Development are the articles, usually interviews, which discussed famous actors' and singers' careers and their personal insights into the job. These types of jobs are limited to the entertainers and performers, with no mention of their support staff.

- Political/World Issues

    Throughout the year the percentage of Political/World Issues was 0 percent (See Appendix 1). Like the Home Category, there are no articles in any monthly issue that would fall in this category. As discussed earlier, the personal stories of readers were not placed here because they did not make larger connections to the similar experiences of other girls, but treated each story as an isolated incident. Why are there no articles of a political or world nature? It may be part of an assumption that young women are not interested. It may also be due to young women's increase in television viewing where these topics are presented in a more dynamic and visually stimulating medium. Or could it be due to a larger focus on the self and not the world outside? (Cobb-Walgren, 1990, p. 341)

- Other

    The Other Category includes sections of the magazine that the studies of *Seventeen* excluded. They were added in this study because they still participate in the deliverance of the overall message of the magazine. The Other category accounted for 8 percent of the total magazine for the year, which made it fourth after Ads, Appearance, Male-Female Relations and Self-Development (See Appendix 1).

Examples of the monthly standards include the "Letters From the Editor," and the "Letters From Readers." These features are important because they help to set the tone of the magazine. Both have a large dose of male content either praising an article that has already been published, or the male content of the current issue.

Also included in this section is the "Say Anything" page where readers write in their embarrassing experiences. They are rated "*Glad it didn't happen to us, ** Your friends are still talking about it, *** Utter and total embarrassment, and **** Ultimate supremo humiliation" (May, p. 22). This section is for entertainment value, but it may also be setting up a dynamic where a young woman hearing about another's embarrassment may feel better or worse about their situations. Entertainment that was not coded into the Male-Female Relations Category, which includes movies, CDs, or television shows were labelled Other. A regular feature entitled "Fanclub," where readers send in their fan mail, was also placed in this category.

"Horoscopes" and "Numerology" were placed in the Other Category, but they could have been placed, just as easily, in different categories. The "Horoscopes" page is divided into five sub-categories after the zodiac sign: mood, love, friendship, life, and lucky days (December/ January, p. 96). If you are a Gemini, your horoscope for February was as follows:

Mood : When you get time alone, you'll do tons of intense soul-searching.

Love: A secret admirer will leave notes in your locker and your books.

Friendship: A close bud will gossip about you, and you'll call her on it.

Life: Your favourite team will bring home a trophy from a big game or tournament. (p.96)

The horoscopes always seem to be in relation to others, whether it is a potential boyfriend, family member or friend. They seem to "encourage readers to define themselves in relation to others" not in relation to themselves (Evans, 1996, p. 396). The only predictions involved are promises of future relationships with boys and better relationships with friends.

The "Numerology" page is similar to the "Horoscopes" page in that it focusses on relationships with others. It could have been included in the Male-Female Relations Category because the numbers are also there for the readers' boyfriends or crushes. For example, in the June/July issue it states if he is a 5 "though he'll be mega-moody in June, he'll be ready to play in July," or if he is a 8 "put the moves on him in June and by July he'll crave your cuddles" (p.122). The "Numerology" section is not to be read by guys, but read by girls to better understand their guy and therefore could have been coded as Male/Female Relations, however, the section for girls are diverse: covering moods, relationships, and feelings. Together they did not belong in one set category so they were placed in Other.

- ## Advertising

This section warrants a study of its own due to the sheer number of advertisements found in a given month. In 1998, advertising comprised 42 percent of the magazine (See Appendix 1); it never dropped below 38 percent and it peaked at 50 percent in the September issue. These pages of advertising do not include the complementary texts addressed earlier. Some of the advertisements that *YM* contained were for subscriptions to their magazine, or telling readers where to find the fashions in the editorial pages. *YM* also runs an ad telling readers about *YM* sponsored events at local malls and chain stores.

Conclusion

YM "is only a small part of the huge entity called media and a small part of the socialization of teenage girls, but in conjunction with those other parts, it can be a powerful reinforcer of the traditional ideology of womanhood" (Peirce, 1990, p. 499). This traditional ideology is the assumption that young women are focussed on their appearance and behaviour to gain the approval of young men with the intent of getting a boyfriend.

YM magazine, like other teen magazines, has the potential to send out very positive, feminist messages to young women. There is the potential to prepare young women to continue their education, to enter careers they find stimulating, to value themselves without a prescribed notion of beauty, to have meaningful relationships with friends and family and not to focus so much attention on sexual relationships.

Instead, we find a magazine that is suffused with advertisements and complementary texts telling a young woman that in order to be beautiful she must change the parts of her appearance that deviate from the norm the magazine presents. Studies have shown that young women are not successful in negotiating the standards of physical beauty that the media presents them. (Duke & Kreshel, p. 65)

Furthermore, the images presented are often of young tall, slim, white girls; any other race that is represented is also very light skinned. Women are not encouraged to determine their own standards of beauty; the message is to conform.

Male-Female relations are also very prevalent, where young women are taught not to please themselves, but act and dress in a manner that will please a boyfriend. It is this boyfriend that will give the young women popularity and not her on her own merits. This is perpetuated by the magazine every time an article excludes a single female from participating (Schlenker et al, p.147). Furthermore the entire focus is on heterosexual relationships, no other relationship is considered or discussed.

Health and exercise are important for a growing teen and the magazine does provide valuable information. Yet this information does not express the health benefits from exercising, but the beauty benefits. Articles like "Look Hot Even With a Cold" (December/January, p. 26) undermine the health message by placing the emphasis again on beauty. There is also no mention that a healthy body requires a lifetime commitment, not the "one month" regime that the magazine promises and encourages.

The potential for the magazine is seen, not in the articles that are written, but the ones that are missing. Where are the articles talking about young women and education? Where are the articles that show examples of hobbies, interests and career possibilities? Why is there not a larger concentration on creating connections instead of competition between girls? Why not explore other forms of expressing beauty or developing one's own sense of style? Until advertisers break their hold on editors and more editorial pages are freed of complimentary texts there will not be a change in the traditional, stereotypical messages presented to young women.

References

Akande, A. (1993). Sex differences in preferences for ideal female body shape. *Health Care for Women International*. Vol 14, 16-27.

Cobb-Walgren, C. (1990). Why teenagers do not 'read all about it.' *Journalism Quarterly*. Vol 67, No2, Summer, 340-347.

Duke, L. L. & Kreshel, P.J. (1998). Negotiating femininity: Girls in early adolescence read teen magazine. *Journal of Communication Inquiry*. Vol 22, No 1, 48-71.

Evans, W. (1996). Divining the social order: Class, gender, and magazine astrology columns. Journalism & Mass Media Quarterly, 72, no. 3, 389-400.

McLean, C. (1998, April 20). The teen gutter press: Parents question the morals and motives of sex-drenched juvenile magazines. *Alberta Report*, Vol 25, p.18.

Peirce, K. (1990). A feminist theoretical perspective on the socialization of teenage girls through *Seventeen* Magazine. *Sex Roles*, Vol. 23, No 9/10, 491-500.

Schlenker, J. A., Caron, S.L., & Halteman, W.A. (1998). A feminist analysis of *Seventeen* Magazine: Content analysis from 1945 to 1995. *Sex Roles*, Vol. 38, No ½, 135-149.

Steinem, G. (1990). Sex, lies, and advertising. *MS. Magazine*. Rpt. In J. Kitchen, M. Kechnie, & A. Levan (Eds.), *Introduction to Women's Studies WOMN 1005/EA/EB/EC*. Toronto, ON: Canadian Scholars' Press.

Ulrick's International Periodical Directory 35th Edition. (1997). New Providence, NJ: R.R. Bowker.

YM Young & Modern No Risk Offer. Po Box 1051, Fort Erie, On L2A 6K7

YM. (1997-1998, December/January).

YM. (1998, February).

YM. (1998, March).

YM. (1998, April).

YM. (1998, May).

YM. (1998, June/July).

YM. (1998, August).

YM. (1998, September).

YM. (1998, October).

YM. (1998, November).

YM. (1998-1999, December/January).

Young Women Speak Out. (1992) Symposium Report. Ottawa: Canadian Advisory Council on the Status of Women.

Appendix A

Table 1: Monthly Breakdown of *YM Magazine* into Various Categories

Total Pages by Month	Categories *(listed as percentages)*							
	Appear-ance	♂♀ Relations	Home	Self-Dev.	Career Dev.	Political/ World Issues	Other	Ads
Dec./ Jan. 116	20%	23%	0%	8%	3%	0%	7%	39%
Feb. 104	22%	25%	0%	9%	0%	0%	8%	36%
Mar. 120	18%	20%	0%	12%	2%	0%	7%	41%
Apr. 124	22%	12%	0%	16%	0%	0%	5%	45%
May 132	20%	15%	0%	13%	3%	0%	8%	41%
June/ July 134	18%	16%	0%	10%	4%	0%	7%	45%
Aug. 142	21%	16%	0%	4%	4%	0%	7%	48%
Sept. 164	17%	9%	0%	13%	3%	0%	8%	50%
Oct. 134	19%	20%	0%	12%	0%	0%	8%	41%
Nov. 110	18%	13%	0%	12%	3%	0%	14%	40%
Dec./ Jan. 108	21%	18%	0%	10%	0%	0%	13%	38%
Totals 1388	20%	17%	0%	11%	2%	0%	8%	42%

The Stones, Roses, Gold, and Fires of Reclaimed Territory

Si Transken
Sudbury, Ontario

Abstract

This paper is an update to the book Reclaiming Body Territory, written by Transken in 1995. The author traces her own experiences of a childhood of sexual, physical and emotional abuse and how she was able to map out a journey for herself filled with self-love and self-compassion for others. Today, she is filled with empowerment based on her own body, her strength, her intellect, her emotions, her soul. Transken describes the current phase of her "spiralling journey" through prose, poetry and journalling. In this paper, she describes how our bodies tell us a story, and how as a feminist therapist she is helping other women discover the beauty of their own bodies and soul.

> my body is not a cite
> of ritual sacrifice; neither is this
> a vacant parking space nor a snarling dust storm
> instead this is a terrain of
> pulsing spiralling soulmuscle friendly
> to itself & others; lovely tingling loved
> from many locations
> internal & external

STONES

Stones are solid and immobile but even they are reshaped and moved by time and by the rushing of warm water. Some of the moments in this process have been like being with stones. Other dimensions of this are about being with spirals. The spiral process of reclaiming continues. Schiwy (1996) in her book *A Voice Of Her Own*, describing creativity and writing suggests the spiral is the way of women's lives. She says,

> Many women describe the course of their life's journey as a
> spiral. Circling back to the familiar before sweeping ahead to

the unknown, the spiral moves forward by moving backward, goes up by going down. In contrast to the relentless forward drive of the masculine 'line,' the spiral incorporates periods of returning to our childhood wounds before proceeding ahead with fresh insight and energy. (p. 44)

My paper is about moving backward and forward along another curving portion of the spiral of my life. This is about finding voice and sharing it.

For a long time it was impossible for me to begin writing this "update" to the 1994 *Reclaiming Body Territory* (*RBT*). *RBT* was a description of a childhood of sexual, physical, and emotional abuse by my father; and collusion with his oppression of me from the educational and medical system. Outwardly, for many years, my body and my intellect appeared healthy; they were "seen" by the educational and medical system as fully functioning. These forums have only limited ways of seeing women's wholeness. My wholeness was discovered through a long diffuse process.

Feminist therapy and creative writing were two interrelated mediums through which I have reclaimed the territory of my whole self.[1] The course I completed in 1992 with Dr. Roxana Ng inspired me and encouraged me to use the journal keeping process as a healing tool and a way of finding my voice. Since that time I have intermittently continued that practice. Dr. Roxana Ng validated my right to bring creative writing and my life body into the cold serious marble halls of academia. Others such as Charmaz (1999); Johnston (1996); Metzger (1992); Razack (1993); & Schiwy (1996) have affirmed within their contexts that only through mixing the insights and text from journal writing, poetry, and scholarly material can we find a process which multi-dimensionally (and thus more accurately) expresses some of our truths.

Emma Goldman was an activist, a healer, a scholar, and feminist. She said something like, "If I can't dance at the revolution then I don't want to go!" and my spin on that theme would be "If I can't bring poems and my breathing body to my scholarly papers then I don't want to write!" Initially, I couldn't bring myself to re-read the text that I'd written in the early 90's. That essay was written in fits and starts and during disassociative and grounding moments. It seems that my body has gone through a chaotic array of miracles, tragedies, shut downs, shut offs, evacuations, examinations, and—reclamations.

At thirty-nine I am in the midst of my mid life journey. As Bolan

(1994) a psychotherapist says, this is a time when women want to both let go and grip more firmly; when we want to know specifically, "which particular piece of the songlines that keep the soul of the earth alive" (p. 31) belong to each of us and how our voice dis/harmonizes with other voices. During the last ten months, I have left my partner of 13 years, purchased a new home, found new love, had surgeries, and noted and responded to changes in my body. I have dis-covered, explored, and accepted new aspects of myself. I have been wrestling with waves of avoidance and denial while trying to sit my body, mind, and spirit down to write this update to *RBT*.

The most major recess in the wrestling match between my inner self's urge to silence, and my inner self's urge to speak loudly and clearly reminded me about the diffuse essences and meanings of safety. Safety must be created in our bodies, our classrooms, our neighbourhoods, our minds, and our homes. This recess helped me begin writing. An insight came to me while riding a bus that was leaving my hometown behind for a few days. On the bus I was able to once again open the pages of *RBT*. I'd been carrying the book, unopened, for weeks. I had not read its contents for at least three years.

While rereading it surrounded by anonymity, my impressions were of satisfaction and pride that I so vigorously told the sharp—and blunt-edged truths. Also, my impressions were of horror and repulsion that I had lived those ugly experiences. I had forgotten where my body had been and how it had been treated. I'd wanted to forget. It became clear to me while sitting on that bus that the reason I had not been able to write this update was because I did not want memories of that despairing time to intrude into my life again and leave their shadow in the new home or the new "time and energy zone" I feel I am now in living in. Reading *RBT* in a safe public and meaningless place like a bus meant that I didn't have to go too deeply into my feelings. The spill-over didn't matter. No "bad karma" stains would be left on my private and precious furniture, carpet, air, or mirrors.

As I reread *RBT* I was reminded of things I'd really put quite out of my mind. In the following paragraphs of spiralling text I will try to be as honest and brave as I was in the first assessment and declaration of my body. Academia and age may have given me more bravery and more techniques for expression, but may have also taught me how to wear more masks. I may have too effectively internalized some of these masks. I invite the reader of this to judge for themselves.

ROSES

Roses need compost so that they may exist. They offer up their stems, leaves, petals for the soil around them to bring forth new life and expanded life as the timing is appropriate. The poem that *RBT* opens with talks about whiteness and being cut down and consumed. It talks about touching my own body for my own sake and trying to accept and possess pleasure from this place I wanted to call home. My past is compost.

Now I do own pleasure and joy from this location I'm centred in. I try to pass on: to teach what I learn. How have I done this pleasure finding and pleasure embracing? There are a multitude of day-to-day behaviours, thoughts, feelings that have changed. Most of them are continuations and extensions of the processes begun during the year I completed Ng's course and began integrating her ideas (Ng, forthcoming). She suggests,

> . . . our understanding of our bodies is mediated by systems of knowledge, including medical knowledge, available to us to make sense of our experiences of health and illness. Thus how we know our bodies changes as our knowledge base shifts. The second assumption is that different systems of healing allow, encourage, discourage, and prevent us from understanding our bodies in definite ways. (Forthcoming, p.3)

During that same time in my life I discovered many other scholars, activists, and/or healers similarly- or compatibly-minded to Ng (Aaron, 1996; Bartky, 1990; Bolaria & Bolaria, 1994; Brown, 1994; Butler, 1991; Dua, 1994; Smith, 1999). I absorbed their information into my personal and professional life.

For the last three years, in gradually increasing intensity and complexity, I have been exercising this wondrous place I get to live in. My life-home-body is mobilized. I can sweat and savour the experience! At this time I do about an hour almost every night of sit-ups, treadmills, muscle building, dancing, stretching (in addition to my hour of creative writing). As Heywood (1998), a woman who has become a professional body builder says, there is something in our core identity that shifts when we feel physically fit and strong. Great joy and satisfaction often come to me when I look in the mirror. I have mirrors all over my home, my office, and my private practice as a political act. I see accomplished mature ripples and rises on my arms and on my belly. The vulnerable concave that my belly once was — or the swollen, hurting and always-too-stuffed belly — is most of the time now a display of strength and comfort. It is a place that harbors excellent wholesome and holy (as in vegan and nonviolent) food. It is a place that knows how to move and dance to its own rhythms and impulses. It is a place that does not always have to be covered up in public.

What is the whiteness referred to in the poem in *RBT*? The whiteness meant vulnerability and anger to me. It meant a sensuality that was other-defined and other-centred. I used to feel that I was a white page onto which the coarse consuming male gaze could project its preferred images. The whiteness of this body has, at times, been so pale that the anaemic blueness of veins could be seen through the skin. Seeing through my outer layer made me feel that my internal organs were too close to the surface — too slashable — too removable. My body is now tanned, healthier looking, more protected. I have created more "barriers". I have become less transparent. I now have a layer of gilding. This means only those who are **invited** to be so near are able to know the pulse and the breathing patterns of this flesh and bones person. I choose who gets close enough. I am the gatekeeper to a potential Eden (an Eden that was before the "fall"; meaning I reject the male-voiced definition of "sin" and the blame put on women for that exile from the garden of purity and innocence).

My body and my whole personhood are still profoundly committed to that process of "testimony" and justice seeking. I have completed my doctorate and have been teaching for two years in a school of social work. The classes I teach include social work theory; family and couples counselling, social welfare, advanced intervention techniques, and I supervise placement interns in a variety of settings.

Most recently I have been teaching "Sexuality and Social Work." These everyday mindfulness and interactional opportunities mean that I am able to bear witness to many contexts in which women's vulnerable bodies are treated with less empowerment, respect, dignity, compassion, and resources than they deserve. I am able to bring a particular knowledge and courage to my students. Each student who's consciousness I open a little wider — or who's experience I validate and offer comfort to — feeds back to my body a type of nutrient. We fortify each other. We continually add iron, calcium, and compassion to the marrow in our bones. Together we construct and insist upon bigger spaces for our own bodies and the bodies of the clients we encounter. We listen to each other and it makes the spiralling journey through lives cluttered with the dangers of patriarchy, capitalism, and sexism (and other oppressions) easier. My pedagogical approach is to encourage the daily asking of "How Are You?" to be done with soulful mindfulness.

> HOW AM I?
> some hours are smoother than others.
> some aches i can be distracted from.
> some memories fade.
> some people phone
> often enough saying enough kind things
> & keeping some promises made.
> some bills get paid
> with unbouncing cheques.
> some soul remains ebbing, desiring, living.
> some nights i sleep till morning
> & some dreams i remember & want.
> sometimes i bother to say
> some of these things when
> someone says, 'how are you?'
> & sometimes they stand still long enough to
> somewhat substantively
> & sincerely listen

We are embodied pedagogy. We teach each other how to live boldly and in womyn-loving ways in this world that is too often a woman-hating world. Turner (1999), a social work professor, emphasizes that we "define ourselves" in our clinical private practice and that this then shapes the profile of our client load. Partially as a result of *RBT*, I have been defined as having a particular therapeutic approach (feminist, expressive arts centered, as a survivor/thriver). This orientation or cluster of attributes brings clients to me who have been body-damaged and body-alienated. In my private practice I work with victim/survivors of many types of abuses: incest, sexual assault, homophobia, physical assault, poverty, racism. These women also benefit from some of the accomplishments of my journey and I from theirs. We build wisdom together.

Our bodies lean into each other as we tell of our stories, or wishes, or dreams of a different world. We breath each other's air of knowing and resisting. As feminist therapists advocate, (Cantor, 1990; McLead, 1994; Miller & Stiver, 1997) I listen to my clients' knowledgeable testimonies and in honoring them I feel my own body breath more fully, more compassionately and more deeply. An example of how I bring discussion of the body into our work is to give guided images such as this:

> Imagine the person you most love on this planet . . . Imagine this person in a place they would adore . . . What would you love to have here in this magic space for this person you love so much? What would you provide for their well-being, for their comfort, for their body's needs? Now imagine yourself as that person. What does that feel like? What happened when you exchanged yourself for the loved person?

Many women feel an initial shock at the idea of providing so abundantly for themselves. We are often so accustomed to deprivation and abuse that abundance and joy are alien. As in 1992, I remain convinced that there has been, and continues to be, an epidemic of abuses against women's bodies. Our deprivation and oppression remain almost as common now as in the 70's.

It is even possible that in some ways we are slipping backwards, in that there is now a backlash against the provision of women's services and supports (Armstrong & Armstrong, 1994; Transken, 1999). There is high unemployment, and poverty among some vulnerable populations. There may be a sense of "been there" and "done that" regarding the uplifting of women. Some people are suggesting that feminists' quest for women's equality has now been achieved, and thus our movement should be disassembled or ignored because we are no longer relevant or necessary (Friedman, 1992; Dineen, 1996; Pattai, 1998).

Equality for women has not been achieved, but some of our supports are being disassembled or weakened. Efforts continue to be made to silence us. For example, the National Action Committee on The Status of Women has had its funding drastically reduced in the last year. The State and its institutions sometimes now declare: Women are equal—Women have arrived! Then any woman who still feels disempowered has simply **chosen** to not reach out for the empowerment available to her. "Get over it" and "get on with it" seem to be the theme songs of the day. In the original *RBT* I talked about how the medical profession, the educational system, and the wider community intersected and colluded to maintain my oppression. These forces continue in their predispositions, although possibly in altered formats, changed costumes, and/or showing different faces.

A therapeutic intervention technique called Brief Solution Focussed (BSF) is one of the newest ways that the violence against women and girls is being colluded with. Elsewhere, I have talked about the dangers I see in therapeutic approaches that fall under the explicit or implicit category of BSF (Transken, 1999). Assumptions built into BSF approaches are that in eight to ten sessions major change should take place in a woman's life and world-view. These approaches often reject or make invisible the realities of structural oppression and herstoric patterns. These BSF approaches return us to only the psychology of the here and now and rugged individualism — rather than the history/herstory, the sociology of oppression, and the necessity of collective activism. There is a possibility with these approaches to blame women when they haven't healed. In BSF approaches, when full healing has not been arrived at after ten sessions there is a sense of : "Well, you've had your chance now and obviously you are an **unmotivated** victim who is somehow benefitting from playing the victim card."

In this context, not only has a woman been violated, but then she is implicitly reprimanded for requesting too many resources in her process of healing. A message is being sent: she is selfish for wanting to take up so much space and time. This is the new format, costume, face of collusion taking place in the social service delivery system. While I was being abused as a child the theme was, "incest doesn't happen" and now the theme might be "it does happen and there's so many services that if a woman has not done her healing work then it is her choice."

Women and girls not only want and need safety, but also comfort and pleasure. My body has been learning about taking up space, resources, time, opportunities, pleasure. I have been trying to budget in a minimum of two hours out of every 24-hour cycle to care for my body. I insist upon these moments of leisure and self-care time daily. Women's self-care time and resources are our birthrights but they are rights often trampled upon by academia (hooks, 1994; Frost & Taylor, 1996; Ng, forthcoming), patriarchy (Bartky, 1990; Brown, 1994; Butler & Rosenblum, 1991; Nelson, 1997), and capitalism (Allison, 1994; Steinberg & Figart, 1999).

This act of claiming every day is revolutionary. This claiming includes doing the exercises my precious body desires; finding, purchasing, preparing, eating and savouring the foods that this body wants and needs; entitling myself to a variety of supplements (life-enhancing substances such as gin sing, bee pollen, B6, B12, folic acid, a multivitamin, kava kava, wild yam, etc.); bathing my body as though it were a rare treasure (rather than a wheel thrown off a transport truck); and using aromatherapy oils such as eucalyptus and peppermint to feel more energetic through the day, and vanilla and lavender to feel more relaxed in the evenings.

My revolutionary reclaiming activity also involves my decision to constantly process and explore my relationship with food. Food is a substance of torture for many women (Lawrence, 1987; Orbach, 1979; Poulton, 1996). In *RBT* I describe the tension and consequences of compulsive overeating. I now try to eat when I am hungry and try not to eat for any other reason (not to please people, to comfort myself when I'm frightened, to be polite, because it is free, because it tastes good, because I'm lonely, etc.). This struggle continues every day. Much of my work with clients also centres around food issues.

GOLD

Gold is often hidden by nature's rubble so that this precious metal is not treated casually. Many of us know that humans have also hidden gold from each other and used it as a currency that leaves some starving and exiled and others overfed and over controlling. In the original paper, I talked about a socialist-feminist world where more would be available to us and remain committed to that world view. But, I have gone more deeply into what I mean by "resources being available to us."

Spirituality is one of those resources and I have found great solace in some of the women-centred voices from Buddhism (Cabezon, 1992; Chodron, 1991, Chodron, 1994; Tomm, 1995) and from Ecofeminists (Eichler, 1995; Griffin, 1995; Griffin, 1980; Macy 1991). Now I would place a greater emphasis on all the luxuries and glories of life: accessories for play, music, time to read fiction, soul-development from a woman-centred perspective, cinnamon for your coffee, curtains on your windows that let the sun come in just the right way, the beauty of stained-glass so that the colours of the world mark themselves out on our floors, money for long-distance calls, so that when your friends move away seeking employment you can remain emotionally connected to them. These are the gold nuggets and gold dusts of life. These resources are the nourishments and they are central to keeping women's bodies healthy. These resources are significant to fully reclaiming our body territories.

I have become more greedy in the years since the first publication. I am actively, and in the impassioned soap-box voice of a revolutionary Emma Goldman, saying to my clients, my students, my community: we want the bread, the roses, an elegant gold-edged vase for the roses, and we want the time to sit with the roses in front of a fire-full hearth. Women want to be adored while we adore our roses and eat our multi-grain bread! We want more and more and more. Ng's course material said, "different systems of healing allow, encourage, discourage, and prevent us from understanding our bodies in definite ways." Yes. The chairs we sit in while we admire our roses, the heating and lighting that is available in that room, the size of the room to dance in or not, the right to privacy or the right to company—all shape how we experience our bodies and their healing/their illness-becoming.

While I was writing the first portions of this paper two comrades in my community died.[2] They died of cancer. They were not that many years older than I. My guess is that their deaths could have been delayed or prevented had they had more resources of every type available to them throughout their whole life cycle (especially sleep and pleasure). This is the kind of reclaiming of body territory I now quest for, and demand space for, in our world. I want a reclaiming that is not done from a minimalist stance. I want us to be loudly requesting more. A First Nations friend of mine once said to me "White feminists have been advocating to be equal with men. Why should we settle for so little?" Her point was that we want to go beyond what men have been giving themselves. Some women have been taking up the male-stream practice of living in our bodies, in that we have begun working 60 hour weeks, smoking, drinking, overeating, undersleeping, overstressing—and now we have the new equality of dying from stress related illnesses. This is not the reclaiming that I want to advocate for.

FIRES

Fires need to destroy so that their flames might exist. Fire also kills disease in a forest. Fires leave ashes which are soaked back into the soil. Roses grow from the soil and return there. Gold is found under and within soil. The nutrients released by fires are necessary. My body has had fires of destruction and fires of warmth and most recently fires of lust, passion, and creativity. This is a healthy body fed with righteous essences and substances. I let in different resources now.

In *RBT* I listed symptoms of the abuse that still lived in my body. Today I still struggle with stomach ailments but have largely controlled those through careful monitoring of my diet. Abandonment is still a triggering and destructive emotion for me. This is a poem that documents some of the aspects of that struggle.

THESE UNGOOD MOURNINGS

waking up
the morning-after-the-night-you've-left-town
is confronting my soul's scars
& touching all the accumulated
cuts bruises absences deprivations
of 38 years of toughlife
& this is about my confronting pain alone.

getting out of bed
my headache surveys where it will be staying
for the next few days & is resentful
that it can't spread itself out more extravagantly;
aggressive leather-clad uglyangry
it awaits opportunities to fist me
taking pride in its street-wise
unpredictable power.

proving for the 1000th time
that compulsive overeating
won't return you to here
or sooth me adequately
or accomplish anything
dirty dishes displayed everywhere sulk
& add to the drudgery
of cleaning up the drudgery
of waking-up-the-morning-after-you've-left-town.

The poem communicates how sometimes I slip backwards when too much stress, grief, and pain find its way into my life. One of the mediums through which I have made enormous progress is that I'm almost completely a vegan (I had been a vegetarian at the time of the *RBT*). I avoid fats and excesses of spice. Almost everything that goes into my body is a fresh fruit, a fresh vegetable, a whole grain: something from the earth that still has some connection to the life it lived while evolving itself. Migraines still make their claim on me, as do bouts of insomnia, but I manage them more than they manage me. Maybe they are early warning systems hard-wired into me now? Maybe they send intelligence to me letting me know that major disruptions are on the horizon preparing to attack me and I need to make a change or make a decision. I am somewhat accepting of their role in my life. I try to pay attention. I try to teach clients and students to pay attention to these warnings and symptoms.

Having reassessed the meaning of "appetites" my body has expanded what it wants on the menu! Allison (1994) talks about how gawky it is for many women to begin deeply and authentically knowing and then writing about their own eroticism (pp. 83-91). hooks echoes those ideas regarding how central to well-being it is that women name and own their desires (1993, pp. 113-127; 1994, pp.191-99). In *RBT* I identified as heterosexual. One part of myself that I have since claimed is an identity as a bisexual woman. I had sexual experiences with girls and women earlier in my life, but did not fully own those experiences. Somehow I had in my mind that if you were not a "practicing" bisexual then you were not a bisexual. Of course, our erotic attractions and sensations are complex (Firestein, 1996; Jackson, 1990). I now note how I am drawn to certain women and men. I differently value those "friendships" I had with women. I remain open to my desires' messages. I try to teach others to hear their truest internally authored messages and to speak with their authentic multi-pitched voices.

Each person we come into contact with during our spirals through life has the potential to teach us many things. I have had the privilege in this last year to have a lover who taught me marvellous lessons. The following are some journal comments about him and the energies he inspired in my body:

> At this moment I am in love. I am in love with someone who knows how to love my body in a way that is beyond the

flesh/blood/bones. He is the first person I have felt impelled, honored, trusting enough to make eye contact with while fully physically and emotionally naked — while being touched, kissed, intimate. Naked and without shame, fear, inadequacy. My body/my personhood feels gratitude, sparkles, desire — bold lust — joy towards his body/personhood. There is a new danger here that I am discovering. A danger that involves having someone **stop** touching me too soon and/or facing the fear that someone could chose to leave me emotionally/physically when I powerfully want their presence. Soulful sex can bring a profoundly different type of pain or vulnerability into the room. This is new territory to reclaim. This is my new strata of experimentation and learning. I feel exuberance towards the universe that this lover exists and is sharing himself with me. I sleep peacefully and wholly when I feel his presence embracing my life. My body has found rest and sanctuary. This love is like the love I should have had at 15 had I not been imposed upon by predators. I am in eye-wide-open wonderment with an androgynous and sometimes awkward curiosity. My skin/flesh/bones/heart/mind/soul is wanting magical adventure and muscular playful possibility — with this person and at this time I am able to gluttonously reach out for these experiences.

This love has taught me about gratitude and bliss. Many of us lose our bliss in our early years (Wolf, 1997) and many of us never have bliss for a moment from our flesh, bones, skin, soul. I am dedicated to helping my students and clients discover what their bliss is, and then validate them in their quest for partner/s who can help them experience their bliss. It is a revolutionary practice to expect women to not only become survivors but to expect them to continually experience **glittering joy** in their bodies.

My relationship with my mother and with my own mother-energy has evolved since the *RBT* book was written. Mother and daughter relationships are complex (Abbey and O'Reilly, 1998; Kaplan, 1992) . This complexity and our tangled feelings have meaning for how we feel in our bodies. In the original paper I discussed the meaning of mothering/motherwork/the body's memory of being mothered. It is fascinating to me that the call to write this paper came to me from

Roxana Ng at the same time that the call came to me from the hospital to have a tubal ligation (I'd been on the waiting list for months). These two activities autonomously synchronized themselves. My stitches were healing as I typed the first spiralling paragraphs of this paper.

I now know that my destiny is to do my motherwork for my clients, students, comrades, community, and the natural environment. My nurturing capacities have become bigger and more robust than could be centred in one child, at one time, in my one home. There was some grief and mourning in knowing I would never have a biological daughter, but there was far more comfort in letting go of biology being my destiny. Had my childhood been different, maybe I would feel differently about this. My childhood was what it was, and I am what I am, and my destiny is what it is. This experience too, of finding my specific place of comfort on the motherwork continuum, I have shared with students, clients, my community. Maybe I am role-modelling another version of motherhood that also needs to be displayed as one option. Women's bodies can gestate, birth, feed the next generation in multiple ways.

Disassociating and segmenting were discussed in the original *RBT*. Segmentation? My ownership and experience of my body is now integrated, elegant, sophisticated, more harmonious. My hands, mouth, throat, shoulders, breasts, belly, legs, usually love their existence and each other and my inner self. Here is a description of how my body can now feel, flex, flourish, and integrate. Inspired by a comment heard on the radio,

" . . . beauty is only the start of bearable terror . . . "

UPON SEEING YOU THERE IN THE HALL . . .

    my frontal lobe slants dangerously
        central cortex shifts oddly
            eyes widen & fixate
        mouth dries &
        its fleshy components connect
            dis jointedly & dis appointingly
    the back of my neck tingles & tightens
                on an almost-amphetamine-alert
                    awaiting
                the never-yet-received imprint of

              your tongue-teeth-lips
my shoulders straighten   &   spine   stretches

my muscles thicken against my chest wall & i notice
       the constricting of
           lungs
          & the expanding
             of joy
             in my belly

(I don't dare describe the dangerous
delightful declarations made in the space
between my navel & thighs
but I will state
that the back of my knees
becomes vulnerable to collapse &
feet forget forwardness)

      all this   just as you walk towards me in this too-public hallway.

I now know the power of desire. It is a form of muscular spirituality. It is the backbone of a strong life-force.

I love the muscles in my back, and these days I can feel them when I bend down to pick something up. I know the muscles in the back of my legs. My breasts are smaller than they have ever been. They are strong and lean. I weigh just about what I weighed when I was 15. This weight is the naturally balanced size of my body. I am proud of myself for all these accomplishments of reclamation. They are my victory list. These are my presents to myself. These are my offerings to my students, clients, comrades, lover—each of these declarations is an Amazon call of fierce hope. My process of holding my body a certain way as I walk through a room: head held up, shoulders back, muscles fluid, feet large and strong, eye contact direct, lungs full of righteously owned air, is a flag to the world. One side of my flag says: Sovereign territory: no trespassing! The other side of my flag says: I am a river of love, health, abundance and maybe we want to share?

As described in *RBT* wedding rings have had many meanings through the years. I am not wearing a wedding ring. I am not afraid to be seen as unattached and unprotected by one man. I feel strong enough to attend to my needs, protect myself, detect and avoid danger. Wearing a ring in the recent past communicated committed affections—described my sense of an aligned love—not a warning against predators. My class vulnerability still sits messily and angrily with me sometimes. Most women remain conscious of their material vulnerability and this shapes all the other dimensions of their life (Allison, 1994; Armstrong and Armstrong, 1990; Cohen, 1987; Waring, 1988). I am economically fragile at this exact moment having left a long term relationship, but I am also professionally skilled and all signs point in the right directions that independence and, soon enough, some security will be mine.

This body does not have to be primarily assessed and valued in regards to its sexual use-value. It never leaves my consciousness though that I am fortunate in this regard. Almost every waitress I make eye contact with and every sales clerk I see reminds me that I could have been as "disposable" in this world as them. Their outward appearance in itself still opens or closes certain opportunities for them – my "credentials" now will open or close most opportunities for me. My body/personhood is still sexed and classed, and that has implications for my worth and marketability in academia and in professional circles, but that is another conversation for another paper.

Now I wear a gold ring that was custom crafted for me. It is an athletically thin gold band with a feminist symbol attached to the band through a larger than necessary, circle of gold. The feminist symbol dances when I move my hand. It catches the light and bounces the light back at the world. Today I feel that I am married to the Women's Movements and to the vision that every day brings real gold into my life. Activism is what my time is wedded to. I love, honour, and obey my inner voice as it dialogues with feminist insights and practices.

> AN ELEGANTLY &
> MILITANTLY VERTICAL WOMYN
>
> yes,
> nonetheless,
> & not without substantial stress
> i'm still vertical
> functional

mobile
& resisting.

vertical
in spite of the
barriers,
limited birthrights,
men,
floods of destructive details,
costs,
absences & longings,
pain,
drudgery of dailiness,
contrasts
between my ideologies
& ideologies
equally
tenaciously owned
by others
around me.

vertical
because
many minor mercies
have come to me &
i've chosen
to gluttonously
& gratefully
cling to
every precious one them.

so,
nonetheless,
elegantly & spitefully
i am vertical,
lonely & resisting,
in a circle of vital

womyn-created
womyn-centered
light.

In the original *RBT* I described being unable to hear the language of grace-of-physical-movement that others speak with/hear with a form of lightness and smoothness in their body. There are still lapse moments. I am quite proud though, that I now use some psychodrama techniques (Aaron, 1996) with my clients, such as acting out roles or posing my body to express an emotion I think they are trying to communicate. In the classroom teaching I attempt to let my body dance into the themes and discussions. My arms move, my legs skip and march and stomp with a fluidity that matches the discussion at hand. My voice can carry around the room with lots of intensity and power. My body and my whole spirit can laugh often, and both childishly and wisely. I can be spontaneous. The bigness of who I am is noticed.

In the beginning of this paper I described how it was not initially possible for me to write this in my new home. I could not open the old text and read it because it seemed like it would reinvite old "bad energy" into my life. Subconsciously, it seems, I was feeling that reading *RBT* would free the vicious ghosts to haunt my new space. As always, I have faced them and survived. I thank my out-of-town friend who let me write the first draft of this in her office. This was not the first time her matriarchal powerfulness disappeared my ghosts. The writing and the sharing of this latest series of loops in the spiral of my journey has been, like the first writing, both excruciating and delightful.

Again I want to declare my affection to the academic mentors (especially Roxana Ng and the students who forwarded her ideas), my therapists, friends, my ex-partner, and my lover who helped bring the wholeness of an ever-evolving body-conscious and body-connected me to this moment. All of these people and all of these experiences somehow have imprinted themselves upon and embedded themselves within this body. The body remembers. Through their acts of hard work, tenderness, tenacity, and enchantment they have created trails and layers of beauty and courage within this body. Through my own engagement I have risen to accept and integrate their gifts.

Creativity is a fire that is moving my life force through my body now. I am involved in poetry and story writing circles, using play therapy with my clients and students, using my soul to lead my life. Art therapy has an enormous potential to bring us to the gold, the roses, the primitive and soul-touchingly/soul-expanding stones of our destiny. As one of my associates in my psychotherapy practice, Carole Trépanier (1999), says in her educational handout about art therapy, this process heals on many levels. This process heals us physically in that it enhances our

> relaxation; release of endorphins which alleviate pain; mindfulness of certain areas of the body and increases blood flow; increase in nutrients, oxygen, and killer T-cells in affected areas; ease of breath; immune system enhancement to fight cancer and infection; hormones which shift the body to healing mode and this has lasting effects; self-healing mechanisms are released.

Trépanier continues by describing the benefits of art therapy to our mental state, including " increased focus and concentration; increased use of right brain; use of concepts, imagery, metaphor; learning new techniques and various art forms; freeing of obsessive, repetitive, negative thought patterns."

When we fully invest our creative potential in the world around us then our emotional well-being is strengthened. Expressive arts increase our freedom of expression of difficult feelings. Our spiritual selves are deepened and strengthened through the use of art therapy. Trépanier adds: " inner power is released; many people experience profound mystical understanding; many come to terms with their life purpose and calling; many have visions of spirit guides, helpers." It is a privilege to do this kind of expressive arts therapy with our clients and with our students. This is embodied learning.

Living my life creativity and encouraging that creativity in my clients, students, peers, and friends involves inspiring them to nurture and promote their inner artists; motivating and giving "permission" to them to organize and insist on a space and the freeing up of time for their inner dynamic energy to manifest. Also, each person must choose a medium or forum or format of self expression that delights and ignites them. I invite people to make art about topics and themes that they feel intensely connected to and inspired by (versus what they initially think they "should" be making commentary on or what they feel they are "entitled" to make commentary on).

It needs mentioning that there are burns and ashes that can come about when we are playing with fire. My creativity assists me to construct containers for my ashes. The following is a commentary from a journal entry that is discussing my jealousy. During all the years when my body was numbed out it was not probable that I would feel jealousy or the lusty urges of wanting to possess as "territory" someone else's body. Here is the kind of pain that can happen when we are a wild flame dangerously burning for someone:

> I feel absolutely poisoned with jealously. It is like some type of red biting ants are trapped beneath my skin around my rib cage area and they are running in chaotic circles and eating my flesh. There is no way to remove them and there is absolute certainty that they will continue their carnage. You knew this. You saw that in my eyes even as you said what you said. You said these things anyway. You were testing me. There was something you wanted to examine in that moment. And you may deny that you were testing me or you may say you were testing me but that it is okay to do so. What is this testing about?

Discovering and shaping my responses to the "burn" factor and ashes is the place I am at in the spiral of life's journey right now.

One of the resources for strengthening has been my spirituality. Discovering a sense of the meaning of my life has helped take the "kinks" out of the spiral. It has helped me walk through the fire. I now refer to myself as a "messy amateur Buddhist." Buddhists often talk about kindness being a prayer and a practice. There is always a emphasis on "nowness" and non-imposition. The following is a quote from a Buddhist Nun that resonates deeply for me:

> That light touch of acknowledging what we're thinking and letting it go is the key to connecting with this wealth that we have. With all the messy stuff, no matter how messy it is, just start where you are—not tomorrow, not later, not yesterday when you were feeling better—but now. Start now, just as you are. (Pema Chodron, 1994, p. 35)

At each loop in the spiral I want to pause, reflect, integrate, document and move on.

Reclaiming Body Territory was a significant turning point in my life. Through writing and having it published I found and affirmed my voice. The process of writing this essay has been healthy and engaging. I am grateful for this opportunity to think/feel/breath my way on and forward from where I was in my body territory almost a decade ago. The horizon before me is gorgeous and beckoning. I see acres of necessary and beautiful fires, wild and tamed roses, gold nuggets and gold dust and I know how stones feel and I know how to respond to them. The process of creative writing and creatively learning from the body's messages and using that knowledge to enhance my personal, professional, and political life has been a gift. I do my best to pass on the gifts of roses, gold, fire – and voice.

Endnotes

1. Ongoingly I thank Beth Zwecher and Erma Howe, two of my feminist therapists. Also, I continue sending gratitude and affection to Maria Biasucci my massage therapist. Thanks go to those brave passionate people who always help me feel and think and become larger: Morgan Gardner, Teena Lacoste, Ginette Demers, Melanie Robitalle, Carol Trépanier, Robert Kominar, Marnina Gonick, Diana Gustafson. These kind people have motivated me to continue living and lusting big.

2. Marilyn Calmain and Nancy Riley were social workers and feminist activists within many circles and contexts. There are now unfillable spaces in some organizations or groups where these women once breathed life, hope, and excitement.

References

Aaron, S. (1996). Basic Bodywork And PsychoDrama Certificate Program [class handouts and notes]. Toronto: C.M. Hinks Institute.

Abbey, S., & O'Reilly, A.(Eds.). (1998). *Redefining motherhood: Changing identities and patterns.* Toronto, ON: Second Story Press.

Allison, D. (1994). *Skin: Talking about sex, class and literature.* Ithaca, NY: Firebrand Books.

Armstrong, P., & Armstrong, H. (1994). *Take care: Warning signals for Canada's health system.* Toronto, ON: Garamond Press.

Atkinson, M. (1984). *Our masters' voices: The language and body language of politics.* London: Methuen & Co. Ltd.

Bartky, S. L. (1990). *Femininity and domination: Studies in the phenomenology of oppression.* New York, NY: Routledge.

Bly, R. (1990). *Iron John: A book about men.* Toronto, ON: Random House.

Bolaria, B. S., & Bolaria, R. (1994). *Women, medicine and health.* Halifax, NS: Fernwood Publishing.

Bolin, J. S. (1994). *Crossing to Avalon: A woman's midlife pilgrimage.* San Francisco, CA: Harper.

Brown, L. S. (1994). *Subversive dialogues: Theory in feminist therapy.* New York, NY: Basic Books.

Butler, S., & Rosenblum, B. (1991). *Cancer in two voices.* Duluth, MN: Spinsters Ink.

Cabezon, J. I. (Ed.). (1992). *Buddhism, sexuality, and gender.* New York, NY: State University of New York Press.

Cantor, D. W. (Ed.). (1990). *Women as therapists.* London: Jason Aronson Inc.

Charmaz, K., & Paterniti, D. A. (1999). *Health, illness, and healing: Society, social context, and self.* Los Angeles, CA: Roxbury Publishing Company.

Chodron, P. (1991). *The wisdom of no escape and the path of loving-kindness.* Boston, MA: Shambhala Publications.

Chodron, P. (1994). *Start where you are: A guide to compassionate living.* Boston, MA: Shambhala Publications.

Dua, E., & FitzGerald, (Ed.). (1994). *On women healthsharing.* Toronto, ON: Women's Press.

Eichler, M. (Ed.). (1995). *Change of plans: Towards a non-sexist sustainable city.* Toronto, ON: Garamond Press.

Eichler, M. (1997). *Family shifts: Families, policies, and gender equality.* Toronto, ON: Oxford University Press.

Firestein, B. A. (1996). *Bisexuality: The psychology and politics of an invisible minority.* Los Angeles, CA: Sage Publications.

Fox, M. (1999). *Sins of the spirit, blessings of the flesh.* New York, NY: Harmony Books.

Frost, P. J., & Taylor, S. M. (1996). *Rhythms of academic life: Personal accounts of careers in academia.* Los Angeles, CA: Sage Publications.

Gallop, J. (1988). *Thinking through the body.* New York, NY: Columbia University Press.

Gallop, J. (Ed.). (1995). *Pedagogy: The question of impersonation.* Bloomington, IN: Indiana University Press.

Goffman, E. (1981). *Forms of talk.* Philadelphia, PA: University of

Pennsylvania Press.

Griffin, S. (1995). *The eros of everyday life: Essays on ecology, gender and society.* New York, NY: Doubleday Dell Publishing Group.

Griffin, S. (1980). *Woman and nature: The roaring inside her.* New York, NY: Harper & Row.

hooks, b. (1994). *Teaching to transgress: Education as the practice of freedom.* London: Routledge.

hooks, b. (1993). *Sisters of the yam: Black women and self-recovery.* Toronto, ON: Between The Lines.

Heywood, L. (1998). *Bodymakers: A cultural anatomy of women's body building.* Fredericton, NB: Rutgers University Press.

Jackson, C. (1990). Confronting Heterosexuality. *Resource For Feminist Research,* Fall. Toronto, ON: OISE Printing Services.

Jennings, S. (Ed.). (1997). *Dramatherapy: Theory and practice 3.* London: Routledge.

Johnston, A. (1996). *Eating in light of the moon: How women can let go of compulsive eating through metaphor and storytelling.* Toronto, ON: Canadian Manda Group.

Kaplan, M. M. (1992). *Mothers' images of motherhood.* New York, NY: Routledge.

Macy, J. (1991). *World as lover, world as self.* Berkeley, CA: Parallax Press.

McLead, E. (1994). *Women's experience of feminist therapy and counseling.* Buckingham: Open University Press.

Metzger, D. (1992). *A guide and companion to the inner world: Writing for your life.* San Francisco, CA: Harper.

Miller, J. B., & Pierce Stiver, I. (1997). *The healing connection: How women form relationships in therapy and life.* Boston, MA: Beacon Press.

Nelson, H. L. (1997). *Feminism and families.* New York, NY: Routledge.

Ng, R. (Forthcoming) Old wisdom in the new age: Exploring health and the body through Chinese Medicine. In *Toward a pedagogy of embodiment: Reflections on health, healing and the body from an Eastern perspective.*

Razack, S. (1993). Storytelling for social change. In *Returning the gaze: Essays on racism, feminism and politics.* Toronto, ON: Sistervision Press.

Ricciutelli, L. (Ed.). (1994). Women and health. *Canadian Women's*

Studies, Summer, Vol. 14, No3.

Ricciutelli, L. (Ed.). (1998). Looking back, looking forward: Mothers, daughters, and feminism. *Canadian Women's Studies* , Summer, Vol.18, No2.

Roman, L. G., & Eyre, L. (Eds.). (1997). *Dangerous territories: Struggles for difference and equality in education.* New York, NY: Routledge.

Ronai, C. (1997). *Everyday sexism in the third millennium.* New York, NY: Routledge.

Schiwy, M. (1996). *A voice of her own: Women and the journal-writing journey.* New York, NY: Fireside Press.

Smith, D. E. (1999). *Writing the social: Critique, theory, and investigations.* Toronto, ON: University of Toronto Press.

Steinberg, R. J., & Figart, D. M. (Eds.). (1999). *The annals of the American academy of political and social science: Emotional labor in the service economy.* London: Sage Publications.

Tomm, W. (1995). *Bodied mindfulness: Women's spirits, bodies and places.* Waterloo, ON: Wilfred Laurier University Press.

Transken, S. (1997). Personal, professional and political roles: Struggling with empowerment and burnout. *Equity And Justice.* Montreal, PQ: Universite du Quebec a Montreal.

Transken, S. (1995). *Reclaiming body territory.* Ottawa, ON: Canadian Research Institute For The Advancement Of Women.

Transken, S. (1995). *A sexual assault treatment program: Responding rapidly and holistically to victims.* Sudbury, ON: The Sudbury General Hospital.

Trask, H-K. (1986). *Eros and power: The promise of feminist theory.* Philadelphia, PA: University of Pennsylvania Press.

Turner, F. J. (1999). *Social work practice: A Canadian perspective.* Scarborough, ON: Prentice Hall Allyn and Bacon.

Weston, K. (1991). *Families we choose: Lesbians, gays, kinship.* New York, NY: Columbia University Press.

Wolf, N. (1997). *Promiscuities: The secret struggle for womanhood.* Toronto, ON: Random House.

Women in Isolated Communities

Bonding Behind Bars: How Incarcerated Women Forge a Sense of Community

Margo Little and Ursula Sauve
Sudbury, Ontario

Abstract

Margo Little's personal experience as a teacher at the Sudbury Jail and Sudbury Youth Services serves as a backdrop for this paper. She demonstrates how the prisons are havens for abuse and rejection and that incarcerated women have only each other to depend on for the daily support needed to survive prison life. She addresses this issue and elaborates on strategic mechanisms these often dysfunctional women use to survive their often long stays in prison.

T hose of us who enjoy liberty and express ourselves without restraint often take our freedom for granted and forget that others are not so fortunate. That's why its important to give voice to a group of women who remain invisible to many of us. This poem, entitled "Behind These Bars", articulates a collective plea for acceptance, recognition and respect.

Behind these bars we are helpless
To them we are numbers, useless.
Feeling we have no control, in or out
Our self-esteem, dignity taken from us.
We are human beings, we have mothers
And children out there the same as you.
We are talked about and looked at, like scum of the earth.
They don't realize that we have suffered sexual, mental, and physical abuse.
That is what had led many of us to this lifestyle
of drugs, the streets and jail.
All we ask is to be treated with respect,
And to be truly listened to, not pushed away.

While it is true that all northern women face immense challenges to personal well-being because of isolation and government cutbacks, women in jail are doubly challenged. Prison is a unique community where women are forced by circumstances to bond and co-operate in order to survive. Although the lifestyle behind bars may appear unhealthy, foreign and dysfunctional to an outsider, incarcerated women have invented their own version of a caring community.

As Karlene Faith points out in her book *Unruly Women: The Politics of Confinement and Resistance,* "prisons are small totalitarian societies with rules and regulations affecting every intimate detail of life"(151). Women have to survive the stigma of incarceration, the claustrophobia of confinement, the deadly boredom and the limitations to physical movement. They also need to cope with the devastation of losing their children, family networks and sometimes their spouses. Other challenges include lack of privacy, interminable line-ups, sleep deprivation, depression and anxiety.

The following poem further illustrates that women behind bars struggle with intense feelings of grief and loss:

To Free Oneself is Nothing
It is Being Free That is Hard

Sitting here alone, wondering, what do we seek?
Happiness, yet we still feel blue,
We are mothers, sisters, daughters and wives
We were conceived and born like all humans in life
What happened to the way things used to be?
Freedom, dreams and happiness
We all make mistakes, that's how we learn, yet we are
Looked down upon with disgrace.
We have children who love us, families who care
Hearts that are broken beyond repair.
Concrete walls everywhere we turn
A better life is all we yearn
Steel bars have blocked our view
Which have kept us from each one of you.
Whatever the reasons, we represent loss,
Loss of self-esteem
Loss of respect
Whatever the reasons, we must cultivate the inner strength to go on,

To ask for forgiveness,
To start to rebuild,
For ourselves, our families and friends, we need to go forth.
Rejoice in today
Look forward to tomorrow
Love each other
Rebuild for tomorrow.

To put this neglected female population in perspective, it is necessary to look at the number of women serving time in Canada. According to Karlene Faith, women make up less than 3 percent of all federal Canadian prisoners. Approximately 4 percent of provincial prisoners are women. At any given time approximately 25 women are serving life sentences in Canada. The prisoners tend to form, "one or a few close friendships which become their refuge in what they perceive to be a generally hostile environment"(158).

It is important to note that Native women are radically over-represented in prison populations. Native women enter the prison system early; many of them are younger than 20. In provincial jails up to 90 percent of the incarcerated women are Native. Of course, the majority are mothers as well. This picture holds true for the local Sudbury Jail.

Although personal identity can be in danger of erasure in the prison atmosphere, many women manage to help each other salvage their basic humanity. Those who have been incarcerated many times eventually begin to understand, "the value of community and collective consciousness as resistance against the oppressiveness of the prison environment"(159). This reality is also emphasized in the 1990 report from the Federal Task Force on Federally Sentenced Women. In the report, entitled *Creating Choices*, the authors acknowledge that women experience hardship and "significant emotional upheaval" asa result of incarceration (31). They note that lack of mental health services in prisons leads women to rely upon each other. It is an accepted fact that women in jail suffer "the burden of memories" associated with rape, sexual abuse, battering and family violence. Because they mistrust corrections authorities, women help each other to avoid suicide, slashing and other self-destructive behaviour. It becomes imperative for women to forge life-saving links inside because positive links to the outside world are lost (64).

One woman who has witnessed this essential bonding process is

Carla, a 24 year old inmate of the Sudbury Jail[1]. *Carla,* a single mother and self-described drug addict, has been in and out of prison since age 18. She acknowledges that women who would be separated by class distinctions or geography on the outside are drawn together in jail. "You get very close to them", *Carla* says. "You get to be good friends. As cell partners you comfort each other and you become very attached. My cellmate was like a sister. I could cry in front of her and we could talk one on one. When she was released I felt lost. I was very broken up when we were separated. I won't ever find anyone that close again".

The following poem evokes the strength and endurance of women's attachments forged behind bars:

> The day has come for us to part
> For you, my friend, it's a new start
> I sit and stare at those bars
> Praying to the Lord for strength
> The strength I need to carry on
>
> I think of all the days that passed
> This all seems so very fast
> In my heart that's where you'll stay
> You've been a friend and always will be
> For that I thank the Lord so kindly.
>
> Only hours till we part,
> And many months till my new start.
> My dear friend, I promise you that I will always be there for you.
> Your time is served, and now you must go,
> For you helped me stand tall and grow.
> Our friendship I will always cherish
> For one like ours will never perish.

It is very evident that, for *Carla,* one of the most stressful aspects of her situation was the threat of losing her children. She credits a friend on the range with helping her to change her point of view and starting to think positively. When she received disturbing news, she was feeling very emotional and crying a lot but her cell partner helped to ease her mind with encouraging words. "Look ahead; the kids will be there when you get out," her confidante said. "They won't keep you in here forever; your kids will be waiting for you".

Carla was grateful for the reassurance that she still had options. Her cellmate reminded her that even getting arrested had a positive side because it forced her to consider treatment. Soon *Carla* started viewing her sentence as a rescue instead of a penalty. Now she had to take action to recover from her addiction and prevent her children from being adopted.

Carla's experience is verified by another young Sudbury Jail inmate. *Donna*, a 19 year old mother and drug addict, has been on the streets since she was 14. She reports that she was attracted to the other women on the range as friends as soon as she walked into the jail. For her there's a "sense of family in jail". She characterizes the jail setting as "more nurturing" than the youth jails where she spent much of her teen years.

Donna's personal crisis came when she was informed that her 2 year old stepson had tested positive for Hepatitis B. "That was hard to deal with", she says. "The baby contracted the disease from a dirty needle". Other women on the range helped her in a variety of ways. One older woman offered "some kind words, a time to talk and her friendship". She also arranged for *Donna* to acquire information pamphlets on Hepatitis B so she could educate herself about the condition. The older woman's mature and calm role modelling also helped *Donna* to control her anger.

Her cellmate also encouraged her to call a crisis centre to receive counselling and advice. With the help of her cell partner she began to get the message: "there's nothing you can do to change it; it has happened and you have to be strong and accept it". She also finds the time they pray together every evening very consoling. "I never prayed in jail before", *Donna* says. "Praying is remarkable; seeing the chaplain has been very comforting".

Betty, one of the matriarchs of the jail system, is one of the elders the younger ones like *Carla* and *Donna* rely upon when they first arrive on the range. First incarcerated at age 24, *Betty* has served time in prisons from British Columbia to Ontario so she has learned the protocol, traditions and taboos of prison life. "I cried my eyes out back then", she recalls. "But I'm a veteran now. I sometimes give advice to the younger ones. I tell them to reach out and keep in touch with family. That's your support line. I tell them what to say to the doctor. The young one don't always know the ropes so they pick up street smarts from the older ones. It is certainly an education inside; you even learn a lot about medical things in jail".

Newcomers are given lots of leeway to ease themselves into life on the range, according to *Betty*. She tells the first timers to ask lots of questions. "That's how they learn", she says. "The first timers look out of place. It's easy to feel sorry for yourself and get down. The old timers tell them what to expect and help to orient them".

The guards in the women's section often warn the current inmates ahead of time "to take it easy" on a novice who is coming in. "Yesterday a 61 year old came in", *Betty* confides. "She was very upset and crying; it was her first time in jail. The guards told us that she was in a very delicate condition. I brought her a magazine and told her to see the doctor to get something for her nerves. I gave her a crossword puzzle to get her mind off of it. I told her, 'Don't worry about it; we're all in here together. Just grab your cup and have some tea, read a book. It's scary the first time. Nobody's going to jump you. The worst part is over'".

Years of experience have taught *Betty* that women need to draw upon their own inner resources in order to maintain their health and equilibrium. She shared her knowledge about breathing exercises and relaxation techniques so the newcomer would not be lying awake all night. After a while the newcomers get into the groove of the jail and get more comfortable with the routine. Soon, according to *Betty's* account, the novice was pushing a broom, doing her part to keep the range clean and trying to fit in.

Another inmate who prides herself on providing motherly advice is *Karen*. She is 43 with grown children aged 22 and 26 as well as a 2 year old grandson. She sees her role as the peacemaker, the one who serves to counteract any of the negative behaviour of the 19 to 24 year olds on the range. "Most people adjust and get along", she says. "We know we'll be with each other for quite awhile so there's no point in hating each other. We are in confined quarters so we have to see each other; we can't avoid each other in here. It makes the time go forever if you fight and make conflict".

After seven months on the range *Karen* has observed most of the common reactions to imprisonment. "Some go through some very hard times", she says. "Some don't care; some cry all the time. I try to say some calming words to the newcomers. I tell them they can't be on the phone to relatives all the time so they have to learn to take comforting words from others on the range. Sometimes I suggest they call Elizabeth Fry if they are upset. I just try to give them direction and advice".

Karen's spiritual approach is often appreciated by other women. It takes a while to build trust but she tells them "to be strong and to take it one day at a time". She also holds a medicine bag and offers prayers in her supportive and friendly way. If a medicine man is scheduled to visit the jail, she will urge the young ones to meet with him. If another inmate is depressed, *Karen* may say, "don't worry; your time will come up. Stop counting the days; just stay positive. And don't get yourself into any trouble when you get out".

As the conversations with *Carla, Donna, Betty* and *Karen* demonstrate, "people in prison face adversity with resilience and courage"(203). Intimate friendships have the power to "make the prison experience endurable"(185). It has also been observed that prison relationships often give women with histories of abuse their first experience with unconditional love.

One of the most powerful means that women use to celebrate their friendships is through poetry. Incarcerated women have historically converted their loneliness, isolation, ostracism and rejection into poetry and other creative writing. Since space is at a premium on the range, writing is one of the few creative outlets available. And since writing is a very therapeutic activity it is a widespread pastime.

The following poem expresses the universal pain of separation from loved ones:

I love you . . .
My one and only
My knight in shining armour.

I spend the days
All so lonely
Waiting for the night to fall.

Fast asleep
I dream of you
To wake with dreams
I intend to keep.

"I shed a tear
With not a fear
For I know you're the one
Who really cares.

> I live upon the love
> You give.
> I love you . . .
> Don't forget.
>
> Please stay strong,
> It won't be long,
> But for now
> In my heart is where
> You belong."

Connections made during incarceration remain strong even after special friends are transferred:

> "Thoughts of you run through my mind
> I think of you all the time
> I read your letters day and night
> Against my heart I hold them tight.
>
> You're a friend, a friend of mine
> For you're a man who's one of a kind
> I long to reach and hold you tight
> In the midst of the pale moonlight.
>
> We are strangers through faces
> Though you've filled my heart's empty spaces
> You've made my heart so whole
> I feel I've gained all control".
>
> Every time I feel blue
> I read your letters and say "I love you"
> If it is possible that, that could be
> Would you love and take care of me?
>
> For my love I treasure deep
> And that would be yours forever to keep
> My heart has been broken so many times
> Just for once, I wish that thou's heart would be mine.

As the selected writings of incarcerated women illustrate, prisons tend to intensify all human emotions. In prison women often find "shared emotional comfort, social camaraderie, spiritual communion and political connectedness"(215). Cut off from the outside world, many women do indeed find sanctuary in one another. For many on the range it is vital to find a friend to "share dealing with the world. Somebody to face this madness with" (215).

Endnotes

1. All names used in this paper are pseudonyms to protect the anonymity of the contributors.

References

Clemens, Micki. *Justice*. Toronto: McGraw-Hill, 1994.
Creating Choices: The Report of the Task Force on Federally Sentenced Women. April, 1990.
Faith, Karlene. *Unruly Women: The Politics of Confinement and Resistance*. Vancouver: Press Gang, 1993.
Fife, Connie. *The Colour of Resistance*. Toronto: Sister Vision, 1993.

Finding Healing and Wholeness: Spirituality for Women Abused by Clergy

Marie Evans Bouclin
Sudbury, Ontario

Abstract

Bouclin has done an interesting study on the sexual assault and abuse that women have suffered at the hands of the ordained Catholic Ministry. Based on analysis of information gathered in a number of interviews from women who were victims of various abuses, she talks about their pain and their journey to recovery. In this paper she proposes a model of feminist spirituality that can help enhance personal healing.

Introduction

There is a book written by the French psychiatrist Sylvie Portnoy entitled, *The abuse of power makes people sick.*[1] In the Roman Catholic church, the issue of power is at the very core of relationships between men and women. Decision-making power is the exclusive right of men ordained to the priesthood. They are considered the "guardians of all that is sacred", and the intermediaries between God and humanity by way of the Church's sacraments. This gives priests an enormous power over lay people, women in particular, because they are not called "according to Christ's plan for his Church" to be ordained. Using the power of the priesthood in such a way that it is damaging to another person is called abuse of power; it can be physical, sexual, emotional, psychological or spiritual.

This paper discusses the experiences of women who, at least at one time of their life, believed this to be God's plan. This is what they were taught and what was modeled from childhood; at Church, in their homes, and at school. First, I shall illustrate the "unwellness" of women who have been abused by clergy by telling four short stories. Then, borrowing largely from Anne Wilson Schaef's analysis of women living in patriarchal societies, I will describe the characteristics found in women abused by clergy. This is based on stories shared with me by 19 Church women, my consultations with 4 therapists, and with several feminist theologians.

Secondly, I will propose a model of feminist spirituality. A distinction will be made between **religion**, which I understand as a **system** of beliefs, rituals, moral codes; and **spirituality**, a **process** whereby we enter into and maintain a relationship with the divine life-force at the core of our being.

Four Stories

Ellen was a single, 37 year old former teacher who worked as a pastoral assistant in a parish for 10 years. In this full-time position, she earned about $22 000. She has a university degree in psychology, a teaching certificate and has taken several theology courses over the years. When the new pastor came in, he wanted to redecorate the church and remodel the rectory, but the Parish Finance Committee said that there was no money for this. So he dismissed Ellen saying the parish could no longer afford to pay her salary. Ellen is having a great deal of difficulty finding work to support herself and is undergoing psychiatric treatment for severe depression.

Joan entered a convent when she was 18 years old. One day she confided in her confessor that she questioned her vocation because she was struggling with celibacy. The chaplain said she needed regular spiritual direction and had her come to his office. Every week, over a period of two years, he would have her come to his office, undress him, and perform oral sex. Several years later, a physician who was treating Joan for chronic ulcers urged her to seek counselling, suggesting that the ulcers were stress-related. Joan had never told her superiors about the sexual abuse for fear she would have to leave the community.

Angela was 45 years old when her husband Paul was stricken with cancer. Her pastor visited Paul regularly as he was dying at home. The evening of Paul's funeral, after her grown children had left, the priest insisted she come and spend the night with him at the rectory. In spite of her reluctance, it was to be the first of many sexual encounters. One evening, she dropped into the rectory unannounced and found the priest in bed with another woman. Angela created such a scene that the priest called the police and had her taken to a psychiatric facility claiming she was crazy and had been stalking him for months.

Lynn is married and the mother of four children. To supplement the family income she worked as a parish secretary. Don, her pastor, often had her write his homilies because she, "was so connected to the real life of his parishioners." Lynn would have to come in Saturdays to do this, because with all his other duties Don did not have time during the week. Progressively exhausted juggling family, housework and her job, Lynn told Father Don she would no longer be coming in Saturdays to help him with his homilies. He fired her on the spot. Later that evening, Lynn's husband had to rush her to the hospital with a stroke.

Besides suffering from a number of physical ailments: anorexia, obesity, stomach ulcers, hypertension, chronic depression, arthritis and cancer, women who have been abused by clergy have an unhealthy way of relating to themselves and other people. They are constantly seeking validation, acceptance, and the approval of others, whether that is a person, a group, or an institution. They have very little self-esteem and self-confidence (which they sometimes mask with arrogance); they have no personal boundaries (they can't say no) and frequently do not respect the boundaries of others (so they are "controllers"); and they have great difficulty knowing or expressing who they truly are so they focus on the wants and needs of perfectionists, workaholics (Wilson Scaef, 1985, 1986, 1987).

Women Who Have Recovered from Abuse of Power Situations

Women who feel they have recovered from clergy abuse acknowledge that they are still involved in a "work in progress". Recovery from abuse, like any liberation from oppression — we know this from feminist theory — begins with awareness. The women I interviewed were jarred into awareness by a crisis: their health failed, a relationship ended abruptly, they lost their livelihood. From a feeling of total brokenness and helplessness, their journey to healing and wholeness began with the caring support of friends and the help of good therapists. They made a conscious decision to "do whatever it takes" to live, get well, and find meaning in their lives.

Most often, these devoutly Catholic women first sought some kind of "spiritual" help from other priests, because they believed them to be God's instrument of healing. This simply did not work. Women, to use the words of one female theologian, are "not even in a priest's consciousness", and so these women were not understood. Often they were further victimized by the priests. But with the shared experience, understanding, support and nurturing of other women, they were guided into a new spirituality, a "holistic" one, that is an inner process of seeking healing for their whole person: body, heart and spirit. Then, and this is crucial, they give themselves permission to question. They began to question their beliefs about God, Jesus Christ, the Church, and the meaning of life. To do this they were supported by women who a) understood the dynamic of abuse; b) had some solid knowledge of theology and spirituality; and c) were prepared to share with them their own spiritual experience and seek answers with them — not provide them with ready-made ones.

Nine Common Steps

I found, in interviewing these women, nine common "steps" in their spirituality. "However, these steps are not simply linear and sequential, like the steps of a staircase, rather, like steps in a dance, they move backward and forward, encircle, repeat, and move ahead once more" (Schüssler Fiorenza, 1992, p.9).

- Women begin the search for their "self", their centre, the essence of who they are in the silence of their inner being.

All the women interviewed confided that their recovery hinged on having learned to pray in a different way. They wanted to maintain their Christian faith, so they first agreed to try meditating in silence. Some joined meditation groups, others received help from a "prayer partner" or a spiritual counsellor. Still others simply found the help they needed in books on silent prayer.

They all mention, "learning to be silent." All these women prayed. Every day. A few of them had formal theological and spiritual training, but all attended Church regularly. Some had a great devotion to Mary, others focussed on reading and meditating on passages from the Bible. The women who had come along the furthest in their recovery admitted that, in fact, they did not practice real interior silence. One woman, who saw herself as a "church addict" reported that she, "said a lot of prayers" but did not take the time to "listen in inner silence", because all she would hear was an inner "scolding" from God the Father, whom she saw as distant and demanding, much like her own father.

- The "dynamic of silence" requires some effort and has a great deal of impact.

Here is how Noreen, a spiritual director, describes the next step:
To "find silence", we must learn to breathe. It is in following
our breath that we begin to journey inward and become aware
of what is "going on inside". That is where abused women
discover the intense anger they are carrying inside, and which
is at the root, I believe, of their depression.[2] Touching their
anger enables women to come out of denial and speak the
secrets they have been keeping and which are making them ill.
IF they can share these secrets, in their intimate detail, with
someone they trust, they can relive all the emotional trauma
they experienced, acknowledge what was done to them,
recognize this was wrong and that they are not responsible.
They realize that they had no control over those events but can
take some control over their lives now. They empower
themselves to heal.

Exercises can help us learn to breathe (Mariechild, 1987).
According to another respondent:
Silence and breathing helped me listen to the needs of my
body. Little by little, I became aware that my whole body
needed caring. I was extremely tired and had all kinds of
health problems. I believe that the 'silence at the end of each
breath' opened up a way to reach healing, one step at a time,
for my body, my feelings and my soul.

- Finding someone to share the inner journey.

The decision to heal and become whole again is closely linked to
having been heard and believed when the women were telling their
stories, and they were not judged. One woman tells of being under
psychiatric care for suicidal tendencies for years. One day she
mentioned to her psychiatrist that she had intercourse with a priest
when she was a teenager, but that it was a long time ago, and that she
had put it behind her. At the end of the session, the doctor said that he
knew a "good Catholic social worker" that she might consider
speaking to about the priest business, because the social worker might
better "understand this kind of thing" and be of some help. "That
woman saved my life", she said. "I realized that I wasn't a liar and a
tramp, I had been abused."

Finding someone who listens with an open heart and mind, someone who is non-judgmental will often lead abused women to suspect they may not be the ones at fault in what took place. Being able to express out loud their feelings of guilt, and being understood by someone who has had a similar experience (or knows someone who did) validates their own experience. This recognition of their story allows these women to face a very painful truth: they have lost something very precious, and like with any loss, there is a void. To fill that void, they have to grieve.

- Taking to the desert, leaving the past behind.

When there is a loss, whether it is the presence in one's life of a man she thought loved her or the satisfaction of fulfilling work within the Church, it takes on a whole new dimension when women begin to talk about it. It is as if hearing themselves tell their story makes it real — a fact, not just feelings. Every woman I interviewed who recovered from abuse admitted that, in time, she experienced all of the stages of grief : shock, denial, guilt, anger, bargaining, forgiveness, acceptance and serenity (Kubler-Ross).

During their grieving, these Christian women reach out to God for help. They pray to be healed, but they feel in some respects, that they no longer know how to pray. They ask: Can a God-Almighty-Father really help them, the God that they hear about at Church? Then there is grieving for the loss of the Church when they realize how alienated they feel in a Church that has allowed its ministers to abuse them. All of the women who felt that they recovered had, for a time at least, "left the Church" because just being at a Catholic liturgy was too painful.

- They see themselves as gifted by God.

Part of finding one's essence, is to be truly honest with oneself. This involves dropping masks (Psalm 139: 13-14)[3]; discovering reasons to believe in one's personal dignity (Isaiah 43: 1-4); recognizing one's flaws; and appreciating one's gifts. It means becoming mature in one's faith and taking responsibility for growth in that faith (Psalm 62: 2-3). One woman I interviewed, dismissed without warning after working for 18 years in a Diocesan office, describes how she felt after spending many years trying to recover from this abuse of power:

I was completely broken. But little by little, as I became aware of who I was deep down, I also discovered who God was for me, and how precious God's love for me was. It was as if I had been given a new life, and I felt more alive than I had in years, and very comfortable recognizing my talents and gifts. I felt more honest, more content, more energized, more creative, more self-confident and truly joyful about who I am.

- Finding a community of like-minded persons who wish to create new rituals and treat one another as equals.

While none of the abused women showed any interest in forming some new kind of self-help group, they all agreed that they had a circle of two or three close friends. These were other women in whom they could confide without being judged; did not offer them advice; did not feel the need to agree; and were comfortable with even when they disagreed. They were not critical or blaming, and were willing to share their own experience. But especially, they were willing to explore new readings in spirituality and new ways of understanding Scripture.

There are passages from Scripture that take on special, personal meaning for women who have been abused. The passages enable them to enter into a "right relationship" with who they are and who God is for them, based on Jesus's treatment of women. Pondering a favourite passage from Scripture helped them to discover their value in the eyes of God, and to be present to a loving Presence within. This brought them to recognize and celebrate their own particular gifts and talents, and so to be comfortable with who they are, and the conviction of being cherished by God.

- Seeking God by another name.

Part of a healing spirituality means finding new ways of describing or naming the divine reality with whom they wish to be in right relationship. In seeking wholeness, women name different "sacred spaces" where they discover divine presence and activity. It can be in one's deepest self; but also in the love of a partner, the birth of a child, or the grateful smile of someone they have helped.

God is no longer the "almighty father who judges and punishes". Instead, God is identified in terms of Presence, Wisdom, Divine Other. In this context, the Holy Spirit takes on much more importance. As one woman said:

I was deeply hurt by men who claimed to speak for God. So,

in my prayer time, I would seek a feminine God-figure. For a long time I thought it was the Virgin Mary, then I started to read Wisdom Scriptures and female mystics, and discovered Christ and the Spirit could also feel like a female presence . . .

When asked what place Jesus Christ held in their spirituality, most of the women said that they found the person of Jesus as presented in Scripture, to be very attractive, especially in his interaction with women. One therapist summarizes it this way:

What is sacred for these women is their overall well-being. . . they find God in all things, especially in their innermost self. They call that God, Thou or You, Spirit, Presence, Love, Divine Other, and that God teaches them to take care of themselves, accept themselves and love themselves. And the Jesus of the Gospels confirms this, and teaches them how to relate to **that** God.

- Establishing new traditions.

Part of belonging to a small community involves creating new traditions, feast and rituals. Traditional liturgies are centred on a male God (Father, Son and male Spirit), and the language and rituals are exclusive of women (or oblivious or hostile). Therefore, women seeking a new form of spirituality tend to create new rituals or give new meaning to old ones, such as sharing a meal (Eucharist), having a prayer service of forgiveness and repentance. Part of their repentance rituals have to do with ways they have abused the earth and their own bodies. Most find some form of fasting very helpful to raise their spiritual awareness.

- Allowing oneself to be transformed.

The most powerful testimony is from women whose spiritual journey literally transformed them. Their "spiritual exercises" brought them to a place where they found their fear had been replaced by confidence, anger by love, envy by joy, the desire for vengeance by detachment, self-pity by concern for others, shame by self-acceptance, and inappropriate guilt by a sense of true responsibility for "doing what they could" for their own well-being and that of others.

Part of their transformation is that they take time to put things into perspective. Rather than worry or obsess about everything, these women strive to be "in the present moment", more conscious of what they are saying, doing, thinking. This helps give them a sense of inner peace. It also helps them make clearer, more objective decisions for themselves, and allow others to do the same. They also find that their hypertension and many physical ailments have significantly diminished.

All of the women I interviewed stated that their lack of personal boundaries goes back to an incident in their childhood where they were helpless in a situation with someone who had power over them. Their person, be it in their body, their sexuality, their skills or capabilities, was appropriated through violence, humiliation or shame (Beatty, 1995, 215). They now realized that as adults, they had to reclaim their power and see themselves no longer as victims, but as responsible for establishing healthy personal boundaries.

Also, they learn to speak for themselves, stop trying to please others, and see to their own needs and wants. They come to take personal responsibility for protecting themselves against abuse. They can identify sexual abuse and harassment, name them, and they have decided not to tolerate them ever again.

Their person has become a sacred reality, an inviolable space inhabited by the divine. They refuse to be ashamed (that feeling of always being wrong, not good enough, fundamentally unworthy and inferior), and know the difference between guilt and responsibility. One respondent explains it this way:

> I was ashamed because I didn't refuse to have sex with the priest. I thought it was my fault, I should have said no. Now I realize how vulnerable I was, and that he was the one who took advantage of me. He is the guilty one. I am responsible to not let this happen again.

Women who were unfairly dismissed initially believed they were the victim of a misunderstanding rather than an abuse of power. They were convinced that they must have done something wrong. They forgave almost immediately the injustice done to them because, "Jesus taught us to forgive" and "the Gospel commands us to forgive". When they ended up at the doctor's office completely burned out, or in a state of deep depression, they did not immediately agree that the abuse of power was what made them ill.

Progressively, these women came to understand the difference between the "Gospel imperative" to reach out to the truly needy; and "caretaking" which is doing for others what they are capable of doing for themselves. For many of them, this meant saying no to unpaid work. A very common away of crossing women's boundaries is to appropriate their time and talents, and decide for them when and for whom they will do volunteer work. "As adult Christians", said one woman, "we are the ones who discern for ourselves how we will respond to the Gospel." Interestingly, these women also have a better grasp of the boundaries of others, and avoid guessing or claiming to know what others think or want.

Conclusion

Due to the religious beliefs instilled in them, it is very difficult for many Catholic women to address the problem of abuse of clerical power in the Church. Criticizing the Institution is tantamount to denying the faith. Most often, at least at the outset, abused women do not distinguish between a *problem* in the Church as a man-made *institution* which *claims* to be founded by Jesus Christ, and a community of equal believers who strive to live according to the *teachings* of Jesus Christ. Becoming aware of this distinction is very often the point at which women abused by clergy decide they want to explore new spiritual avenues to wellness.

In his book entitled, *The Holy Longing: The Search for Christian Spirituality*, Ron Rolheiser states ,"long before we do anything explicitly religious at all, we have to do something about the fire that burns within us. What we do with that fire, how we channel it, is our spirituality"(1999, p.9). Finding that fire is the process by which we discover within ourselves the sacred, that divine presence and inner activity which make us feel loved, valued and fully alive.

Endnotes

1. Portnoy, Sylvie. *L'abus de pouvoir rend malade: rapports dominant-dominé*. Paris: Éditions L'Hartmann, 1994.

2. For more information on anger turned inward read Lois Frankel, *Women, Anger and Depression*, 1992.

3. Bible references are taken from *The New Oxford Annotated Bible with the Apocryphal / Deuterocanonical Books*, edited by Bruce M. Metzjer and Roland E. Murphy, New REvised Standard Version. New York: Oxford University Press, 1991.

References

Beatty, Melody. (1994). *Vaincre la co-dépendance*. Montréal: Editions Sciences et culture.

Carlson Brown, Johanne & Bohn, Carole R. (Eds). (1989). *Christianity, Patriarchy and Abuse: A Feminist Critique*. New York: Pilgrim Press.

Cummings, Louise. (1994). *Eyes Wide Open: Spiritual Resources for Healing from Childhood Sexual Assault*. Winfield, BC: Woodland Books.

Fortune, Marie Marshall. (1994). L'inconduite du clergé: Abus sexuels dan les rapports ministériels. *Concilium*, 252, février, 145-154.

---. (1983). *Sexual Violence, The Unmentionable Sin*. New York: Pilgrim Press.

---. (1992). *Clergy Misconduct: An Educational Curriculum for Clergy and Religious Professionals*. Centre for the Prevention of Sexual and Domestic Violence.

--- & Poling, James N. (1994). *Sexual Abuse by Clergy: A Crisis for the Church*. Decatur, Journal of Pastoral Care Publications.

Frankel, Lois P. (1992). *Women, Anger and Depression: Strategies for Self-Empowerment*. Los Angeles: Health Communications Inc.

Griffiths, Josephine. (1997). *Seeking Sophia: Meditations and Reflexions For Women Who No Longer Go To Church*. Toronto: Novalis.

Harris, Maria. (1991). *Dance of the Spirit: The Seven Steps of Women's*

Spirituality. New York: Bantam Books.

Hoffman, Virginia Curran. (1991). *The Codependent Church.* New York: Crossroad.

Johnson, Elizabeth A. (1993). *She Who Is: The Mystery of God in Feminist Theological Discourse.* New York: Crossroad.

Mariechild, Diane.(1987) *The Inner Dance: A Guide to Spiritual and Psychological Healing.* Freedom, California: The Crossing Press.

Pellauer, Mary E., Chester, Barbara & Boyajian, Jane (Eds). (1987). *Sexual Assault and Abuse, A Handbook for Clergy and Religious Professionals.* San Francisco: Harper & Row.

Portnoy, Sylvie. (1994). *L'abus de pouvoir rend malade: rapports dominant-dominé.* Paris: Éditions L'Harmattan.

Radford Ruether, Rosemary. (1985). *Women-Church.* San Francisco: Harper & Row.

Sands, Kathleen. (1994). Secret Heartaches: Priestly Celibacy and the Women It Touches. *Escape from Paradise.* Minneapolis: Fortress Press.

Scaef, Anne Wilson. (1986). *Codependency: Misunderstood-Mistreated.* San Francisco: Harper & Row.

---. (1987). *When Society Becomes An Addict.* San Francisco: Harper & Row.

---. (1985). *Women's Reality: An Emerging Female System in a White Male Society.* Minneapolis: Winston.

Schussler-Fiorenza, Elisabeth. (1992). *But SHE Said.* Boston: Beacon Press.

The Internet and Its Impact on a Small, Rural Japanese Village

Yuko Komatsu and Naokoto Kogou
Japan

Abstract

Through a project designed to empower the small community and to enforce the traditional communal spirit of self-help, every family in Yamada-Mura was given a personal computer and an Internet connection in the summer of 1996. Now, Yamada-Mura is being computerized by making effective use of various kinds of support from people outside of the village. In this process, many women and elderly people in the village also seem to have their lives greatly enriched by using the computer. Our presentation will briefly outline Yamada-Mura's history, and describe the project itself from its planning stages to the present day.

What kind of place is Yamada-Mura?

Historically, the main sources of income in Yamada-Mura have been agriculture and tourism. The landscape of the tiny village has always been dominated by rice farms, while hot spring resorts and ski lodges have also become important to the local economy. Demographic trends, such as the rapid aging of the population and the migration of younger people to urban areas, have affected Yamada-Mura greatly in the recent past. At present, about 25% of the population is sixty-five years of age or older.

Features of Computerization

From its inception, the project aimed to take advantage of Yamada-Mura's communal spirit, and enable the villagers to enrich themselves by giving them the means to increase their interaction with the outside world through the use of the Internet. And, another purpose was to close the information gap in the village. Yamada-Mura suddenly attracted public attention when it distributed personal computers (PCs) to all households in the village. A steady stream of people from the media, people doing research on the village, and administrative organizations came to the village almost every day. The village was forced to take action because of the sudden computerization by cooperating with various people to help the villagers understand computers. The village adopted this approach in order to solve its problems. However, it has since led to an unexpected regeneration of Yamada-Mura and a change in the consciousness of each villager.

The background and history of this regeneration and change are as follows:

(1) The village has long been based on a spirit of communal self-help. This is the basis of the community because the villagers typically help each other out on a day-to-day basis.

(2) Young people and those interested in encouraging the spread of the use of computers have donated their time to help make this goal come to fruition. They came from all walks of life: university and college professors and students as well as business people.

(3) A new festival in honor of the advent of the information age was held by villagers and non-villagers. Volunteers had participated in the past in similar community events sponsored by the village such as the "Yamada-Mura Friendship Festivals" and/or "Courses On Electronic-mail", and they took a strong interest in the information-oriented community. They have been supporting the village residents since then in the computerization of the village.

(4) A cyber network and real network were developed simultaneously. The use of e-mail and e-mail mailing lists have probably had the greatest impact on the lives of the villagers along with the presence and support of the volunteers. The exchanges of messages by subscribers to the mailing list have been playing a significant role in the revitalization of the community, helping people organize a variety of community events to attract more people to the village.

(5) The use of computers has become more popular, and this has resulted in more economic activity. Since the whole village was revitalized thanks to the exchange with non-villagers, Yamada-Mura has attracted attention from throughout Japan. As the result, the village was visited by the Prime Minister and succeeded in obtaining further economic support from the government.

(6) The distribution of PCs motivated the community members

and spread of the use of computers by villagers.

While the use of computers has been promoted in the village, the use of PCs by the elderly, which was the original purpose at the outset, has not progressed as well as had been expected. Recently, however, village women have improved their image by helping to support the elderly and understanding their thoughts and needs.

A Volunteer Support Network for the Elderly

Yamada village started a PC school for the elderly one year ago. When this school was first set up, some of the elderly people actively started to enjoy using computers. In this case, it was women volunteers, consisting mainly of housewives who lived in the village, who provided assistance in this effort. But, they faced a number of challenges in the PC school.

Support in the PC School for the Elderly

The PC school for the elderly is held twice a month. Village women help the elderly to use the computers by providing them with individualized instruction. This school is basically intended to provide long-term and continued support at the pace of each elderly person.

- Change in women

When computers were installed in the village, almost all of the people who were put in charge of promoting the use of computers were village men. However, the hard work of the women was overwhelmingly responsible for the successful introduction of computers to Yamada-Mura. Village women then used the Internet in their own lives through various exchanges with non-villagers and began to widen the various networks among women. The flow is a big factor influencing Yamada-Mura's development afterwards.

Initially, the assistants sought to teach PC use exclusively to the elderly. A history of how the support progressed showed how hard it was for the elderly to use computers, including the use of the keyboard and mouse. Half a year later, the assistants began to value the special learning needs of the elderly, and responded by writing guidelines based on what they had learned from their interactions with them. Sometimes the assistants just watched what the elderly did. In these teaching efforts, the assistants began to realize that they were also learning during the process of their teaching work.

- Change in the elderly

According to our investigation, the reasons why the elderly did not use computers were exemplified by statements such as: "I want to use a PC, but I don't know how to"; and "My children or grandchildren tell me that an old woman like me cannot understand how to use a PC even if I am given private lessons." At an early stage of the PC school, many of the elderly were passively taught and in a condescending manner. However, as the elderly started to teach the assistants something about the wisdom of life as well as other knowledge that they had learned, their attitudes gradually started to improve. The elderly now show a strong desire for learning, a willingness to learn, and confidence. In particular, e-mail, which the elderly have recently begun to use, has become a great tool for facilitating conversation, revitalization, and exchanges among the elderly.

Positive New Changes

- Mutual support

The personal computer classroom is useful because the relationship between village women and the elderly has changed from that of teacher and student to one of mutual cooperation, learning and respect. Some of the elderly use one PC together and help to teach each other. In other cases, the elderly, village women, and the instructor pull together to solve various problems. Many times, an elderly person helps out another elderly person to help solve various problems.

- Positive selection and use of support

At the beginning, the PC school was the only place for the elderly to learn about PCs. However, the elderly gradually came to use the assistance of their family members, which has long been a delicate issue, and to rely on the help of the leader of their group, or to study at other facilities. They thus try to select the most suitable means of support for themselves. Little by little the elderly have begun to become more active in their own lives.

Social Support

As mentioned above, the changes in the assistants and the elderly through the PC school for the elderly remind us of the following axiom: "We study and work in cooperation with others through most of our lives, and not by studying or working individually as desired in many schools." The computerization of the village can bring us a wide variety of information even while we are not aware of it. The relationship between the elderly and village women has developed into one of mutual support in their daily lives through the PC school. When the elderly, who tended to be left behind in the village, found the need to lean on someone, they found support locally, from the women of the village. In any community, people must often take action with the support or cooperation of other people and must understand matters. Problems in our daily lives can, in many cases, be solved in association with the environment or other people. This is a natural process, yet studies on this kind of support have not been highly valued.

Defining Women's Health from Diverse Perspectives

Living and Thriving with Brain Injury: What You See Isn't Always What You Get

Sharon Dale Stone
Thunder Bay, Ontario

Abstract

As a survivor of a brain haemorrhage, Stone explores how the invisibility of this injury can or cannot be a mixed blessing. On the one hand, someone with invisible disabilities can evade the stigmatization that tends to be experienced by those with visible disabilities. On the other hand, the very invisibility of the disabilities means that it is very easy to attach a negative moral judgement to someone's apparent lack of willingness to do all that others expect. Using her own personal experiences, Sharon elaborates on these issues as well as the implications for the creation of caring communities where differences can be recognized and respected.

Introduction

Most people are not aware of how common brain injury is. Nor are most people aware that there are many different kinds of brain injury, so that there is wide variation in how survivors are affected. In this paper, I discuss brain injury caused by haemorrhagic stroke and reflect on my own experiences of surviving a haemorrhagic stroke at age 12. Before turning to my focus, however, it is useful to briefly review some facts about traumatic brain injury (TBI), which has in recent years received increasing public attention.

Usually, TBI is the result of an accidental blow to the head. Laws requiring the wearing of bicycle helmets, motorcycle helmets and seat belts are related to attempts to prevent TBI. Still, there are about 150 new cases of TBI per 100,000 people *every year* (Higenbottam, 1998, p.8). For Canada, this translates to about 56,000 new cases every year, and about 16% of these people become significantly disabled (p.8).

Women, of course, are often victims of TBI, but the prototypical survivor of TBI is a young man. Indeed, it is difficult to find literature, whether academic or popular, that pays attention to women's experiences *as women* of surviving TBI. The academic literature includes: Linge (1990) which offers a man's personal account of recovery from serious head injury; and Webb (1998) which discusses men only in considering the consequences of TBI. Nochi (1997) considers the experiences of both men and women in dealing with the consequences of TBI, but in so doing, does not consider the significance of gender as a mediating factor. In popular literature, a book on living with brain injury (Acorn & Offer, 1998) includes survivors' stories written by men, but none written by women. Refreshingly, women's experiences *are* included in a guidebook for living with TBI (Stoler & Hill, 1998), but as with Nochi, there is no attention paid to men's and women's differing experiences. Nowhere in all of these publications is attention paid to the role played by gender in mediating experience. But gender **does** mediate experience in important ways, for example, in terms of expectations and assumptions that others make, or, in terms of resources available for developing a new understanding of one's own body.

A similar situation exists when it comes to literature about haemorrhagic strokes, though here an even bigger problem than the lack of information about women's experiences is the lack of information about the experiences of young people. Haemorrhagic stroke is also known as a brain haemorrhage, and I am specifically interested in a type called subarachnoid haemorrhage (SAH). All of these terms are refinements of the more general term "cerebral vascular accident"(CVA). Subarachnoid haemorrhage is less common than TBI, which is perhaps why most people have never heard about it, but this does not mean that it is a rare occurrence. In fact, SAH happens to people rather commonly, with an incidence of approximately 1-5% of the population, or 6 per 100,000 people (Broderick et al., 1993). What's more, it is far more likely to be experienced by someone under the age of 65, so it is clearly not an experience that is typical of old age (Biller et al., 1987; Broderick et al., 1993). In fact, it is rather rare in old age.

I experienced a brain haemorrhage when I was 12 years old, caused by an arteriovenous malformation (AVM) that ruptured. In describing what happened to me, the most comfortable term is brain haemorrhage, because that is how I was taught to name what I experienced. I learned the term CVA a few years later, and I learned about subarachnoid haemorrhage after I read my medical records, but I did not learn that it is also called haemorrhagic stroke until about 10 years ago, when I stumbled across a narrative written by a woman who had experienced a brain haemorrhage when she was 24 (Robbins, 1986). There are two points I want to make about this narrative.

My first point is about how she named what she had experienced; she used the term "stroke" which I was surprised to see applied to what had happened. No one had ever used that term with me. This got me thinking about all sorts of issues. In particular, it led me to wonder about the assumption (which I had previously shared) that stroke is a common experience for old people, but not for young people. After investigation, I learned that there are two general types of strokes: ischemic and haemorrhagic; both types likely are to leave the survivor with similar disabilities. Moreover, even though ischemic strokes are more common (Mayo Clinic, 1995) and more likely to happen to an elderly person, they certainly can happen in younger people.

On the other hand, there is comparatively little attention paid in both the medical and social science literatures to haemorrhagic strokes which, as noted above, is more likely to be experienced by someone under the age of 65.[1] Indeed, the scholarly focus on elderly stroke survivors, which often includes a statement about the commonality of strokes for this population, leaves the false impression that stroke is not something that younger people are likely to experience. Thus, I have recently taken to telling people that I survived a haemorrhagic stroke at age 12, instead of telling them that I had a brain haemorrhage. I'd like to shake those assumptions about who experiences a stroke.

My second point about the narrative that I found is that I was absolutely fascinated by it. The writer talked about her experience of the actual haemorrhage, and detailed her experiences of recovery and rehabilitation. What she wrote brought back many memories for me about my experience when I was an adolescent. I had never before known anyone who had experienced what I had, and I felt a kind of kinship with this woman whom I had not met.

For most of my life, I had assumed that what had happened to me was not only a rare occurrence for people in general, but especially rare in someone who was not yet an adult. But after I read about the woman who experienced haemorrhagic stroke at age 24, I began to wonder whether the experience was as unusual as I had been led to believe. Then I discovered a support page on the internet for survivors of brain aneurism and AVMs [AAMS], where hundreds of people, mostly women, have posted their stories,[2] and I began to get an inkling of the magnitude of the silence about haemorrhagic stroke.

My current preoccupation is with breaking the silence about young women who become brain-injured as a result of haemorrhagic strokes. Not only do I want to raise awareness about how frequently it happens, I also want to raise awareness about the invisible disabilities with which survivors are usually left.

The degree and types of disabilities that result from haemorrhagic strokes vary dramatically, but as often as not, survivors tend not to be visibly disabled. Typically, we are left with varying degrees of hemiplegia,[3] aphasia,[4] and a pronounced tendency to tire easily. So, unless one is trained to recognize the signs, it can be hard to tell that someone is a survivor.

One might think that the relative invisibility of disabilities is a good thing, allowing as it does for survivors to participate in mainstream society and be treated just like everyone else. From the perspective of survivors, however, the invisibility of disabilities can be a mixed blessing.[5]

There's not a lot of literature about the lives and experiences of people, whether men or women, who've survived a haemorrhagic stroke.[6] On the one hand, I find this lack of attention amazing, since haemorrhagic strokes are actually so common. On the other hand, I find this unsurprising, since brain injury is not only extremely stigmatizing, but it is also extremely easy to (mis)interpret resulting disabilities in terms of personal inadequacy.

To appreciate why it's so easy to misunderstand brain injury, you might find it useful to know something about my own story. Because of my relatively young age when I had a haemorrhagic stroke, it often feels to me as though I've lived with disabilities my whole life.

Immediately following the stroke I went through about six months of intensive physical and occupational therapy, and regained about 75% of the physical abilities I had before the injury. I've never regained more than that and never will, and this is the usual case for people who have a haemorrhagic stroke. In fact, I was extremely lucky that I was as young as I was: my youth allowed me to recover relatively quickly.

By the time I returned to school, I was walking and using my body as well as I do now (even better, actually, since I had youthful energy to rely on). I was acutely aware of my disabilities in those days, everyone called them handicaps, though I don't think many others were aware of my difficulties. I think I was so aware of them for two reasons. The first had to do with my experience having been so recent, and the second had to do with my home life. Not only were my parents constantly reinforcing for me that I was handicapped, but my relationship with my younger sister had changed dramatically, so that we were not as close as we had been beforehand. Without these circumstances, I'm not sure that I would have been so aware of my disabilities. Maybe I've repressed it, but I don't remember reflecting on my lost abilities. I remember accepting my physical limitations, so that they quickly became part of my identity.

When I entered the paid labour force and was asked to fill out employment application forms, I always gave information about my handicaps. I didn't do this because I felt particularly handicapped, but my parents had so impressed upon me that I was handicapped, that I was just being honest. By my early 20s, though, I began to realize that when employers asked about handicaps, they were really asking about factors such as the ability to see or walk that could seriously impinge upon ability to fulfill employment duties in an unaccommodating workplace. I could type, take shorthand, answer the phone, and keep the files organized, and that was all that really mattered. They weren't really interested in my difficulties with fine motor skills or my poor balance. After all, I wasn't applying to be a waitress. So I stopped declaring my handicaps, and it didn't take long for me to stop thinking about myself as handicapped. My youthful energy meant that whatever difficulties I had could be easily masked. I became good at lying to myself.

When I was faced with difficulties that I could not ignore or that could not be masked, I thought of them in terms of my own personal inadequacies. Certainly I did not know anyone else who had been through what I had, and this made it a lot easier for me to castigate myself for my failings. It would be years before I would come across the feminist insight that "the personal is political," and even a few years more before I would apply that slogan to my own life with disabilities. To do that, to understand my personal troubles as originating in and exacerbated by political life, I needed to become acquainted with the disability rights movement and the feminist wing of that movement.

My growing political awareness took place within the context of living with my aging body, so that my disabilities were more and more impinging on my ability to negotiate daily life without effort. Along the way, I also acquired new disabilities such as arthritis, which can seriously impinge on my ability to engage in unaided mobility.

By the time I was in my mid-30s, I was primed for accepting and promoting a radical disability rights philosophy. Since then, I have grown increasingly frustrated with popular attitudes towards disability in general, and with the profound lack of awareness that exists about invisible disabilities in particular. I have, over the years, moved from seeing my own disabilities in terms of handicaps that made me not quite whole, to denying that I had any handicaps or disabilities at all, to finally embracing and even celebrating an identity as a woman with disabilities. It's a journey that I feel privileged to have had the opportunity to take.

For many years now, I have become angered when people praise me for "overcoming" my disabilities to earn my PhD and become a university professor. This attitude angers me because I know that my disabilities have made me who I am today. My achievements have happened not *in spite of* my disabilities, but *because of* my disabilities. Yet, I also know that I am extremely privileged to have disabilities that are not always obvious, and I frequently pass as able-bodied, even when I would rather not pass.

Over the years, I've become acutely conscious of the unusualness of my perspective on disability. Outside of the disability rights movement, I've come across very few people who understand my attitude. For the most part, when I say that I am proud to call myself a disabled woman, I could be speaking from the planet Neptune. The tragedy theory of disability is still hegemonic, and there's still a long way to go before the disability rights movement begins to permeate public consciousness in the same way as the feminist movement, for example, or the lesbian and gay movement to use another example.

There's an even longer way to go, it seems to me, before awareness of invisible disabilities begins to permeate public consciousness. Not many people can understand why someone who can hide her disabilities would want to claim them.

Yet I know, from personal experience, the tremendous costs of hiding. My disabilities are an important part of who I am, and anyone who refuses to acknowledge that is refusing to acknowledge me. Others may not always be able to see my disabilities, but they are always with me. And it is the very invisibility of my disabilities that can cause me the most difficulty. Because I don't fit normative conceptions of what someone who is disabled is supposed to look like, I find that others make all sorts of assumptions about what I can do. But because of my disabilities, I either cannot fulfill expectations, or else I must do so with a great deal of effort. Sure, it would be a lot easier if everyone would just accept that disability carries no particular "look." Invisibility is certainly a mixed blessing.

To give one more anecdote illustrating misunderstandings that can arise when dealing with invisible disability: during the fall of 1999 I underwent an operation to fix an ankle that had been causing me considerable pain for many years.[7] The problem was not directly related to my stroke, but in a roundabout way it was exacerbated by the disabilities I have as a result of the stroke. The ankle problem was a mostly invisible disability, so that acquaintances were generally shocked to learn about the operation. This reaction bothers me. To me, it implies that disability per se is shocking, something that one doesn't talk about in polite company. It feels like I'm being told that I am myself shocking. I feel set apart, as though I shouldn't really bring all of myself to everyday interaction.

It seems to me, though, that we'd all be better off if we started acknowledging that disability is part of the human experience, and just because someone doesn't "look" disabled, it doesn't mean that she can meet the taken-for-granted expectations of others. It seems to me that if we are to create communities that are truly caring, we'll stop "othering" those who can't, for whatever reason, meet the expectations of others. In my utopian world, no one makes assumptions about anyone else, and no one assumes that what you see will necessarily be what you get. A tall order, perhaps, but one that I think is well worth striving for.

Endnotes

1. Regarding the medical literature, my own investigation of the journal *Stroke*, which involved searching articles published between 1970 and 2000 for the keywords "haemorrhagic," "arteriovenous malformation," and "aneurysm," indicated a relative lack of interest in haemorrhagic strokes as compared to ischemic strokes. A similar search of the (US) National Institute of Health databases of funded research also shows that there is comparatively little research done on haemorrhagic strokes. Moreover, my selective review of abstracts of articles published in *Stroke* over the past 10 years indicates that it is common for researchers to use the term "stroke" when studying only ischemic strokes, and it is common for researchers to study only those over the age of 65. As well, at the National Stroke

Association's annual conference held in Toronto at the end of August 2000, paper presentations overwhelmingly focussed on the elderly survivors of ischemic strokes.

Regarding the social science literature, there is a wealth of information about elderly survivors of ischemic strokes (e.g., Anderson, 1988; Becker, 1993, 1994; Becker & Kaufman, 1995; Kaufman, 1988a, 1988b, 1988c; Pound et al., 1998), but compared to the medical literature, there is even less attention paid here to haemorrhagic stroke.

2. My own story is posted at: <http://www.westga.edu/~wmaples/stone.html>. It is important to keep in mind that this site is not about survivors of TBI, who have experiences that are in many respects quite different from those who survived haemorrhagic stroke. It is also important to recognize that this site is only accessible to those who have access to the internet and the patience to search for information. Thus, it does not replace information written on paper, and it is no contradiction to say that there is widespread silence about haemorrhagic strokes.

3. Paralysis of one side of the body. In my own case, the haemorrhage was located in the left hemisphere of my brain, leaving the entire right side of my body totally paralysed. With intensive physiotherapy, I regained part of my former abilities.

4. Difficulty with understanding spoken language and/or difficulty with verbally expressing one's thoughts. Interestingly, aphasics are usually well able to express themselves in writing.

5. Compared to what has been written by those with visible disabilities, there is little written about the experiences of those with invisible disabilities. First-person accounts of invisible disability that I have to varying degrees found to resonate with my own experiences include: Field (1993), Lloyd (1987), Peters (1993), Todoroff and Lewis (1992), and Todoroff (1993). My own reflections on living with invisible disabilities can be found in Stone (1990; 1993).

6. I am not aware of any stories written by or about women who had a childhood stroke, and there are few by women who were

adults at the time. Bonnie Sherr Klein's autobiographical story about her own haemorrhagic stroke (1997) is one of the few published accounts that exist. Klein's stroke happened when she was in her 40s and she was left with visible disabilities. As well, actress Patricia Neal was well into adulthood when she had a brain haemorrhage; her story can be found in Farrell (1969) and her autobiography (Neal, 1988).

7. I wore a cast for about 2 months and used a cane for a short while afterwards. As I write this almost a year later in late summer 2000, I find that I am still recovering from the operation in that I still experience occasional pain when walking. Yet, because I no longer show visible signs of disability, I find that others seem to expect that I am totally recovered.

References

[AAMS] Aneurysm and Arteriovenous Malformation Support: <http: /www.westga.edu:80/~wmaples/aneurysm.html>.

Acorn, S., & Offer, P. (eds.). (1998). *Living with Brain Injury: A Guide for Families and Caregivers.* Toronto, ON: University of Toronto Press.

Anderson, R. (1988). The quality of life of stroke patients and their carers. In R. Anderson & M. Bury (Eds.), *Living with chronic illness: The experience of patients and their families* (pp.14-42). London, UK: Unwin Hyman.

Becker, G. (1993). Continuity after a stroke: Implications for life-course disruption in old age. *The Gerontologist* 33(2), 148-58.

---.(1994). Age bias in stroke rehabilitation: Effects on adult status. *Journal of Aging Studies* 8, 271-290.

Becker, G., & Kaufman, S.R. (1995). Managing an uncertain illness trajectory in old age: Patients' and physicians' views of stroke. *Medical Anthropology Quarterly* 9(2), 165-187.

Biller, J., Toffol, G.J., Kassell, N.F., Adams Jr., H.P., Beck, D.W., & Boarini, D.J. (1987). Spontaneous subarachnoid hemorrhage in young adults. *Neurosurgery* 21(5), 664-667.

Broderick, J.P., Brott, T., Tomsick, T., Miller, R., & Huster, G. (1993). *Journal of Neurosurgery* 78 (February),188-191.

Farrell, B. (1969). *Pat and Roald*. New York, NY: Random House.

Field, J. (1993). Coming out of two closets. *Canadian Woman Studies* 13(4) (Special Issue: Women and Disability), 18-19.

Higenbottam, J. (1998). What is a brain injury? In S. Acorn, & P. Offer (Eds.), *Living with brain injury: A guide for families and caregivers* (pp. 7-19). Toronto, ON: University of Toronto Press.

Kaufman, S. R. (1988a). Stroke rehabilitation and the negotiation of identity. In S. Reinharz, & G.D. Rowles (Eds.), *Qualitative gerontology* (pp. 82-103). New York, NY: Springer.

---. (1988b). Toward a phenomenology of boundaries in medicine: Chronic illness experience in the case of stroke. *Medical Anthropology Quarterly* 2, 338-354.

---. (1988c). Illness, biography, and the interpretation of self following a stroke. *Journal of Aging Studies* 2, 217-227.

Klein, B. S. (1997). *Slow dance: A story of stroke, love, and disability*. Toronto, ON: Knopf.

Linge, F. R. (1990). Faith, hope, and love: Nontraditional therapy in recovery from serious head injury, a personal account. *Canadian Journal of Psychology* 44 (2), 116-129.

Lloyd, B-A. (1987). No longer silently disabled. *Healthsharing* 8(4), 26-28.

Mayo Clinic. (1995). Stroke. *Medical Essay* (a supplement to *Mayo Clinic Health Letter*): June.

Neal, P. (1988). *As I am: An autobiography*. New York, NY: Simon and Schuster.

Nochi, M. (1997). Dealing with the "void": Traumatic brain injury as a story. *Disability & Society* 12 (4), 533-555.

Peters, S. (1993). Having a disability "sometimes". *Canadian Woman Studies* 13 (4) (Special Issue: Women and Disability), 26-27.

Pound, P., Gompertz, P., & Ebrahim, S. (1998). Illness in the context of older age: The case of stroke. *Sociology of Health & Ilness* 20(4), 489-506.

Robbins, D. (1986). Stroke: A personal perspective. *Women & Health* 10(4), 9-31.

Stoler, D. R., & Albers Hill, B. (1998). *Coping with mild traumatic brain injury*. Garden City Park, NY: Avery Publishing Group.

Stone, S. D. (1990). My invisible disabilities. *Transition* (November), 3-4.

---. (1993). Must disability always be visible? *Canadian Woman Studies* 13 (4) (Special Issue: Women and Disability), 11-13.

Todoroff, M. (1993). 'You think I want to make fuck with you':
Travelling with a disability or two. *Canadian Woman Studies*
13(4) (Special Issue: Women and Disability), 28-30.

Todoroff, M., & Lewis, T. (1992). The personal and social
implications of 'passing' in the lives of women living with a
chronic illness or disability. In H. Stewart, B. Percival, & E. R.
Epperly (Eds.), *The more we get together: Women & disAbility*
(pp. 29-38). Charlottetown, PEI: gynergy books.

Webb, D. (1998). A 'revenge' on modern times: Notes on traumatic
brain injury. *Sociology* 32(3), 541-555.

How Sick is "Normal": Lifestyles of Chronically Ill Women

Diane Driedger
Winnipeg, Manitoba

Abstract

This paper will explore the barriers imposed by society on women with chronic illness, such as chronic fatigue, fibromyalgia, diabetes and colitis. Women in particular are called upon to fulfill many roles in society and some may contract stress-related illnesses. While people with other disabilities, such as paraplegia, blindness and deafness most often have stable health, this is not true of those who are chronically ill. So, not only does society not understand, neither does the traditional disability movement. Driedger has included the views of four Winnipeg women with physical chronic illnesses and will address how women's groups have contributed to some of the stigma associated with identifying barriers for women who have some of these illnesses. Recommendations on how society, the women's and disability movements need to adapt workplaces, families, and the pace of life will also be included.

Introduction

People don't like me when I'm sick. People don't like it when I have to change plans and not go out with them or come over because I am too tired or in too much pain. For seven years I've had fibromyalgia, a kind of arthritis of the muscles as I call it. Some friends have left, deciding that I was too hard to have as a friend. My family believed I didn't want to see them because sometimes I just could not leave the couch to visit.

For seven years I've dealt with the stigma of chronic illness. What does sick mean? I went to the disability movement where I had worked for 12 years – and found it doesn't like sick people either. Then I went to the women's movement where I had been involved almost as many years, and they don't like sick people there either.

I became determined to evaluate why our society does not like sick people. Who are chronically ill people? Those who have a continuing battle with sickness like AIDS, multiple sclerosis, fibromyalgia, chronic fatigue, diabetes, epilepsy, including four Winnipeg women with physical chronic illnesses that I have interviewed. This paper will also identify the barriers for women with chronic illness in society and how both the disability movement and the women's movement in Canada have contributed to the stigma. Finally, a new paradigm for living with sickness will be proposed.

Society's View

First, what does sickness mean in my life and the lives of other women? When a person is sick they are expected to play the "sick role." This means that the person who is sick is not responsible for everyday adult roles and activities. The person is not expected to work, care for others or to live an independent life. You are dependent physically and emotionally. You don't work because your role is to spend full time getting better. As Jim Derksen (1980) reinforces: "The 'patient' or 'sick' disabled person is allowed and even expected to behave in a child-like manner. Like a child, however, he must follow orders; in this case the orders of doctors and the agents and proxies of doctors"(p.5).

I've been doing that. I have visited this practitioner and that trying to get better. My poem (1999) "Give my Regrets" explains my feelings after a few years:

> I'm having a party
> of third parties
> you see they keep coming
> into my life
> the physio the acupuncturist the herbalist
> the GP too
>
> it's called see my body
> it's not quite right
> pin your tail on
> the diagnosis
>
> it's a formal affair
> I'm usually dressed
> in a paper gown
> with a slit
> in the back
>
> no need to call ahead

just show up
with several others in tow
ready to give a second opinion

I have found that if three years pass and you're still not better there is hell to pay. Your family maybe doesn't believe you. Many women with chronic illness report that their families just think they are doing this to avoid them, that they are not really sick, that it's all in their heads. After all, "you look so good." The medical profession may not believe you if they can't cure you. Their role is to get it done – you are a bad patient if you don't get well.

Basically, chronically ill people are on their own – there is no formula for living with chronic illness, surprising because our technology has ensured that we will live longer and with more chronic illness: AIDS, MS, Fibro, cancer, diabetes, high blood pressure etc.

Society Sees Work as God

Society wor(k)ships hard work and productivity. As a chronically ill person you may not be able to work like you did before or maybe not at all, or maybe it changes with your health. You have the added stigma of being seen as lazy and unproductive.

The problem is that the capitalist system was founded on the productivity of workers. Sick and disabled people, may not be able to produce what "normals" do, as Marta Russell (1998) says in *Beyond Ramps: Disability at The End of the Social Contract*: "In capitalist jargon we become part of that immoral concept, the surplus population in company with the elderly, the unskillled, those injured on the job . . ."(p.61).

Why are sick people immoral? Russell states that "we in America have come to equate morality with financial productivity and immorality with laziness or non-productivity"(p.61). Of course, this comes from the owning classes' definition of productivity that our society buys into and operates upon.

As a Mennonite with an ingrained work ethic, I know that lying on the couch to rest periodically is not acceptable. Andreas Schroeder (1999) writes about this in his short story, "Eating My Father's Island":

> His daughters 'danced around on his nose', everybody knew that, and this wife spent most of her life in bed another decidedly un-Mennonite trait so their garden was always

choked with weeds and their herd records in disarray. In fact, most people visited the Sawatskys just to feel better about their own neat farms. (p. 39)

Survival of the fittest is indeed the case. Luckily the social welfare state in Canada has mediated this through social supports for people with disabilities and those with chronic illness. These efforts have been realized by disabled persons, their parents and advocates, especially since the Second World War. But the system has been eroding since the 1980's, as Barbara Murphy (1999) reiterates in *The Ugly Canadian: The Rise and Fall of a Caring Society:*

We blame unemployment on the unemployed, the aging population on the elderly, and the demand for health care on people who are so anxious to sit for hours in doctors' waiting rooms that they make appointments even when they don't need them . . . We see nothing on the horizon to disturb our new value system.(p.133)

Society: Sick People and Sickness are not Beautiful

Another barrier for people with chronic illness is that sickness is seen as a prelude to death – and we are a death-defying culture. We are at dis-ease with death and the disintegration and aging of the body. We are a youth culture. As Victoria, a woman who has experienced irritable bowel syndrome says, "Because we have so much fear surrounding the body we also tend to separate and segregate those who are ill whether it be in hospitals or organizations."

People do not want to be like chronically ill people. Perhaps it is catching of course, most chronic illnesses are not.

The Disability Movement's View of Chronically Ill People

Quite simply, the disability movement does not like sick people. Marilyn, who has had diabetes since childhood, says of her involvement in the disability movement:

People with disabilities are really loathe to be perceived as sickly. There is a view that there is a lack of independence for a sick person and even to make decisions about your life direction. So they don't want to align themselves with sick people. But they can't say that in the movement. But it is subtle, especially in how they schedule meetings, not respecting people's fluctuating energy levels. They just don't have the patience to be flexible. The person with a physical limitation that is stable says, 'Hey, I can still function in the world what's your problem?'

I know that as a person who went from being temporarily able-bodied (a TAB) to being chronically ill, my experience was of marginalization in the movement. The message was that the "real" issues are of people in wheelchairs and to some extent blind persons and then those with invisible disabilities.

Sickness is denied in the movement. The movement's leaders have always decried the supercrip image: they are not superhuman because they live like everyone else. But, in reality the supercrip image is upheld, especially by most leaders whose adage is: work till you drop. The expectation is that if you are dedicated to the movement you will sacrifice your health to it.

To come in to work when you are sick is a badge of honour. But, here is the difference: many people with mobility impairments have a stable disability, so they can come in with a cold and still function. Someone with a chronic illness, who has the same cold, will be floored for a whole week in bed if they come into work and do not look after themselves. Chronically ill persons in the movement are said to not be trying hard enough and this has been my own experience.

Generally recognized in the disability movement in Canada is that if there is an informal hierarchy of disability in the movement the stars are those in wheelchairs. This opinion is held in a movement that has said for 20 years that it wants to speak in a unified voice, representing all people with disabilities, because then we are stronger. Yes, we will be when all are included.

The disability movement has advocated that all must have access to jobs, but the reality is that some disabled people with chronic illness may not be well enough to ever work a part-time job, let alone a full-time job. There are, of course, many disabled persons who can. The disability movement, again, has wanted to divorce itself from its nonproductive members, who may cast a bad light on the productivity of other disabled persons.

The Women's Movement

The women's movement has historically had the same view as the disability movement: we must be strong as women, show no weakness. We can fit in, with supports such as proper day care, but there is no acknowledgement of women who are sick.

This would cast a pall of weakness over all women. In the women's movement, again, you must be dedicated and this means bone-crushing fatiguing work . . . the enemy is always out there! We must be vigilant!

Marilyn, who has diabetes, says of her women's movement involvement:

> The women's movement really worships strong women. There's a revulsion for anyone sick or weak. Those not able to weather every storm are excluded from the circle . . . the 'I can't make it today because I'm not well,' doesn't work with them.

Grace, a woman with several chronic illnesses adds,

> I still feel the women in the women's movement feel they have to be superwomen. They're always looking for women with lots of energy. If you're in the women's movement, you'd better be able to do lots of work or don't bother.

The women's movement has also glorified the experience of the body, not the beauty myth of society, but it's own emphasis on owning your body and feeling it entirely. Susan Wendell (1996), in her book *The Rejected Body,* reiterates that the feminist movement has not wanted to transcend the body, due to traditional theology that devalues the body, especially women's. This is a male fear of being merged with matter. Wendell states, "feminists have also argued that the dominant forms of Christian theology . . . represent the body as a major source of the desires and weaknesses that lead to sin, and overcoming the body as an essential ingredient in moral perfection" (p.165).

Wendell points out that most feminist theory does not recognize another motive for wanting to transcend the body, that is pain and illness of chronically ill women like herself who has chronic fatigue. Women with chronic illness need to go on and not wallow in all the workings and meanings of our bodies because it can be a source of frustration, suffering and even torment; it may never reach our expectations and certainly not those of society and the industrial machine.

Wendell further points out that she has to overcome the chronic pain of her body to do anything, like writing an article, adding that "when [she] began to develop the ability to observe [her] symptoms and reduced [her] identification with the transient miseries of [her] body, [she] was able to reconstruct [her] life" (p.175).

A New Paradigm of Living

How then do we deal with women who are chronically ill in society, the disability and women's movements? There needs to be a new paradigm of living: sickness and disease are part of life, and this means we must also accept that death is part of life to get over the fear.

Wendell says that we must begin to talk about bodies that are full of pain. We should not just glorify and celebrate women's bodies, although that needs to be done too.

The experiences of all women need to be recognized in the women's movement and sometimes women who are chronically ill will request accommodations such as longer rest breaks, maybe a couch at the office, maybe the request to work at home, maybe more breaks at meetings to rest.

In the disability movement the same kinds of accommodations need to be made. The image of supercrip has been decried for years, but for a lot of disabled people that's just lip service, because they believe they must push themselves to measure up in the movement, to pull their weight and to work like everyone else and those who don't do that are a black eye on the movement.

Part of being human is weakness; when we face up to that we will become a more caring and inclusive world. As Jean Vanier (1998) says in *Becoming Human*:

> A society based on the Darwinian 'survival of the fittest', where we are to fend for ourselves, has serious disadvantage. It promotes a strong, aggressive attitude, and the need to win. It can paralyse the development of the heart, prevent healthy cooperation among people, and promote rivalry and enmity. It tends to marginalise those who are weak and even those who reject individualistic principles and want to live in and for a society based on truth and justice for all.(p.51)

Indeed, a society that includes and acknowledges the worth of ill people will be truly human.

References

Blackford, K. A.(1993).Feminizing the Multiple Sclerosis Society of Canada. *Canadian Woman Studies*, 13, 124-128.

Derksen, J. (1980). *The disabled consumer movement: Policy implications for rehabilitation service provisions.* Winnipeg: COPOH.

Driedger, D. (1989). *The last civil rights movement: Disabled Peoples' International.* London and New York: Hurst and St. Martin's.

Driedger, D. (1999). *The Mennonite madonna.* Charlottetown: gynergy books.

Driedger, D. (1999). Interviews with four women with chronic illness in Winnipeg, Fall.

Israel, P. & Odette, F. (1993). The Disabled Women's Movement: 1983 to 1993. *Canadian Woman Studies*, 13 , 6-8.

Lyons, R. F. & Meade, L.D. (1993). The energy crisis: Mothers with chronic illness. *Canadian Woman Studies*, 13, 34-37.

Marris, V. (1996). *Lives worth living: Women's experience of chronic illness.* London: Harper Collins Publishers.

Murphy, B. (1999). *The ugly Canadian: The rise and fall of a caring society.* Winnipeg: J. Gordon Shillingford Publishing.

Russell, M.(1998). *Beyond ramps: Disability at the end of the social contract.* Monroe, Maine: Common Courage Press.

Sontag, S. (1988). *Illness as metaphor and AIDS and its metaphors.* New York: Doubleday.

Stone, S. D. (1993). Must disability always be visible? The meaning of disability for women. *Canadian Woman Studies,* 13, 11-13.

Stone, S. D. (1992). Notes toward a unified diversity. In H. Stewart, B. Percival & E. R. Epperly (Eds.), *The more we get together: Women and dis/ability* (pp.21-28). Chartottetown: gynergy books.

Todoroff, M. & Lewis, T.(1992). The personal and social implications of 'passing' in the lives of women living with a chronic illness or disability. In H. Stewart, B. Percival & E. R. Epperly (Eds), *The more we get together: Women and dis/ability* (pp.29-38). Charlottetown: gynergy books.

Vanier, J. (1998). *Becoming human.* Toronto: House of Anansi Press.

Wendell, S. (1996). *The rejected body: Feminist philosophical reflections on disability.* New York: Routledge.

Attention Deficit Disorder:
Is it a deficit? Is it a disorder?
Women university students' experience

Sonya Corbin Dwyer
Regina, Saskatchewan

Abstract

This paper presents the experience of eight women university students diagnosed with Attention Deficit Disorder (ADD) in their own voices. In themes emergent from the data, the women question many issues including: when symptoms become an impairment; how people with 'real' ADD can be distinguished from those who do not 'have' it; how distinctions between 'abnormal' and 'different' can be addressed; what the focus on weaknesses instead of strengths, the negative rather than the positive really means; how the blame is placed on the individual for not fitting into society's expectations; and what the effects of being given a label are. The women in this study also question the terms "deficit" and "disorder" in the label Attention Deficit Disorder, but did not challenge the term "attention". "Attention" is not a pejorative. Finally, these issues are addressed in the context of whether this label promotes a healthy lifestyle and creates caring communities.

Introduction

This paper is based on my doctoral research in the study of adult women diagnosed with Attention Deficit Disorder (ADD) (Corbin Dwyer, 1998). I chose adult women for my research because the number of females being diagnosed with ADD is rising and most research has been conducted on male children. This discrepancy has resulted in limited understanding of the disorder in other populations, particularly females and adults (Schaughency, McGee, Raja, Feehan, & Silva, 1994). Some practitioners recognize that women with ADD have different experiences than men with this disorder because of the socio-political context in which they live (e.g., Solden, 1995; Nadeau, 1996). Current information about women who are diagnosed with ADD is primarily anecdotal, based on clinical observation. This study is an attempt to begin to address this need for more information about women's experience of ADD.

Before proceeding, the terms ADD and AD/HD (Attention-Deficit Hyperactivity Disorder) require clarification as both are currently used by clinicians, often interchangeably. Brown (1995) noted that it was not until the publication of the DSM-III in 1980 and the inclusion of the term Attention Deficit Disorder that this disorder (or the label "ADD") could be used with children with and without hyperactivity. When the DSM-III-R was published in 1987, there was a lack of research to support the notion that the disorder may occur without hyperactivity. As a result, the diagnosis was re-named Attention-Deficit Hyperactivity Disorder (AD/HD). The diagnosis used to indicate the presence of ADD 'without hyperactivity' was replaced by Undifferentiated ADD. This new label had no diagnostic criteria, thus raised questions about the validity of such a diagnosis. Since that time, many research studies have documented this disorder with and without hyperactivity and, as a result, three subtypes of AD/HD are listed in the DSM-IV (APA, 1994). The three subtypes are Predominantly Inattentive Type, Predominantly Hyperactive/ Impulsive Type and Combined Type. There is also a variability of degree of impairment (as perceived by self and others) among people with these three types.

Keeping this preliminary background of ADD in mind, I will introduce the eight participants in my study; outline one of the themes arising from my interviews with them; and, look at some of the implications of the theme for developing caring communities.

Participants

In this study, eight university women were interviewed using a qualitative research methodology. All of the participants in this study used the term ADD, therefore this term is used throughout the paper to reflect its use by the women. Some demographic details, as well as the topics that pertain to each woman's individual experience are described in what follows.

- Robin

Robin was 25 years old, a third year, undergraduate student. In the year prior to the first interview, she was diagnosed with dyslexia and ADD, the characteristics of which she viewed as one and the same. As a child, Robin was hyperactive but she had since grown out of the hyperactivity. Thinking of her diagnoses as more of a learning style, she was concerned about the accuracy of the term "Attention-Deficit/Hyperactivity Disorder". She disliked the label because of the negative connotations of having a "disorder", preferring instead to explore her strengths and weaknesses rather than simply use a label.

- Dagny

Dagny, at age 21 was in her fourth year of an undergraduate degree. She was diagnosed with ADD at the age of six, although she did not personally become aware of it until about age eighteen. Growing up, she came to the conclusion she was stupid because it would take her twice as long as her peers to complete her work and her work would not be as 'good' as her peers. She became discouraged and passive, but noted that she grew out of both traits. She described herself as a private person and commented that her mother did not know how much she struggled in high school because she retreated to her room rather than talk to her mother about her situation.

- LJ

LJ was in her mid-thirties. At the time of the first interview, she had been diagnosed with ADD for about a year and was a university student taking some graduate courses as an unclassified student. She had already earned two undergraduate degrees, one of which was a professional degree. After completing the second degree, LJ was employed in her field. In retrospect, she said she chose to quit this job because of the ADD symptoms, although she was unaware that she had the disorder at the time.

- Michelle

Michelle was 37 years old and was diagnosed with ADD within a few months prior to the first interview. She described herself as having a "sporadic, interrupted university career." Michelle went to university after high school but did not achieve the high marks she had expected based on her secondary school training. This experience caused her to question her ability and generate possible explanations. Michelle thought that since she was a woman of colour, that perhaps her high school teachers had pushed her through, not wanting to be perceived as discriminatory, a type of reverse discrimination. She dropped out of university after one and a half years and worked in a variety of jobs that she did not enjoy, for approximately two years. She then went back to university and completed an undergraduate degree. After applying to one graduate program and not getting accepted, Michelle obtained a summer job and returned to university to improve her marks in order to get into a professional faculty. She was not accepted into this faculty and went to work full-time. She decided she really did not enjoy the work and returned to university again to upgrade her marks. She was completing this second degree when we initially talked.

- Christine

Christine was a forty-one year old, divorced single-mother of two children; both diagnosed with ADD. She was in her fifth year of an undergraduate degree. She was diagnosed with ADD about three years prior to the initial interview, as a result of her children being diagnosed. She described her initial reaction to her diagnosis as feeling overwhelmed and devastated, as well as feeling guilty that her children inherited the disorder from her. She did research on ADD for a course she took in university and this research helped put things into perspective for her. She had come to terms with the diagnosis and tried to focus on the positive, while acknowledging the negative aspects to ADD symptoms. She said that it is sometimes easier to blame things on the ADD than it is to take responsibility for them.

- Suzie

Suzie was 20 years old, in her second year of university and had been diagnosed with ADD when she was sixteen. The diagnosis facilitated a deeper self-understanding of her actions and motivations and also helped Suzie to change her behaviour. Initially, Suzie was not aware that ADD affected areas of her life other than learning. She had always had and continued to have social difficulties, particularly with relationships and making friends. Possessing a quick temper, she reacted quickly to others but sometimes her interpretation of their actions was inaccurate. She realized that she reacts impulsively to others and her parents, her main support system, were helping her become more aware of these situations.

- Dawn

Dawn was in her mid-twenties and her second year of university. She was diagnosed with ADD a year before we met. Initially, Dawn did not think she was smart enough for university but she wanted to prove to herself that she was. She found that she studied all of the time and had no social life. Although Dawn worked really hard and got 'B's, she thought she was not living up to her potential and could do better.

- Sue

Sue was in her late forties and was a divorced single mother of two children. She was diagnosed with ADD a couple of years ago after her oldest child was diagnosed with the disorder. Sue completed an undergraduate degree in the mid-1970s and had just returned to university where she was enrolled in a diploma program. She was really enjoying university this time as she understood herself and her needs better because of the diagnosis. For example, she found that her hands did not move quickly enough to keep up with her thoughts and now had strategies to deal with this issue. As well, during her first degree, Sue spent all of her time studying, having to work ten times harder than her peers but back then she did not know why.

From three interviews with these eight women, the following theme emerged: Is ADD a deficit or a disorder? In the following sections the question will be examined more closely, as there is more to unravel than may be apparent at first glance.

ADD: Is it a Deficit?

Michelle:
> The kinds of reactions . . . caused me to reflect on whether or not it's a deficit. We think of these kinds of things as drawbacks or disabilities or deficits and I guess I kind of question whether or not that's a valid way to look at it or not . . . I mean, is this a manufactured deficit or is it really a . . . deficit?

Scholten (1997) coined the term 'Attention Deluxe Dimension' because as she describes it, the symptoms of ADD relate to an abundance of attention rather than a deficit of attention. She points out that in certain situations, people diagnosed with ADD may 'look' as though they are inattentive when, in fact they were actually attending to a number of different things at the same time. Furthermore, she believes in matching people's natural abilities to environments which allow them to develop their potential.

ADD: Is it a Disorder?

According to the dictionary, the term 'disorder' is defined as "an abnormal mental condition" (Merriam-Webster, 1993). While deviating from the norm or from the average does not necessarily mean that something is unfavourable, the connotations of "an abnormal mental condition" are quite negative. As well, the issue of whether all of the characteristics that come under the term 'ADD' are a deficiency or impairment was raised by some of the women in my study.

Some questioned the appropriateness of the label:

Robin: I think it's important to look at the strengths and weaknesses and ask yourself whether it's a disorder or not . . . I think they're just going about it the wrong way. The way they're perceiving it is as a disorder and they're not going to find the answer because I don't think it is.

LJ: I see it as an impairment but I'm not sure how much of an impairment it is.

Dawn: The scale is just so wide . . . I definitely have some signs of ADD but I don't think I have the severe ones.

ADD in the Broader Social Context: ADD as a Socially Constructed Phenomenon

Robin: For the first time in my life, I'm realizing that I do things differently, like little different learning styles than the norm. It never occurred to me that not everyone could do that.

Michelle:
        It's not that I have doubts about whether or not I exhibit these kinds of behaviours and characteristics so much as resisting the psychiatric categorization...being aware of the implications behind some of the questions that are

asked…the implications of those questions are that it's wrong to do that.

In her discussion of feminist philosophical reflections on disability, Wendell (1996) raises a number of topics which speak directly to the issues brought forth by women diagnosed with ADD. I offer them here as questions to consider: Is there a culturally neutral definition of disability? How much physical/mental suffering is inherent in the difference itself, i.e., how much suffering could *not* be eliminated by any social arrangements, no matter how supportive they might be to the lives of people with these differences? Is the drive to find 'cures' for disabilities an attempt to wipe out difference? Can we, should we, how do we perfect nature and humanity?

"Cures" . . . for what?

Physical and/or mental differences are usually perceived as 'abnormality' or 'pathology' and consequently, cures are typically sought (Wendell, 1996); ADD is no different. There is much emphasis on 'cures'(typically called 'treatment') but little recognition of the potential and value of these people's lives. The message that some of these women heard was that they were not good enough until they were 'cured.' Such a message places the self-respect of people with ADD in conflict with any desire to be treated; they may want improved marks and social skills but how does this fit with the attitude that they need to be treated/cured? Having ADD is a part of who they are . . . so does this mean they are not whole, are defective? Wendell (1996) suggests that the search for treatment is accompanied by insulting implications.

Does This Label Promote a Healthy Lifestyle?

Michelle:

> [Giving the person a label is] almost like blaming the individual when they don't fit into the norm that is expected. We tend to be one of those societies that looks at **individual** accomplishments and **individual** responsibility…The person who functions best with communal support in order to live becomes this special need.

When thinking about the question "does this label promote a healthy lifestyle?", the women's questioning of whether ADD is a disorder or a deficit is of key importance. The label focuses on the negative symptoms by containing those two words, "disorder" and "deficit," and must be considered in this light. The purpose of this label appears to be to place the blame on the individual and exonerate all others, where society plays a role in creating and maintaining the concept of ADD.

Michelle:
> Why does everyone have to fit into one definition of 'normal?

Robin: I think the way schools are set up is really damaging to someone with so-called ADD . . . because they tend to process things differently and they do want to have things more hands on . . . It's sort of like the other way around — if [people without the diagnosis of ADD] were to learn in an atmosphere that was set up for someone with ADD . . . all of a sudden they would have the disorder and they probably wouldn't pay attention either.

Some of the women addressed the negative aspects of the diagnosis directly:

Sue: Who wants to know that they have ADD? There's too much negative literature out there.

Dawn: There's still a stigma about ADD and I'd just rather not go through that . . . I don't really tell a lot of people . . . I pretty much keep it to myself and to my family.

Other women spoke of the general population's lack of information, or misinformation, about ADD:

Dagny: Do you tell people because unless you know someone else has it, you're going to get the same idea — 'you don't have it, you're just lazy.'

The women also discussed how they 'redefined' themselves after getting the diagnosis, and label, of ADD. In light of this new information, they were able to put their characteristics in context. This is an important issue to explore when considering whether the label promotes a healthy lifestyle that was addressed by most of the women:

Michelle: The diagnosis has helped me in some ways because it makes me stop thinking that there's some internal character moral flaw that I have.

Christine: It didn't happen overnight — it took me a long time to get where I'm at, to feel good about being me and feel okay about having faults and having ADD and it's not the end of the world.

Sue: It was traumatic at first but now the news is really empowering . . . because I now understand why I do the things I do and why I have done the things I've done and it's really putting things into perspective for me.

Dagny: That's helped a lot with self-esteem — just being aware that I'm different and that I'm not slow.

Dawn: The fact that if this is what I have gives me a little relief in that I'm not an idiot . . . that I can do it but this is the reason why I'm having such a hard time doing it.

LJ: [A diagnosis] definitely would have made a difference in terms of emotional mental health because I think there would be less guilt . . . you'd understand what was going on rather than blaming yourself or having others blame you for not being typical and normal.

Implications for Creating Caring Communities

What are the implications of questioning whether ADD is a deficit or a disorder? In the following section, three areas are considered so that we may help create caring communities: focusing on strengths, embracing diversity and differences, and valuing cooperation and collaboration.

- Focusing on Strengths

Robin: I think you need to recognize the negative aspects of all things but emphasize the strengths because that's really important—for someone to believe that they are capable of doing things and that they do have a lot of potential and how they can build on that strength because so much of it goes unrecognized.

People diagnosed with ADD are often seen in terms of their deficits. If caring communities are to be created, individuals need to be seen for their strengths. Since the label focusses on weaknesses, these individuals' strengths are often invisible to others and even to themselves. 'Treatment' tends to focus on deficit areas, but as one woman pointed out "You still have strengths and just because you have this one set back, you do have other strengths . . . work within these strengths, work within your parameters".

- Embracing Diversity and Differences

Dagny: How many people want to admit they're different?

As a caring community, we need to be willing to learn about and respect ways of being and forms of consciousness that are unfamiliar...including cooperative and collaborative ways of accomplishing tasks rather than methods which emphasize independence and autonomy. We need to seek out and respect the knowledge and perspectives of people with disabilities. We need to give up the quest for perfection (Wendell, 1996). We need to focus on strengths, rather than weaknesses, what a person *can do*, not what they cannot do. The women in this study learned to embrace their differences.

> Dagny: You've got low self-esteem because you're not normal. I mean, I hate to say 'normal' and unusual or weird or different, because I see them as differences—it should be different, it shouldn't be a wrong or a right . . . I've learned over time to change my perception and that's helped a lot with self-esteem—a lot!
>
> Robin: I guess that's how I perceive it, more as a learning style, and I try not to emphasize so much having a disorder because how would you have any confidence to do anything? I don't think I would get through university if I was so worried about having a disorder . . . whether I have a disorder or not, it doesn't matter—it's more how I

perceive it and how I can deal with it.

Further, the women in this study even began to question whether the label even encapsulates the phenomenon of ADD and the experience of ADD.

- Valuing Cooperation and Collaboration

Caring communities would also value different approaches to accomplishing tasks. In conjunction with an emphasis on independence and autonomy, collaborative methods would be appreciated and rewarded. Instead of concentrating on how to cure or 'treat' individuals diagnosed with ADD, caring communities would support these individuals' strengths and learning preferences. Ways to support the learners could include teaching effective communication skills for all people and all styles and offering peer and cross-age tutoring and cooperative learning experiences in both school and work settings.

As members of caring communities, we need to be aware of people 'disconnecting' from our communities because of shame/guilt over not fulfilling society's expectations, as well as embarrassment (e.g., over their lack of organization). Listening to the voices of individuals with differences is an essential foundation for building a more inclusive future; these women remind us that we all need to be treated as individuals.

Summary

This paper explored the label "Attention Deficit Disorder" from the perspectives of eight women with the diagnosis of ADD. Many questions regarding its accuracy were raised. When the question of whether the label promoted a healthy lifestyle was examined, the women talked about the negative focus of the label including the blame it places on the individual while exonerating all others. However, the label has also allowed the women to redefine who they are because it offered new information. Implications for creating caring communities included the importance of focussing on strengths, embracing diversity and differences and cooperating and collaborating.

References

American Psychiatric Association. (1994). Attention-deficit and disruptive behaviour disorders. *Diagnostic and statistical manual of mental disorders (4th ed.).* (pp. 78-85). Washington, DC: Author.

Brown, T. E. (1995). Differential diagnosis of ADD versus ADHD in adults. In K. G. Nadeau (Ed.), *A comprehensive guide to Attention Deficit Disorder in adults: Research, diagnosis, treatment* (pp. 93-108). New York: Brunner/Mazel Pub.

Corbin Dwyer, S. L. (1998). *The experience of women university students diagnosed with Attention-Deficit Disorder.* Unpublished doctoral dissertation, The University of Calgary, Calgary, Alberta, Canada.

Nadeau, K. G. (1996). *Adventures in fast forward: Life, love and work for the ADD adult.* New York: Brunner/Mazel, Pub.

Schaughency, E., McGee, R., Raja, S., Feehan, M., & Silva, P. (1994). Self-reported inattention, impulsivity and hyperactivity at ages 15 and 18 years in the general population. *Journal of the American Academy of Child and Adolescent Psychiatry, 33* (2), 173-184.

Solden, S. (1995). *Women with Attention Deficit Disorder: Embracing disorganization at home and in the workplace.* Grass Valley, California: Underwood Books.

Wendell, S. (1996). *The rejected body: Feminist philosophical reflections on disability.* New York: Routledge.

Structural Barriers to the Advancement of Women with Disabilities in a Mid-sized Japanese City

Ryoko Yanagihara
Toyamo, Japan

Abstract

Rocco House Toyamo Community Work Shop for the disabled is a special community project in Japan that started in 1979 with the idea that disabled persons have a right to live in mainstream society and not be shunned in institutions. In this study Yanagihara shows that in advanced nations we are moving away from the idea of large institutions yet the contrary exists in Japan. Little or no government funding is available to house the disabled in an area where they can live freely and enjoy the same basic rights as the rest of society.

Problems Confronting People With Disabilities in the Local Cities

Toyama City, the prefectural capital, has a population of 320,000 people and is situated alongside the Sea of Japan. Racco House Toyama Community Work Shop for the Disabled started 11 years ago with 2 mildly intellectually disabled people and one staff member in a small house close to the centre of Toyama City.

In 1979, the Japanese Government established compulsory education systems for severely disabled children. Following this, the parents of those disabled children began the next movement. This movement was based on the observation that after basic public education was obtained, disabled people would need to continue to learn social skills in order to be affiliated into their communities. Parents individually organized small workshops for their children in their respective communities.

Since then 20 years have passed and there are now about 5000 workshops for people with disabilities in Japan. They are not completely sustained by governmental funds; therefore, the funds are raised from outside donations and other fund raising activities. In Toyama City, before Racco House started, people with severe disabilities didn't have the right to choose where they would like to live after graduating from school. The government decided they had to live in large institutions or hospitals. After Racco House started, they were granted the right (small as it was) to live with their family.

Now, Racco House has grown to include 23 disabled people who have severe intellectual and/or physical disabilities, and 5 staff members. Out of 23 disabled people, 14 of them suffer from cerebral palsy (C.P.) and 4 of them suffer from severe intellectual disabilities which they have had since birth. The other 5, suffer from severe intellectual and/or physical disabilities due to accidents which occurred during childhood. Due to their various conditions, they had to be placed into special institutions, where were hospitals, training centres and special schools, until they were 18 years of age. As a result of this, their knowledge of the world; their relationships with other people; their social experiences and their social skills are severely lacking. I believe, these special and often segregated upbringing, made their disabilities seem even more profound.

We, at Racco House, have spoken with general public and with local government officials about the idea of "normalization." The idea of "normalization" is that anyone has a right to live in a mainstream society. However, if the disabled people are lacking in social skills or social manners, the general public would not acknowledge them as the members of that community Therefore, we teach them basic social skills, social manners and common sense.

Currently, in Toyama City, if severely disabled people desire to live in a community, there is no other option than to live with family (particularly parents), there are no small group homes that are equipped with personal 24 hour service. Therefore, the only option available to parents who are not able to personally look after their children, is a large institution. Racco House is trying to lessen the burden placed upon the parents by providing a more in-depth service.

At the moment, Racco House provides such services as a bathing, physiotherapy, respite care, emergency service, a holiday community access service, etc. Some people may also wish to live by themselves or in small group homes, so we are teaching them more useful independent living skills, for example, how to control their own health and other beneficial habits. For now, we need to prepare for 24 hour services. However, now we are receiving no assistance from the government for these services, and we often appeal to them for the creation of such a program.

Within more advanced nations, such as Northern European

Countries, America, Canada, and Australia, the larger institutions have closed down completely or their numbers are decreasing. In Japanese cities, such as Tokyo and Osaka, the movement on behalf of the disabled people is growing. Therefore, in these areas, 24 hour services is available and the number of disabled people living on their own is beginning to increase. However, the number of large institutions is continuing to grow throughout Japan; moreover, the popular opinion is still for disabled people to live in isolation apart from mainstream society. In short, the local government, the general public, and even the people with disabilities themselves, do not recognize the importance of the need for human rights for disabled people.

Racco House upholds the following two principles and the local government and society are presently being informed. One is that all people, even those with severe disabilities, have the right to live freely in society with the least restrictions possible. The other important principle is those people should be able to live a safe, comfortable and productive life enjoying the same basic human rights as the rest of society. In order to create this kind of society, there are two considerations. First, it is imperative to improve public facilities and services such as roads, public transport and building access. Also, service providers and resources must be developed along with additional resources which are accessible to everyone. Secondly, there must be an increase in the numbers and quality of human resources available and provide 24 hour services.

The Problems Facing Females Who Have a Disability Living in Local Cities

In Toyama City, where is a particularly strong conservative trend; not only women with disabilities, but also the general public don't fully comprehend the issue of discrimination. Most people are not even conscious of the fact that discrimination of women is occurring in the general community at all.

Within Japanese institutions, there is no law that supports human rights. I have heard of some ill treatment occurring in some of the larger Japanese institutions, such as cases of disabled females being surgically sterilized, but since these incidents were never publicly published, they may have been nothing more than rumours. Also, another problem is that the number of females with disabilities is about the same as that of males.

However, in places such as Racco House, where the focus is on social skills, the number of disabled males is vastly greater than disabled females. In fact, 80%, or 18 members, at Racco House, are male. Most disabled females and their families believe that disabled females belong in the home, hidden from society.

Japan is still a male-dominated society. Toyama City also still sets maternal roles for its women. Men are taught to play the "role" of the male, women are taught to obey men. These "roles" are rampant throughout Japan, making it next to impossible to step out of these "roles." During the post World War II era, the Japanese government created programs to enhance the equality between men and women, such as in politics, employment, education, and voting. Recently, local city governments have held conferences discussing the role of women in Japanese society. I'm sure it will take some time to change the over all view of Japanese women in society.

Finally, in the conservative local cities, the females with disabilities suffer dual discrimination. Firstly, because they are disabled, and secondly, because they are female.

Conclusion

In this paper I have presented two topics. The first topic broadly relating to people with severe disabilities in a particular small Japanese city and secondly, that of disabled females. These two groups of people have one basic common problem — that being, the lack of human rights found in local cities in Japan. Japan is one of the foremost economically strong countries in the world. However, as a whole, Japan appears to set a very low priority for raising community awareness and for establishing and maintaining a policy relating to human rights issues for all people.

In conclusion, it is my belief that the Japanese people do not fully understand the concept of what a democracy is. Social welfare leads to human rights and a democratic society that demand strong social welfare leadership. Therefore, Japanese people must redirect their focus and pay more attention to human rights for everyone. I believe firmly that if disabled women in Japan (particularly in local cities) are able to participate and be seen as productive members of society, then positive attitudes towards these women would be fostered amongst the general community. This outcome would determine future direction, priorities and shared responsibility for policy makers in

Japan. This being established, Japanese policies can be brought in line with the other more progressive countries in the world concerning the issue of basic human rights.

About the Editors and Contributors

The Contributors

. . . . Armstrong, Pat

Pat is a professor of sociology and director of the School of Canadian Studies at Carleton University. For over twenty years, she has been focussing on women and work, women's work in the health care field, pay equity and other state policies that have an impact on women. She is a strong believer in activist politics and collective work. Her publications have been done with others and with change in mind.

. . . . Barlow, Maude

Political activist, author and policy critic, Maude Barlow is an outspoken crusader for Canadian sovereignty and citizens rights. She is founding co-chair of the Action Canada Network, National Chairperson of The Council of Canadians, a non-profit non-partisan public interest organization supported by more than 100,000 members. She has served as a senior management consultant on employment equity and social justice to all levels of government. In 1991, she was the only Canadian on an international women's peace mission to Iraq on the eve of the Golf War.

. . . . Bernier, Christiane

Professeure au département de sociologie à l'Université Laurentienne depuis 1991. Elle s'intéresse particulièrement aux problématiques touchant les femmes et la famille francophone, la question de l'analphabétisme en Ontario français, ainsi qu'une orientation vers une analyse de l'épistémologie féministe contemporaine.

. . . . Bouclin, Marie Evans

Marie Evans Bouclin has had a life-long interest in the human and reproductive rights of women. She has a MA in theology from l'Université de Sherbrooke. At present, she works as a freelance translator for the University of Sudbury where she has also been a long-standing member of its Board of Regents (active since 1989).

.... Broad, Gayle

Gayle Broad has been an activist/feminist in Northern Ontario for more than 20 years. She has worked with low-income groups, battered women, teens, and many survivors of sexual abuse/assault. She is currently employed as a community legal worker, and is also a PhD student at the School for Policy Studies in Bristol UK, where she is studying worker ownership and participation.

.... Chapman, Marilyn

Marilyn Chapman is a nurse educator in the Collaboration Nursing Program at Malaspina University College in British Columbia. Holding a Master's degree, she has taught nursing for many years as well as worked in the field.

.... Dwyer Corbin, Sonia

Sonia has worked with adults with attention deficit difficulties in many settings. She has worked as a school psychologist and in private practice in Newfoundland. She is currently with the Faculty of Education at the University of Regina. This paper was part of her University of Calgary doctoral dissertation.

.... Driedger, Diane

Diane Driedger is a former board member of CRIAW and has been involved in the disabled people's movement in Canada and internationally for 19 years. She is also an historian, a poet, a writer. She has co-edited two collections by women with disabilities from various countries.

.... Edmonds, Louise

A PhD graduate from Political Studies at Queen's University in Kingston, Louise's expertise is in Canadian Government and Public

Policy and Administration. Her research focus is on the Canadian Health Care Policy, breast cancer, physician communication, child care, and street youth. She has worked at Queen's Park on the personal staff of several cabinet ministers in both legislative and policy capacity.

. . . . Fox, Jane

Jane's background is varied. She holds a BSC in Nursing degree from the University of Windsor, is a registered nurse, and has a certificate as a Canadian Family Educator. Since 1988 she has been facilitating parent groups; she has been involved with the La Leche League for many years.

. . . . Grant Cummings, Joan

Joan is past executive director of Women's Health in Women's Hands Community Health Centre and the 13th president of the National Action Committee on the Status of Women. She is founding member of the Ontario Black Women's Coalition, board member of Intercede (the Toronto organization for Domestic Workers's Rights). As a Bejing delegate, she worked on the Globalization of the Economy (in particular on the issue of counting women's work and the rights of migrant workers), and on Health. Joan firmly believes that the struggle for equality rights rest heavily with the organizing of our movement as a cohesive anti-racist and anti-discriminatory force.

. . . . Hanna, Lisa

Lisa Hanna is a doctoral candidate in the Department of Sociology, Carleton University. In addition to ongoing studies of the coping strategies of informal caregivers of the mentally ill, she maintains a long-standing interest in the sociology of mental health.

. . . . Heggie, Joan

Joan is a PhD candidate at the University of York, England and her research is on the experiences of lesbians in the British Army. Her Master's degree dealt with 'The Feminist Debate on Women in the Military'.

. . . . Jacquot, Lise

Lise. est directrice générale de Nouveau Départ National Inc. a Québec.

. . . . Jaffe, Ellen

Ellen Jaffe was born and educated in New York — she attended Wellesley College and New York University. She's lived in England where she studied psychotherapy at the Tavistock Clinic. She's lived in Ottawa since 1979 combining writing , counselling and working with a women's writing group in Hamilton. She is also a published author who has written for a variety of magazines and anthologies.

. . . . Komatsu, Yuko

Yuko Komatsu works in the Department of Industrial Relations at Takaota National College, Japan. Her specialized field is information engineering.

. . . . Lambert, Clémence

Elle est psychothérapeute et intervenante en santé mentale et travaille sur le projet Transition 50, un des volets de Nouveau Départ National Inc.

. . . . Little, Margo

Margo Little holds an MA in Humanities from Laurentian University and is a Sudbury based writer and educator. She has a background in journalism, social work, and teaching. She is a founding member of various community organizations including the Community Legal Clinic in Sucker Creek and the Sudbury Writer's Guild. Her column on educational issues runs in the *Sudbury Star* bi-weekly. She is also a winner of numerous short fiction awards.

. . . . Meyer, Methchild

Methchild Meyer (M.Ed.) has conducted community-based social research studies with a focus on women and equity for over ten years. She also has extensive experience in training, group facilitation, and the development of educational material. As a principal in Gentirion Consulting, her specialties are qualitative research, curriculum development, cross-cultural and anti-racist training.

. . . . Morris, Marika

Marika Morris is a Research Coordinator for the Canadian Research Institute for the Advancement of Women (CRIAW) working in Ottawa. She co-authored a study involving gender analysis of home care policies and practices soon to be published by Status of Women Canada.

. . . . Parkes, Maureen

Maureen Parkes is a nurse educator in the Collaboration Nursing Program at Malaspina University College in British Columbia. Holding a Master's degree, she has taught nursing for many years as well as worked in the field.

. . . . Rainbow, Kia

Kia Rainbow, who is working on her Master's in Social Work degree, has been a volunteer coordinator and community developer with the Community Resource Centre of Goulbourn, Kanata, and West Carleton for the past 5 years. She is actively involved in numerous committees addressing the special issues and needs of lesbians. She was one of the founding members and past chair of the Lesbian Issues Sub-committee of Ottawa-Carleton. She also has facilitated numerous workshops providing advocacy and education service providers at the local, provincial, and national levels.

. . . . Rukholm, Ellen

Ellen Rukholm, RN, PhD is the Director of Nursing in the School of Nursing at Laurentian University. She has been involved with health promotion and heart health in particular for the last 10 years. She co-chaired the Heart Wise Women Committee, a Sudbury Hearth Health committee that is committed to raising awareness amongst women in our community of their risk for heart disease.

. . . . Stone, Sharon Dale

Sharon Dale Stone is an assistant professor of sociology, Women's studies, and Gerontology at Lakehead University. She is a survivor of childhood brain hemorrhage and is currently writing about the experiences of women who have survived a brain hemorrhage. In Toronto and Montreal, she was active in the DisAbled Women's Network, and she has worked for many years to raise awareness about invisible disabilities.

. . . . Tachinami, Sumiko

Sumiko Tachinami is an associate professor at Nagano Prefectural College, Nagano, Japan. She has also taught at Toyama Women's College and worked as an elementary school teacher in Tokyo and Toyama. In the years from 1994 to 1997 she undertook research and studies at Laurentian University. She has published articles on pioneer techniques in kindergarten and kindergarten teacher training on abandoned children in early modern Japan.

. . . . Thistle, Karen

Karen Thistle just recently graduated with a Master's Degree in Journalism from the University of Western Ontario as well as having an undergraduate degree in Rhetoric and Women's Studies from Laurentian University. Besides Karen's keen interest in media, she is a volunteer leader with the Girl Guides of Canada.

. . . . Transken, Si

Si Transken is a feminist therapist and advocate who owns and operates Trans/Formative Services — an organization that exists to participate in the journey to and struggle for justice: equality, dignity, comfort, and joy in all women's lives. She has taught at the School of Social Work at Laurentian University and is also a certified mediator.

. . . . Watters, Colleen

Colleen Watters holds a Master's Degree in Social Work from the
University of Manitoba. She currently works as a contract researcher
with the Canadian Centre on Disability Studies (CCDS) in Winnipeg
where she works on various projects. She has co-authored two
documents related to disabilities, 'Canadian Initiatives in supporting
self-employment' and 'Urban Business Development and Disability:
Models and Strategies'.

. . . . Yanagihara, Ryoko

Ryoko Yanagihara is a staff member at Racco House, Toyama City,
Japan. She is a social feminist activist, a trained social worker with a
MSW and an advocate for women with disabilities. She has done
scholarly work in Australia where she was able to practice her
English.

The Editors

. . . . Gabrielle Lavigne

Undergraduate degree in Native Studies and currently finishing an Interdisciplinary MA in Humanities: Interpretation and Values at Laurentian University on a part-time basis. The Manager of the Placement Centre/Centre de Placement at Laurentian University, she has been involved in Education/Placement/Youth/Women's committees all of her life.

. . . . Tricia Burke

BA in English at Laurentian University, 1998. She was involved with the Presidential Advisory Committee on the Status of Women and the Women's Centre at Laurentian University for over 6 years. She has also been extremely active in the CRIAW conferences as well as the conference proceedings. Currently she is enjoying where her feminist journey is taking her.

. . . . Manon Lemonde

Professeure agrégée à l'École des sciences infirmières qui travaille à l'Université Laurentienne depuis 1987. She is currently on leave from Laurentian University as a Career Reorientation Scientist at the University of Toronto. For the last ten years she has been involved in women's committees both on and off campus and has also been a representative on the local school board.